The book is wonderful, rich with ideas, pictures, and examples. More important than giving you a treasure of classroom strategies, it is a breath of fresh air in the academic and self-regulation community.

—**Eric Jensen**, neuroscientist, author of
*Teaching with the Brain in Mind* and *Brain-Based Learning*

I truly enjoyed this book. It was one of the best education books I have ever read. *Activate Math!* was eye-opening and motivated me to break away from old teaching habits. Since incorporating movement with math using mats and other hands-on activities, I have seen remarkable changes, especially in one student who previously struggled with his number identification and writing numbers. He used to hide under his desk and refuse to do any work, but now he smiles, participates, answers questions, and can identify numbers he couldn't recognize just weeks ago. Adding movement during math has transformed the dynamic in my classroom; students are excited, engaged, and retaining more information, which makes teaching both easier and more effective. This is a book I believe every educator should read.

—**Vicki Watkins**, kindergarten teacher, Canaseraga Central School

*Activate Math!* is the kind of book teachers immediately want to put into action. Koontz and Schoephoerster show how purposeful movement can transform math from something students sit through into something they experience. Grounded in research and packed with practical strategies, this is a powerful resource for educators who want energized classrooms and deeper mathematical understanding.

—**Selina Smith**, 4th grade teacher

It is of critical importance that young learners feel confidence and ownership in how to do mathematics and move their bodies. This book has can enable teachers to empower students in both areas. It includes accessible explanations of how movement-based mathematics aligns with contemporary research in mathematics education and neuroscience. It also contains classroom activities that incorporate movement into a wide range of mathematical topics and only require affordable materials like chalk, tape, and index cards.

—**Meghan Riling**, assistant professor of the Practice of Mathematics, Department of Teaching and Learning, Vanderbilt University

I had the opportunity to visit and participate in math and movement activities in person and witness the joy the students experienced. The time spent was purposeful, deliberate, and fun. It gave valuable insight into the importance of adding movement for my own students learning math concepts. Students were excited to learn and do more. I look forward to using more of the strategies from *Activate Math!* into my future classes.

—**Mary Yuhas**, 3rd grade math teacher, Pittsburgh Public School District

*Activate Math!* highlights the numerous advantages and connections between building a positive math mindset, engaging in physical activity, and utilizing evidence-based practices. Educators at any level will gain insight into the power of movement-based instruction and how to apply the catalysts to improve student understanding and their relationship with math.

**—Elizabeth Kraemer,**
Instructional Resources Team Math Coordinator, Erie 1 BOCES

In this post-pandemic, technology-saturated world, this approach is a much-needed breath of fresh air. Combining math and physical movement takes the anxiety out of math instruction and replaces it with active engagement, deep learning, increased mathematical fluency and an understanding of scaffolded math skills. I have seen the positive effects of this firsthand after just a short time of implementation with our students.

**—Kerri Bianchi**, principal, Carrie E. Tompkins Elementary School

*Activate Math!* is a practical, energizing guide that reimagines how students learn. It highlights how physical activity can deepen understanding, boost student engagement, and build confidence. With practical strategies, real classroom applications, and an inclusive perspective, it serves as a valuable resource for forward-thinking educators working with diverse learners across grade levels.

**—Dr. Lynn Allen**, Deputy Superintendent,
Putnam Northern Westchester BOCES

After reading *Activate Math!* it affirmed what I've long believed: math can be joyful. Growing up as a young girl in the 1980s, I had an underdeveloped math identity and gravitated toward subjects that told stories. But when math is active, it tells stories too. As a principal, I supported teachers that brought math outside by measuring flowerbeds, counting with sticks as 10s and pebbles as 1s. When we create core memories through movement and relevance, we help students build positive, confident math identities that last a lifetime.

**—Dr. Katie Brasley Trepanier**, school administrator and founder of
KTB Innovative Solutions, an Education and Leadership Consultancy

*Activate Math!* is an exciting addition to the field of embodied learning—an evidence-based, practical guide to movement-based math instruction. Suzy Koontz and Kirby Schoephoerster offer clear, concise, and compelling answers to why and how students should be getting out of their seats—and hopefully putting an end to the all too common refrain "I'm not good at math."

**—Jennifer Light**, Bern Dibner professor, MIT

# ACTIVATE MATH!

# ACTIVATE MATH!

## Using Movement to Spark Engagement and Ignite Learning

**SUZY KOONTZ**
and
**KIRBY SCHOEPHOERSTER**

iste+ascd

Arlington, Virginia USA

# iste+ascd

2111 Wilson Boulevard, Suite 300 • Arlington, VA 22201 USA
Phone: 800-933-2723 or 703-578-9600
Website: iste-ascd.org • Email: memsupport@iste-ascd.org
Author guidelines: ascd.org/write

Richard Culatta, *Chief Executive Officer*; Genny Ostertag, *Managing Director, Book Acquisitions & Editing*; Stephanie Bize, *Acquisitions Editor*; Mary Beth Nielsen, *Director, Book Editing*; Megan Doyle, *Editor*; Lisa Hill, *Graphic Designer*; Valerie Younkin, *Senior Production Designer*; Emily Reed, *Senior Director, Publishing Operations*; Christopher Logan, *Senior Production Specialist*; Shajuan Martin, *E-Publishing Specialist*



All links in this book are correct as of the publication date below but may have become inactive or otherwise modified since that time. If you notice a broken link, email books@ascd.org; include "Link Update" in the subject line; and in the message, specify the link, the book title, and the page number on which the link appears.

PAPERBACK ISBN: 978-1-4166-3436-2     ASCD product #125004     n4/26

PDF EBOOK ISBN: 978-1-4166-3437-9; see Books in Print for other formats.

Quantity discounts are available: email programteam@ascd.org or call 800-933-2723, ext. 5773, or 703-575-5773. For desk copies, go to www.ascd.org/deskcopy.

**Library of Congress Cataloging-in-Publication Data**
Names: Koontz, Suzy author | Schoephoerster, Kirby author
Title: Activate math! : using movement to spark engagement and ignite learning / Suzy Koontz and Kirby Schoephoerster.
Description: Arlington, Virginia : ISTE+ASCD, [2026] | Includes bibliographical references and index.
Identifiers: LCCN 2026000280 (print) | LCCN 2026000281 (ebook) | ISBN 9781416634362 paperback | ISBN 9781416634379 pdf
Subjects: LCSH: Mathematics—Study and teaching—Psychological aspects | Movement education—Curricula | Motivation in education
Classification: LCC QA11 .K7735 2026 (print) | LCC QA11 (ebook)
LC record available at https://lccn.loc.gov/2026000280
LC ebook record available at https://lccn.loc.gov/2026000281

35 34 33 32 31 30 29 28 27 26          1 2 3 4 5 6 7 8 9 10 11 12

**To my mom,**
who passed on her timeless wisdom for
helping children learn with joy and confidence.
Your love and teaching live on in all I do.
—SK


**To my teachers,**
whose enthusiastic efforts to prepare me and
my generation to lead with empathy, curiosity,
criticality, and an unwaveringly democratic spirit
deserve endless recognition and praise,
for *faith in democracy is all one with
faith in experience and education.*
—KS

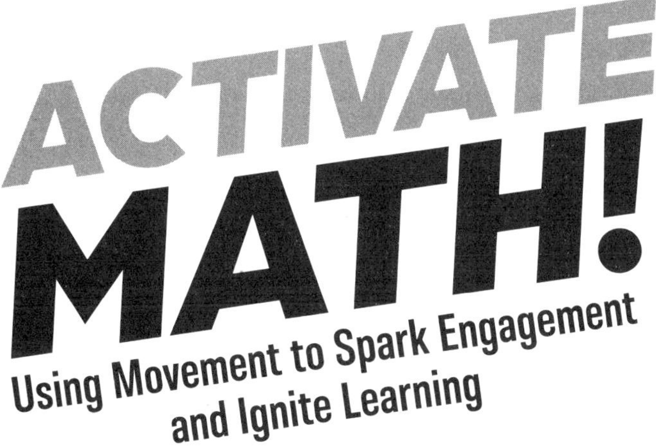


ACTIVATE
MATH!
Using Movement to Spark Engagement
and Ignite Learning

# Introduction: Why Movement *and* Mathematics Matter

Chances are you've heard this statement before: "I'm not a math person." You might have even said it yourself or believe it now to some degree (we will admit that we've felt this way on numerous occasions all throughout our educational journeys). You might have witnessed your own students identify as "not math people" or even heard them reference their parents or peers as "not a math person." More concerning, yet quite common, you might've even overheard a parent position their own child as "not a math person" because that parent, when they were their child's age, was also "not a math person." There's a copious amount of research that's proven how this mindset negatively affects short-term student motivation and learning as well as student identity development and long-term mathematics achievement. The purpose of this book, however, is not to lament the devaluation of mathematics and the prevalence of the "I'm not a math person" attitude. Rather, what concerns us here, and what we're most excited to share in this book, are what we as educators can do in our own *instructional practices* to foster students' positive relationships with mathematics.

Students today face several challenges that directly interfere with their learning of mathematics, and that can have lasting effects on their relationships with classroom content and the whole discipline. From our many years of working with young learners, their families, educators, and school administrators—and informed by research and public perceptions of 21st century math education—we believe that there are three interrelated contributors to our kids' self-positioning as "not math people" in today's classrooms.

First, students are struggling to become "mathematically fluent" with the fundamental concepts. Math is cumulative. When students do not become fluent in early years, it makes the acquisition of math more difficult in subsequent years. There's also a wide-reaching disengagement with math tasks and the discipline of mathematics more generally, which is observable in classrooms as increased instances of off-task behaviors, low motivation to complete assignments, and a rise in questions and statements like "When will I have to do this in the *real* world?" or "It's not like I'm gonna have to use math in *my* job." Disengagement makes learning math difficult for students of all ages. A recent study funded by the Gates Foundation found that 96 percent of parents surveyed across racial demographic groups say they believe that their own child would be more likely to excel in math class if it felt more "relevant" and "engaging." Additionally, parents *and teachers* shared that an "ideal K–12 math education" would be relevant to the real world (64 percent), useful (54 percent), focused on creative problem solving (52 percent), and engaging (50 percent) (Jimenez, 2023). It's clear that something different is not only needed but *wanted* by learners, educators, and communities.

Second, there is a prevalence of *anxiety* among students and adults toward the learning and teaching of mathematics more broadly. Approximately 93 percent of U.S. adults indicate that they experience some level of math anxiety (Blazer, 2011). In 2012, 29 percent of American students "agreed" or "strongly agreed" that they get very nervous when doing mathematics problems; that number increased to 38 percent in 2024 (Schwartz, 2024). As we will discuss in detail throughout this book, the presence of anxiety in the classroom is a significant threat not only to students' general health and wellness but also to their learning in both the short term and the long term, both academically and physiologically.

Third, students are not receiving enough opportunities throughout the school day to be physically active, which in turn is contributing to negative health outcomes physically, mentally, emotionally, socially, and academically (Ward et al., 2019; Brattico et al., 2021; Klamm et al., 2022). The recommended dosage is *at least 60 minutes of moderate-to-vigorous physical exercise per day*, and only 16.1 percent of students were meeting this amount before the COVID-19 pandemic. However, that number fell to 8.9 percent during the pandemic (Raney et al., 2022; Cortez et al., 2023). As of 2021, childhood obesity in the United States includes more than 20 percent of all adolescents (Brooks et al., 2021), and since the COVID-19 pandemic, adolescent recreational screen time more than doubled from 3.8 hours per day to 7.7 hours per day (*not including* school work) (Raney et al., 2022). This is what we educators are facing in the typical math classroom.

## Why Movement Is Needed in Math Classrooms

Exasperated by the COVID-19 pandemic and growing discontent with traditional mathematics instruction, elementary students are underperforming in mathematics nationwide, causing significant concern among teachers, administrators, and parents (Camera, 2019, NCES, 2022). As a result, K–12 institutions and their various stakeholders appear to be more open to innovative math instructional strategies than they were prior to 2020. What is exciting here is that school leaders and educators are actively exploring solutions that can enhance students' math achievement by integrating interdisciplinary concepts and principles, while also prioritizing health consciousness and wellness, in their daily lessons.

For this reason, the publication of this book, we believe, is *timely*. For many educators and administrators, particularly those who do not work extensively with younger students, in physical education, or with student populations with special needs, incorporating movement into classroom instruction *seems* innovative. Historically, however, physical activity and academic achievement have often been cited as complementary if not *inseparable* components of a valuable, impactful education. One such citation comes from the Greek philosopher Plato, who in the 4th century BCE contemplated the "ideal education" for students in book three of his *Republic*:

> And as there are two principles of human nature [emotion and reason], some divine being has given mankind two arts—education and physical activity—which answer to them so that these two principles—like the strings of an instrument—may be relaxed or drawn tighter until they are duly harmonized. [...] The one who mingles education with physical activity in the fairest proportions, and best applies them to the soul, may achieve perfection. (3.411e–412a)

In our modern American, screen-centered educational system, we seem to have lost sight of the holistic impact that physical activity (PA) has on learning, emotional development, and school participation. Thanks to modern science, incorporating PA into daily student activities has been proven to increase overall health, regulate emotions, and support learning by strengthening students' neural networks. The connection between movement and learning is no longer just a theory or a philosophical aspiration but explained by science and evident in the data. Despite the well-researched benefits of increasing PA opportunities throughout the day, and despite the consensus among experts that there is *no evidence* to support the argument that academic performance *decreases* when more time is allotted to PA during the school day (Donnelly & Lambourne, 2011; Sneck et al., 2019; Vetter et al., 2020), few schools are embracing movement-focused programming on a regular basis, much less in the *mathematics* classroom. Why is that?

While sitting in their seats, students often perceive math as scary because there's only one right answer and there are only a few ways to get that answer. Combining movement and math is unique because students physically *become the manipulative* as they move their body from one number to the next. When students get out of their seats and physically use their bodies to determine the answer to math questions and collaboratively solve problems, they learn how to self-correct any errors that may occur, boost risk taking with their learning, and diminish their math anxiety.

Combining movement and math is particularly crucial for learning and applying math concepts because these concepts are often presented and taught *abstractly*, which can be challenging for students to grasp through traditional, sit-down methods. By incorporating movement, we allow students to embody these concepts, making them more concrete and accessible. This movement-based approach is appropriate all throughout a student's learning journey, from early elementary school, where students are learning foundational concepts, to higher grades, where they can use physical activity to explore more complex ideas.

Public opinion around the need to make mathematics more engaging has shifted quite dramatically, especially since the outset of the COVID-19 pandemic. More and more data concerning the long-term negative effects of increased screen time and traditional sit-and-be-quiet methods of math instruction are being published and, in turn, changing minds and attitudes. How we've been teaching math is not working for *today's* students. Movement-based instruction, as we will discuss throughout this book, shows significant promise for reshaping minds, behaviors, and systems in such a way that affords *every* student a chance to engage excitedly in mathematics content. This is what we hope to illustrate to our readers throughout this book.

## Structure and Organization

Chapter 1 will introduce our movement-based instructional framework. We will discuss its underlying concepts (i.e., the Three Teacher Powers and the Five Catalysts of Movement-Based Instruction), define key terms, and supplement with research to set the conceptual and methodological stage for the following chapters. Chapter 1 will also include figures and visualizations to illustrate our moving and learning framework.

In Chapter 2, we will introduce the first of the Five Catalysts of Movement-Based Instruction: *Engagement.* Movement stimulates student engagement during mathematical tasks by motivating participation in the learning process, strengthening focus, and orienting attention and (positive) attitudes toward the task at hand. Movement-focused activities have been proven to increase focus and engagement in virtually every situation.

In Chapter 3, we will introduce the second of the Five Catalysts of Movement-Based Instruction: *Scaffolding.* Teachers have the capacity to script the critical moves that students are to follow to the best of their ability in order to complete an activity and, in turn, build fluency in a particular mathematics concept. A teacher who possesses the Moving and Learning Mindset works to scaffold their lessons by introducing a problem, discussing what is to be done, and providing students with a kinesthetic learning environment in which to solve the problem. In doing so, they provide students with a learning space that supports more structured and deeper comprehension, which in turn mitigates math anxiety.

In Chapter 4, we will introduce the third of the Five Catalysts of Movement-Based Instruction: *Expansion*. We will detail how teachers have the power to broaden the perspectives that their students have toward mathematics both generally and specifically. Within the math classroom, teachers aim to connect learning with other activities and capacities of students, which in turn contributes to the enrichment of learning contexts and demonstrates the practicality of mathematics. Movement-focused activities streamline this process and make the transfer of learning more enjoyable for students.

The fourth Catalyst of Movement-Based Instruction will be covered in Chapter 5: *Enrichment*. Teachers often supplement their lessons with new tools and schematizations in order to accelerate learning while simultaneously addressing the differing needs of their students. The implementation of movement-based math games in a traditional math curriculum helps meet the learning needs of your diverse student body, enriches the concepts being taught, and bolsters student enjoyment and engagement with the material.

Finally, in Chapter 6, we will introduce the fifth of the Five Catalysts of Movement-Based Instruction: *Review*. Teachers should involve their students in active discourse and consistent review of *what* they are doing and *why* they are doing it. Reflection also allows for new orientations and ways of thinking, which could in turn lead to new activities. Movement-based activities in particular offer rich opportunities for students to review and ponder difficult concepts while still having fun.

The Conclusion will include a brief summary of the concepts covered throughout the book, including the Three Powers of the Moving and Learning Teacher and the adapted five catalysts for guiding educational, movement-based learning activities.

## A Call for Inclusive Mathematics

Our book aims to bridge both the science and the practice of movement-based mathematics education, the primary purpose of which is to provide educators with an evidence-based, engaging, and impactful framework to reignite student confidence and competency in mathematics. A secondary aspiration of the book is to enrich *your* attitude toward movement-based learning in general and (ideally) ignite a passion and confidence in applying movement-based math strategies regularly in your own classrooms using your teacher powers of emotional contagion, fostering instructional relationships, and promoting growth beliefs. Each chapter of this book includes a story of real student success either from a Moving and Learning teacher or from our own experiences working with students as interventionists. The stories introduce and conclude each chapter and epitomize the main points covered in the chapter. We hope these stories inspire you as they have us to take these promising practices and run with them!

We believe that the *true power* of movement-based instruction is in its actualization of *inclusivity.* Physical activity, play, and movement more generally are paramount to our development, communication, and expression as humans, thus everyone regardless of background, culture, social position, and economic status can connect to it and experience it. In the classroom, movement is tangible and actionable in how it can bring the abstract into the "experienced." Movement is intricately tied to our cognition (that is, our learning is *embodied*), and it informs how we think and how we make sense of the world around us. Movement has also been identified as a "cure" in how it combats depression, anxiety, and hyperarousal and rewires our brains—and *all* brains—in such a way that sets us up for accelerated learning. Movement is also cyclically reinforcing; when we move our bodies, especially when we move vigorously, we *feel* its immediate effects (e.g., increased heart rate, increased focus and attention span), but we also experience outcomes that nudge us into a positive feedback loop of continuous engagement in movement-based activities (Sanaeifar et al., 2024). When we don't move, we also feel the effects on our thinking and our health—we might feel physically groggier, but we might also think more slowly or struggle focusing. *All* minds, to varying degrees, experience the effects of movement, and *all* minds benefit from increased physical activity. We will delve deeper into these concepts throughout the book.

It is important to us (Suzy and Kirby) that we continue to strengthen the momentum that we're seeing on the ground, among ed funders, and at the policy level around evidence-based kinesthetic education advocacy; we want to support those powerhouse teachers who are finding success and seeking success in reframing how we should be teaching mathematics. For this reason, the proceeds of this book will go *directly* to support the National Math Foundation (NMF). The NMF is a 501(c)3 nonprofit whose mission is to foster exercise, healthy eating, and learning through movement as a means to develop a community of math literate members. The NMF works across the nation to provide teachers with the resources and the technical assistance they need to get their students to grade level in math and reading. The sales revenue of this book will help fund the provision of these resources, programs, and services to school communities across the country. Additionally, the NMF connects with research institutions to lead rigorous evaluations of multisensory math programs that are making a difference in student achievement. It is important that educators and school leaders are aware of what evidence-based options are available to them to support their students.

As it currently stands, there is a notable lack of rigorous, high-quality studies on the impact and implementation of movement-based programming across various student populations and learning contexts. Additional rigorous, longitudinal studies are needed, and the NMF is leading the charge in actively partnering with school districts and educational research institutions to carry out these nuanced investigations. New tools and technologies that center physical activity during mathematics instruction hold significant promise for math learners and instructors. Ongoing evaluations of these tools and the organizations that design and implement them are a necessary step in shifting mindsets and instructional practice.

## How to Approach This Book

We hope you approach this book as an evidence-based, practical guide through the professional discourse of movement-based education; this book will offer you insight into how physical activity supports student learning and what you can do to regularly promote physical activity inside and outside your classroom. This book will provide multiple strategies to help you develop what we call a Moving and Learning Mindset and create active learning environments using our multisensory learning approach. Our approach is informed by research on guiding productive educational play to fit a broader definition of movement-based learning (which will be detailed further in Chapter 1). Each of the book's chapters will delve into ways that movement initiates and/or supports learning in the math classroom—which we have termed *catalysts*. These catalysts offer insights into how movement affects classroom learning. In order to maximize the learning that movement-based learning accelerates, educators can look to these five catalysts to guide their instruction and their activities.

We want to add here as well that this book should *not* function as a tool to diagnose children with Adverse Childhood Experiences (ACEs) or trauma. Instead, we ask you to approach the discourse and dialogues of ACEs and trauma-informed education shared here as complementary to our framework, as it is indebted to ACEs research. As such, we hope these discussions and relevant activities help you enrich the supportive learning environments at your school through a multisensory learning approach.

Although we use *kinesthetic* learning and *movement-based* learning interchangeably in practice, we want to state up front that the movement-based model of instruction we advocate here, although informed by the VARK model of learning preferences, does not ascribe to the learning styles theory. Labeling or categorizing students as certain "types" of learners or enabling their own self-identification as a certain type of learner can actually have negative effects on their learning and limit their motivation and confidence to engage in classroom material (Thomas, 2021). We don't believe that some kids are solely kinesthetic learners and some are not—nor do we believe that it's particularly advantageous to categorize them as such. In reality, students' preferences toward how they best learn is subject to change, and when it comes to providing students unique support, the *more ways* we can get them to interact with classroom content (i.e., the more modalities we can employ), the better learning outcomes we see. Moreover, *all* learners process information better when they are actively (and physically) engaged during the learning process.

We believe that the experiences, evidence, and stories shared in this book are relevant to educators of *all* grade levels and that increased opportunities to participate in physical activity should be offered to every student regardless of age, grade, or achievement level, because physical activity supports the learning of *all* students. This book contains 45 movement-based math activities and games (9 per chapter) that we've developed and implemented in our own programs over years of working with educators and students. The movement-based, math-focused activities can take place anywhere (in the classroom, in the hallways, in the gym, in the library) and at any time (before or after school, during unit or classroom transitions, before or after class).

These activities vary in complexity and appropriateness as they relate to students' skills (both coordination-wise and math competency-wise), but they are intentionally designed to get students to practice their math collaboratively while out of their seats. Some activities might make sense in some contexts with some students and not others; we have intentionally prioritized *breadth* in the type and difficulty of these activities to illustrate a comprehensive picture of how teachers can engage in effective movement-based math instruction. We hope you will use and adapt these activities in whatever ways are most helpful for you and your students, ideally in an attempt to foster long-term healthy habits. The 45 activities are by no means exhaustive. Rather, we have chosen to include activities that we feel most directly reflect the relevant topics and research of their respective section. We hope that these activities can function as *starting points* in the process of making PA a part of your mathematics curriculum and hopefully a habit for your students. Believe us when we say that neither you nor your students will regret it.

It goes without saying that we live in uncertain times, but we cannot let global pandemics, the lack of public education funding, or even the decentralization of health and PA in our curricula stand in the way of our kids reaching their fullest potential. We believe that the approach to learning presented in this book—one that prioritizes the structure and the fun of physical activity—is the spark that will help reignite our students' love for mathematics.

# The Moving
# and Learning Mindset

Our students need to be moving their bodies more often than they currently are and more often than they ever have. But, if we're to actually get our students to move and, in turn, reap the benefits of increased physical activity during the school day, we need to first and foremost understand our students, where they're at, and how movement supports the learning of each and every one of them. In order to change behaviors, build habits, and create environments where every student can connect with math and build up positive math attitudes and identities, we also need to consider how our role within this environment affects our students' learning, how we embody movement-based practices (or not), and how we demonstrate the types of attitudes we want our students to have. Any effort to change how we go about teaching math is very much a *mindset* game. Of course, we have standards to meet and limited time and resources to accomplish all that we want in our quest to meet those standards, but the "how"—the *process*—through which we meet those objectives affords us quite a bit of flexibility to respond to the changing needs of students. Our flexibility within the rigid framework of math standards is limited only by our mindset and our openness to and valuation of change, creativity, innovation, and evidence-based practice.

The purpose of this first chapter is to introduce the Moving and Learning Mindset (our "how") and the research, methodologies, and learning frameworks that ignited its conception and continue to fuel its implementation. In doing so, we will provide the evidence-based foundation for the following chapters, which will delve deeper into practical examples and instructional implications of our movement-based framework. A teacher who possesses such a mindset approaches learning and teaching in a hands-on way by providing an array of multisensory instructional strategies and opportunities for physical activity (PA) during instruction. Before we get into the nitty-gritty of our framework, it is important to first set the context—specifically the context of brain science and trauma-informed education—from which this movement-based approach emerged.

Let's start with a story from Sarah—a student from a small town in upstate New York—who was generous enough to share with us her unfiltered reflections on her own experience with mathematics growing up. At the time of writing this book, Sarah was a university engineering student in Germany. In 3rd grade, she caught the "travel bug" and fell in love with learning about other countries. She also recognized early on that technology and innovation were becoming economic cornerstones in our increasingly globalized world and wanted to be on the forefront of it all. But that love for math didn't arise out of nothing; similar to so many young learners in the United States, Sarah's journey to becoming a vocal advocate for STEM began steeped in anxiety.

> When I was 8 years old, I had the honor of being labeled as one of the "mathematically challenged" kids in class. There were eight of us. It was such a prestigious title that I liked to hide at my desk, pretending not to hear the teachers calling my name to come over and work with them. "Sarah? Sarah?" they'd say, eyes locked right on me while the other "challenged" students gathered around them. And I'd think, *Maybe if I just sit really still and pretend I didn't hear them, they'll forget I exist. Maybe I'll blend in with the smart kids and get to stay here, basking in the glow of non-remedial math.* Yeah… no. That didn't work. Instead, it turned into a whole scene where they

walked over, stood next to me, and made a point of reminding me and in turn everyone around me (including the "smart" kids) that I needed extra help.

Now don't get me wrong—those math boxes were brutal. Math boxes were end-of-lesson independent work where we had to reflect on our daily math goals. I could stare at them for hours and still come up with nothing. I truly did need help. But at some point, something started to bother me. Why did I always need help? Why wasn't I improving? Day after day, I watched the smart kids breeze through their math boxes, practically sprinting up to the teacher to get them graded. They'd wait in line, talking about how easy everything was. Meanwhile, over at our table—the struggling squad—we'd just sit there, silently drowning. Hearing our classmates talk like that only made things worse. Our wounds only grew deeper each time someone said, "That was so easy!"

It's wild how early negative self-talk starts, how fast a kid starts believing they're "just not good at math." That something's wrong with them and that they'll never get it. Those negative feelings grow only stronger when the extra help teachers get fed up with how "dumb" you are. They'd ask the same question over and over again. They'd jab their finger at the question on the paper a thousand times, like somehow the next question—or the next jab of their finger—might magically make me get it. I could practically see steam coming out of their ears. And there I was, sitting there, absolutely clueless. I wanted to guess—maybe just throw something out there—but I was terrified that the wrong answer would turn the steam into full-blown fire.

All I really could do at that point was cry. On many beautiful occasions, I sat at that table, crying into my math boxes, tears dripping right onto the paper. But hey, if crying shifted their focus from how terrible I was at math to trying to comfort me, then—honestly—I counted that as a win. But here's what's important to recognize: I wasn't the only one. There are so many students who feel exactly the same way I did. They miss the basics and then spend the rest of their school lives struggling, right up until their last math class in high school or whenever they finally get to quit.

The thing is… there's no escaping math. It's cumulative and it's everywhere. If you don't understand the fundamentals early on, how can you possibly expect to develop a deeper understanding later? Leaving students behind, ignoring their needs, or failing to find teaching methods that actually work for *all* students (not just the small minority) is more than just a missed academic opportunity. It's a hit to their entire sense of self. It makes them believe they're the problem instead of recognizing the real issue: the system that's failing them.

So what can we do for students who just aren't getting it?

When I started learning through movement, everything began to change. I learned multiplication so quickly by jumping on colorful floor mats with big boxed numbers. As a class, we shouted out the multiples together while jumping along. Then, each student had the chance to physically interact with the mat to answer multiplication questions. It was through that kinesthetic and visual interaction with numbers that my brain finally started to understand what multiplication actually was. We even used those same mats for division—something that had previously been just a big blank void in my brain. But seeing the groups physically laid out in front of me didn't just boost my number fluency—it helped me solve word problems too.

That "lightbulb moment" I had been waiting for came when I used my body as a tool—as a manipulative—to make sense of the math. I'm honestly not sure it ever would have clicked otherwise. And you know what was truly remarkable about that movement-based approach? It worked for all of us. Every one of the struggling students started making progress once we were shown a different way to interact with numbers. We got excited. We moved our bodies and our confidence at the same time. Even the so-called smart kids benefited—or at the very least, they had more fun than sitting in silence, stuck in a chair. I used those multiplication mats to practice my 3s, 4s, 5s, 6s, 7s, 8s, and 9s. I jumped, I wrote, I solved—and eventually, those multiples became second nature, like the ABCs.

This isn't all of her story. In talking with Sarah about her experiences with mathematics as we were writing this book, she shared that she doesn't have a "typical engineering brain," but something clicked for her when her teachers started teaching math using physical movement. She began to see the "rhythm and beauty" in math, and it all started to make sense. We will return to Sarah's story of how learning through movement changed the way she saw math—how powerful that approach can be for not only students who learn differently but for *all* students. As educators, we need to meet the different needs of our students both inside and outside the math classroom. When we understand the richly complex capacities we possess as educators—namely, how our emotional intelligence can quell learning anxiety, how our strong instructional relationships can boost classroom engagement, and how our collective valuation of growth can promote inclusive learning—we all become better facilitators of our students' learning. These powers, coupled with the application of movement-based instructional practices, accelerate mathematical learning and self-confidence to new heights.

## The Science of Stress and the Brain

At the heart of our movement based approach to math instruction lies the holistic principles of trauma-informed education. One of the primary goals of trauma-informed education is to inform educators that each and every student has a complex identity that is shaped by a variety of physical and sociocultural factors, all of which affect how they learn and how they participate in the math classroom. *Trauma-informed* schools prioritize students' mental health as soon as they walk in the door, and trauma-informed teachers offer their students numerous opportunities to learn classroom content while centering reflective discussions and support around their physical, mental, and emotional development. The expectations that we set for our teachers thus require a certain amount of disciplinary knowledge, specifically knowledge of learning science, cognitive psychology, and neurobiology. In other words, educators who embody this movement-based mindset are cognizant of the social, physical, and psychological machinations that drive participation in classroom activities (Thomas et al., 2019).

A *holistic* approach to math instruction is necessary due to the reality of how stress and adversity affect our students and their learning. A large majority of our students have experienced at least one adverse childhood experience (ACE), according to adult surveys conducted by the CDC (2025). More than two-thirds of children reported at least one traumatic event by age 16, according to a survey conducted by SAMHSA. Additionally, of the adults surveyed across 23 states, 25 percent reported that they had experienced three or more ACEs during their childhood. Whether your students have ACEs or not, every student experiences stress, and some stressors are more toxic than others. Sometimes this stress is invisible, and other times it becomes apparent through students' physicality and behavior. Teachers should be aware of the signs of toxic stress in order to effectively regulate, emotionally connect with, and then teach. This instructional pathway from regulating to connecting to instructing is important for how—and when—we implement movement-based activities in the classroom; it intentionally addresses the developmental and operational pathways of the human brain and the realities of stress in which many of our students live.

For simplicity's sake, it can be helpful to think of these pathways as vertically oriented, and although the triune brain model (which has historically depicted the brain in this vertical orientation) has been superseded by a more evolutionary-based *adaptive* model (Steffen et al., 2022; Turnaround for Children, n.d.), the triune model continues to function as an accessible, *visual* introduction for educators unfamiliar with the implications of stress and regulatory interventions on student learning. We have attempted to depict the best of both models here (see Figure 1.1):

1. The brain *develops* from the bottom up, meaning that the lower regions of the brain mature first, yet, as we mature in age, so too does our brain at all levels via their interrelated neural connections:
   - The brain stem begins to develop in utero.
   - The midbrain develops primarily from when we are babies to toddlers.
   - The limbic system develops primarily from toddlerhood to teenhood.
   - The cortex develops primarily from teenhood to adulthood.
2. The brain *operates* across all of its levels when engaged in learning and interaction in the mathematics classroom:

- Our brain stem is constantly assessing our surroundings to identify stimulants and threats.
- The midbrain takes information from the brain stem, processes it through our movements, eyes, and ears, and determines whether those stimulants are threats, and if so, whether those threats are immediate or not.
- The limbic system translates the determinations of the midbrain into particular emotions and behaviors, which are in turn buffered and/or strengthened by the other interrelated systems.
- The cortex acts as a buffer to the limbic system as the source of rational thought and conscious judgment. The cortex of a teenager is still in development, meaning that their ability to make sound judgments that help to counter emotional outbursts requires additional, external support and regulation.

3. Life experiences—both good and bad—have a physiological impact on students' brains. When it comes to traumatic or toxic-stress-related experiences, there is a distinct neurological process that occurs, which can help to explain seemingly inexplicable behaviors. When we encounter stress, that stress takes a different route; our brains actually *become stressed* from the top down:
   - Our cortex first assesses a stressful situation and decides whether we should be calm or alert. Stress that permeates the cortex but is rationalized away is often called *manageable stress*. Stress on the cortex weakens cortical neural networks that underpin cognition and executive function (Arnsten, 2015).
   - If the cortex determines the stress is worthy of alert (or if the cortex is underdeveloped due to toxic stress or trauma experience at the time of its development), the stress moves quickly into the limbic system and manifests itself as alarm. When the brain is in an alarmed state, more emotional behaviors take over to help mitigate the external stressor(s). At this state, the brain is unsure of its safety, asking itself, "Am I safe right now or not?"
   - If the stress persists and becomes unmanageable for the limbic system, the stress permeates into the midbrain; here, alarm turns into fear. At this stage, the brain has determined that it is not safe,

and behaviors become reactionary and emotions more fearful or aggressive.

- If the brain continues to be exposed to stress and the midbrain is unable to mitigate the situation, the brain stem takes over, and an active fight, flight, or freeze response initiates.



## The Regulated and Unregulated Brain

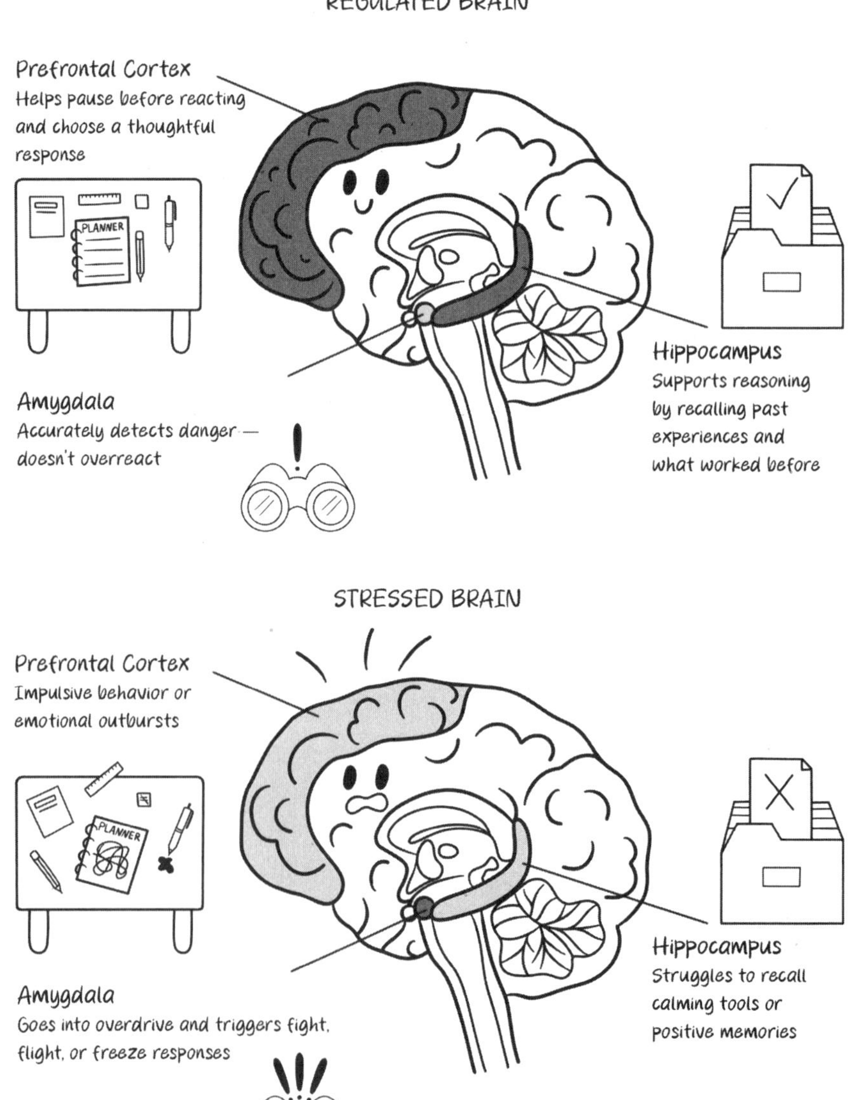

Prolonged exposure to toxic stress is linked to a variety of negative health outcomes that have far-reaching consequences for students physically, mentally, and academically. According to one large-scale study on ACEs by the Substance Abuse and Mental Health Services Administration (SAMHSA) (2024), individuals who experience childhood trauma are 5,000 percent more likely to attempt suicide and have an eating disorder (see also Ihme et al., 2022). Studies have also found that the more ACEs an individual has, the more likely they are to have depression and PTSD in adulthood, and that the more ACEs an individual has, the higher their chance of having long-term health issues such as heart disease, strokes, cancer, and diabetes (Bethell et al., 2014; Center for Youth Wellness, 2014; Herzog & Schmal, 2018). One factor that contributes to this decline in physical wellness is the link between ACEs and immune function; chronic stress disrupts and impedes the immune system from functioning properly.

As educators, it is crucial to understand not only how toxic stress can impact a child's physical and mental health but also how it can affect their *education*. ACEs have been linked to quite a number of negative education outcomes, including higher dropout rates, chronic absenteeism (Stempel et al., 2017), low academic achievement (Blodgett & Lanigan, 2018), and lower school engagement (Bethell et al., 2014). Shockingly, pediatrician and researcher Nadine Burke Harris—California's first surgeon general and one of the most vocal advocates for increasing public attention and knowledge about ACEs—found that students with three or more ACEs are 32 times more likely to struggle in school (Barry-Jester, 2019). Furthermore, a study by the CDC found that children with three or more ACEs are 2.5 times more likely to fail a grade (Idaho Youth Ranch, n.d.). Kaiser Permanente (n.d.) reports that children with three or more ACEs are five times more likely to have attendance issues, six times more likely to have behavior problems, and three times more likely to experience academic failure.

How, then, can we help our students? It starts with *noticing*. Specific emotions like anger and rage are common indicators of this natural descent (Eggleston et al., 2021), so we must be cognizant of students' emotions, how they express those emotions, and what potential stressors could be causing them. According to experts, the best way to address this issue holistically is to approach classroom instruction from the bottom up and in line with how the brain develops and operates. This bottom-up instruction is known among trauma-informed practitioners as the "Triple R" approach:

1.  **Regulate**: We first help our students (and in turn their brain stem and midbrain) realize that they are safe.
2.  **Relate**: When we relate, their limbic system realizes that they are safe. We will discuss the importance of building relationships later in the chapter, but it is important to note that relationships mean very little when students are functioning below the limbic level.
3.  **Reason**: When we reason with students who are stressed, we engage in cortical modulation where the cortex modulates the experiences of the bottom parts of the brain, which is an incredibly important skill that we develop over time through positive relationships and healthy habits within safe and welcoming environments.

When we offer them tools for support prior to and during meltdowns, students can begin to develop resilience and strengthen their brains' upper levels. Where, then, does *physical activity* fit into this bottom-up approach?

## Physical Activity as a Healing Factor

Movement-based learning encourages physical activity, which bolsters cognitive, social, and emotional development (Enloe, 2021), enhances the brain's capacity to retain information (Ratey & Hagerman, 2013), and develops not just one's individual capacities and strengths but also one's self-confidence in those capacities (Moore et al., 2023; Dutrisac et al., 2023). Movement-based activities help students' brains *regulate, relate,* and *reason* because of how physical activity supports neural development and communication. Movement has been shown to increase levels of glutamate in the brain, which is the messenger neurotransmitter responsible for initiating and sustaining the vast majority of the signaling between nerve cells (neurons). In short, glutamate is crucial for brain functioning and complex thought (Maddock et al., 2016). There are many different types of movement-focused interventions that we can do to support students at different levels of brain development and stress management (see Figure 1.2).

**Physical Activity and Brain Functions**

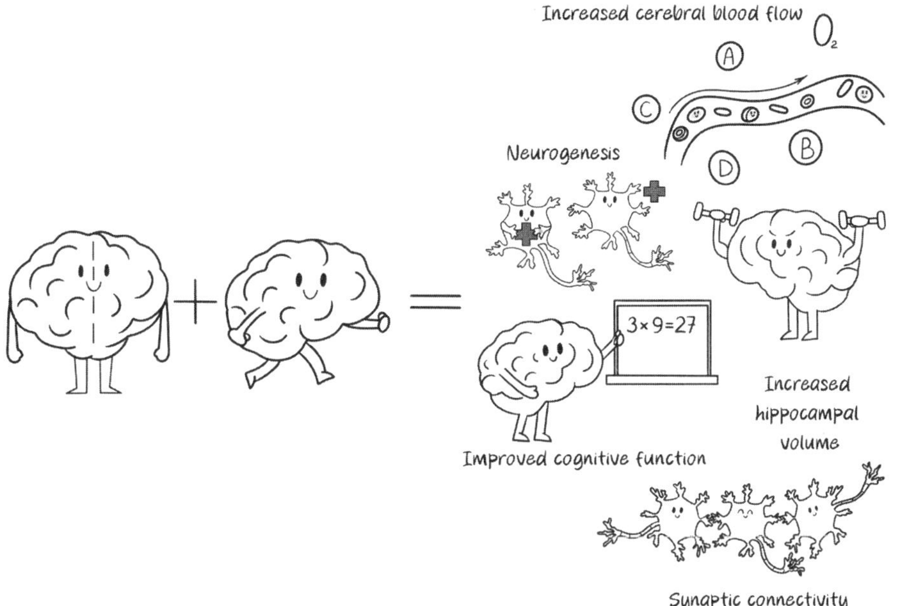



## Crossing the Midline

At the brain stem and midbrain levels, physical movement is a powerful intervention. Stretching, swinging, yoga, rhythmic drumming and clapping, and even martial arts are wonderful interventions that quickly regulate the brain stem. Walking, running, cross-body movements, dance, and most physical exercises involving jumping and hopping that get the heart pumping help regulate the brain stem and midbrain. Physical exercise regulates the brain by increasing the release of small proteins called *growth factors*. These growth factors are key in maintaining the brain's plasticity from birth to adulthood to old age by promoting the growth, maintenance, differentiation, and repair of neurons (Mendez Colmenares et al., 2021). Brain-derived neurotrophic factor (BDNF) is a growth factor that boosts neurogenesis and is particularly enhanced by aerobic physical activity (Ratey & Hagerman, 2013; Brattico et al., 2021; Pickersgill et al., 2022). Moreover, students with maltreatment-related PTSD have been found to possess an underdeveloped corpus callosum, which is the bridge between the brain's hemispheres (Kitayama et al., 2007). A strong corpus callosum allows information to quickly and efficiently pass between the hemispheres.

One way that we can help our students strengthen this bridge and support their developing motor and cognitive skills is to get them up and out of their seats and crossing their body's "midline" (see Figure 1.2) while engaging in complex, aerobically rigorous movements (Jacobs et al., 2018). The ability to cross the midline indicates communication between both hemispheres of the brain, allowing people to efficiently learn new skills. Children who do not consistently engage in midline movements have the potential to experience difficulties—both spatially and academically—later in life (Saidmamatov et al., 2022; Jensen, 2005). As students engage in complex movements that cross their midline, the neural pathways of the corpus callosum strengthen and form new and more complex branches to more efficiently transfer information. In turn, these more robust neural networks fueled by BDNF allow for better learning and easier retention of new information (Ratey & Hagerman, 2013; Sanaeifar et al., 2024). At a neurological level, movement and active play strengthen our brain's neuroplasticity, which benefits *all* students but is particularly helpful for students who live with toxic stress. Studies show that repeated movements (and increasing BDNF) can strengthen neural connections in *all* brains, improving efficiency and learning speed and induce plasticity, especially in children who've experienced childhood adversity (Pickersgill et al., 2022; Notaras & van den Buuse, 2020).

## Fostering Relationships

Helpful limbic system interventions include small-group activities, brain breaks, and calming activities, all of which can include movement-based activities to help build class cohesion, increase engagement, and foster collaboration.

At the relational level, movement and play utilize the many ways that students can learn and in turn enrich social networks (Tate, 2009; Peterman & Ewing, 2019). Through movement-focused activities, teachers are able to strengthen neural connections and foster strong instructional relationships, all while simultaneously improving students' self-efficacy and self-esteem, which contribute to students' retention of important information, how they make sense of the world around them, and how they will engage with higher-level material (Edwards, 2017; Fesseha & Pyle, 2016; Kumaş & Ergül, 2021). When educators supplement their instruction regularly with PA, making and retaining these positive relationships becomes that much easier. For a child whose brain and body have been negatively affected by toxic stress, movement and play can build trust while regulating an overactive amygdala (which is located in the limbic system) by helping it better discern which situations pose an actual threat.

## Improving Cognitive Function

Physical exercise and movement-based play and learning have also been shown to facilitate information processing and memory functions in the prefrontal cortex (Brattico et al., 2021).

According to the University of Georgia, physically moving for just 20 minutes was associated with improvements in numerous mental capacities, including the long-term retention of new information (Tomporowski, 2003). This discovery is incredibly important for children who've faced adversity and been affected by trauma, because neuron generation and forging new neural connections are disrupted by traumatic experiences. All learning eventually ends up in the cortex, so if students are unable to *regulate* or *relate*, they will not be able to *reason* and, in turn, learn! Traditional methods of instruction like note taking, reading, or lecturing require the cortex to work hard. These methods can be extremely difficult for students with underdeveloped lower regions of the brain and impossible for students who are actively functioning at those lower levels.

Movement can also lead to the release of dopamine and adrenaline and, when coupled with the growth factor BDNF, functions as a natural combatant to cortisol, which creates wear and tear on the brain's stress response system when elevated for long periods of time (Harris, 2019; Place, 2021). BDNF has been shown to directly affect the cortex and improve the *speed* of learning. According to Dr. John Ratey, "German researchers found that people learn vocabulary words 20 percent faster following exercise than they did before exercise and that the rate of learning correlated directly with levels of BDNF" (Ratey & Hagerman, 2013, p. 45). BDNF, in other words, is the physical impetus of learning; its structural properties produce the essential building blocks that allow for the creation of new neural pathways, which allow us to learn new things.

Sanaeifar and colleagues (2024) also found that BDNF levels in the hippocampus and cortex are boosted when neural activity is triggered by specific stimuli in an "enriched environment," which provides learning and sensory engagement, social interaction, and physical exercise. What is interesting in their findings is that a positive feedback loop is created when learners participate in such an environment; being in a place where you are physically active, are engaged in learning, and have opportunities to interact with others creates surplus BDNF and activates the mind to *continue to stay* in such an environment and, in turn, continue to enhance BDNF levels. There is also a negative side to his loop. When BDNF expression is interrupted (e.g., by stress, epigenetic factors, diminished sensory engagement, lack of physical activity, and minimized social interactions), our neural activity decreases so as to *continue to stay* inactive and, in turn, continue to reduce BDNF levels (see Figure 1.3). This is particularly relevant to our students, because our provision of physical activities to them (and making the math classroom an enriched learning environment) can disrupt any potential negative spiraling while simultaneously putting their brains on track to produce BDNF and boost neural activity.

When we incorporate movement into our instruction, we provide an intervention that targets and strengthens *every* level of the brain. In fact, a fully developed brain will benefit from regulatory interventions that target any of the three lower regions of the brain (MacNeill, 2019; see Figure 1.4). In an instructional setting such as a math classroom, that means *all* of our students—not just the ones who are functioning at lower levels of the brain— benefit from regulatory interventions involving physical activity!

The brain science and trauma-informed lenses through which educators contextualize their instructional interactions with their unique student body set the parameters for our movement-based instructional methodology, which we will discuss next.

## The Moving and Learning Teacher Powers

We can enter into a Moving and Learning Mindset when we focus our attention on *how* we facilitate inclusive, science-informed learning strategies in the math classroom. As educators, we possess three particularly influential

## The Feedback Loops of BDNF Production

## Physical Activity Interventions

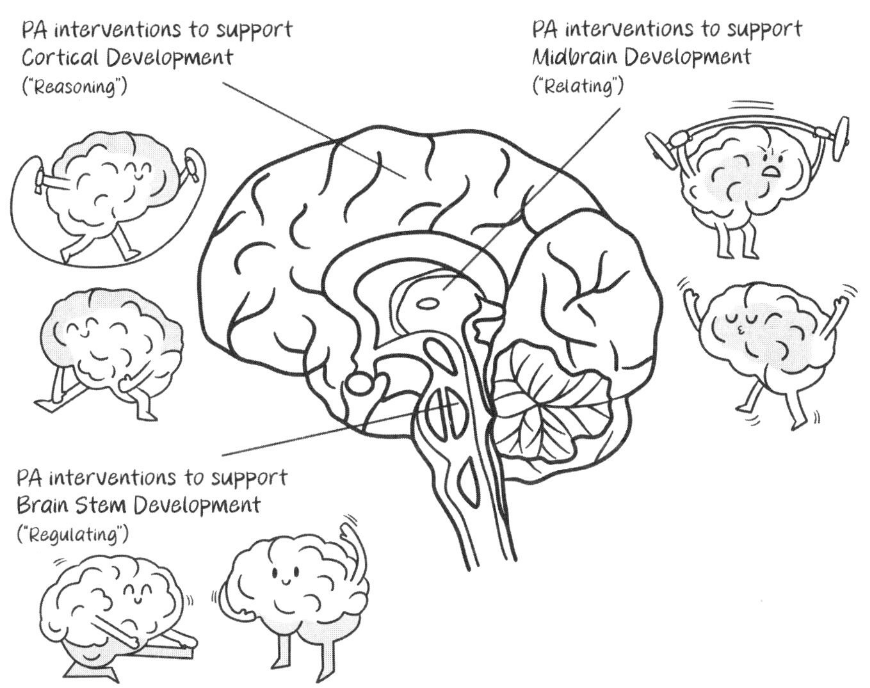

capacities that allow us to nourish classroom communities of lifelong math learners. We call these abilities Teacher Powers:

1. The power of emotional contagion
2. The power of relationship building
3. The power of growth beliefs

Every educator possesses these powers, but not every educator understands their significance or utilizes them consistently to support the development of positive mathematics attitudes. These powers align closely to the pathways of brain development and regulatory interventions discussed in this chapter, but we must note that these powers can and should be embraced at *all levels* of intervention. At a practical level, the Teacher Powers provide a specific framing for more focused interventions that the Triple R approach alone does not. In other words, the Triple R approach answers *what* we are able to do to support all math learners, brain science answers *why* this kind of support is effective and matters, and the Teacher Powers answer *how* we can go about facilitating this effective support.

From our many years of experience working with students, teachers, administrators, and education researchers across the country, we've witnessed firsthand what happens when educators prioritize physical activity in their instruction: teachers are more likely to (1) celebrate and demonstrate positive emotions, (2) develop strong and caring relationships with their students, and (3) foster growth beliefs among all members of their classroom community. In the following three sections, we will describe these instructional powers in detail.

## Emotional Contagion and the Power to Regulate

In theory, educators impart knowledge and skills to their students. In reality, however, teachers hold an influential position of authority as role models to students, particularly those struggling with adversity and who lack dependable role models outside school. Whether or not your students admit it (or are consciously aware of it), they continuously take cues from you, your attitudes, and your behaviors—cues that inform their own attitudes and behaviors in the math classroom. This phenomenon is known as *emotional contagion* and is defined as "students' and teachers' tendency to mimic and synchronize each other's nonverbal behaviors, tone, and ultimately emotional experiences" (Mottet & Beebe, 2000). A review of the literature definitively confirms the reality of emotional contagion in classrooms, and it recognizes strong correlations between teachers' and students' affective experiences (Rodrigo-Ruiz, 2016).

A student's attitude toward a topic like math develops over time through lived experiences with peers, interactions with mentors, instruction, and time spent on task, yet general attitude has been found to be reasonably stable (Bragg, 2007; Hwang & Son, 2021). We have adapted the definition Mazana and colleagues (2019) offer for attitude in our movement-based approach: *math attitude* is the learned tendency of an individual to respond to the study and practice of mathematics, which can either be positive or negative. We can also think of math attitudes as consisting of three components: affect, cognition, and behavior (Mazana et al., 2019; Quane, 2022; Walker et al., 2020). Attitudinal *affect* consists of feelings of self-confidence, anxiety, and enjoyment regarding mathematics, whereas attitudinal *cognition* consists of the perceived usefulness of mathematics, and attitudinal *behavior* consists of students' intrinsic motivation to continue studying math. Under this three-factor model, discussions of emotional engagement with mathematics fall under the *affect* component.

Teachers who embody the Moving and Learning Mindset are in control of their emotions and actively work to foster emotional regulation in their students. Emotional control and regulation is a skillset that is not innate; it is learned over time, and we must practice it if we are able to guarantee that our students will acquire it and, in turn, be able to adapt to change, bounce back from adversity, and respond emotionally to situations in ways that do not limit their potential (Koch et al., 2018).

Emotions like anger and fear have significant potential to lead to what has been termed *math anxiety*. According to Luttenberger and colleagues (2018), math anxiety has been defined as "feelings of apprehension and increased physiological reactivity when individuals deal with math" (p. 312). Approximately 93 percent of adult U.S. Americans indicate that they experience some level of math anxiety (Blazer, 2011), and 17 percent of the U.S. American population suffers from high levels of math anxiety (Ashcraft & Moore, 2009). The 2022 Programme for International Student

Assessment (PISA) found that 38 percent of American students agreed or strongly agreed that they get very nervous when doing mathematics problems, whereas in 2012, the percentage of students who agreed or strongly agreed was 29 percent (Schwartz, 2024). It must be noted, too, that math anxiety is *multidirectional*, meaning that it both affects and is affected by other emotions.

Anxiety levels, self-efficacy, and self-confidence have been linked to students' levels of math achievement later in their educational careers; students with high math anxiety scored significantly lower in achievement than students with low math anxiety (May, 2009). As math anxiety scores increase, achievement scores tend to decrease (Newcombe, 2010). This is in large part due to how math anxiety directly affects students' working memory. Working memory is instrumental in the operational thinking required to carry out fundamental math operations (like multiplication) and also in higher-level mathematical thinking. According to the National Council of Teachers of Mathematics (NCTM), developing fluency requires not only a balance and connection between conceptual understanding and computational proficiency but also guidance from an instructor, which can be enhanced through the gamification of fluency activities (Rutherford, 2015; Allen-Lyall, 2018; Ekowati, 2017; Smith & Smith, 2006). Studies suggest that both students' conceptual understanding of multiplication and ability to compute relies heavily on the efforts of their early educators; when educators make intentional efforts to bolster number sense, to distinguish between counts and quantities, and—interestingly enough—to remain *emotionally positive* toward teaching the subject, math achievement improves dramatically (Smith & Smith, 2006; Watanabe, 2003; Vogt et al., 2018).

## Community Building and the Power to Relate

Through ongoing regulatory support, our power to relate and foster trusting relationships with students is made manifest. To remind students that they're in a safe, welcoming, and active classroom environment that holds high expectations of their effort is the foundational practice of educators who embody the second power of the Moving and Learning Mindset. Just as our own emotions can affect the students' learning, so too can our instructional relationships. For a long time, we've known that personal connections with a caring teacher contribute to a student's improved learning and their development of social skills and more positive attitudes toward school (Curby et al., 2009; Ewing & Taylor, 2009). Yet, only relatively recently have we come to more fully understand the realities of the brain and its relationship to classroom relationship building. Again, in order to gauge where our students are in their thinking, we need to know what is going on under the surface. Once the brain is regulated, we are able to connect with and support our students at a relational level (Lakeside, 2025). How we connect as teachers advocating for movement-based mathematics has a huge effect on how our students participate in class, their connection with the material, and ultimately their success in mathematics later in school and beyond.

There are many ways to go about *investing in connecting* that are in concert with being a positive emotional buffer to students' affective response to whatever happens in the math classroom:

1. Every attempt to build a relationship should always start with setting clear behavioral expectations and boundaries (Eggleston et al., 2021). Students need to know what we—and our classroom community—expect of them so that they have a clear understanding of what is and isn't appropriate behavior.

2. We must convey to students that they are personally responsible for their success through their agency and their choices, all of which have consequences. Awareness of choice is extremely empowering for students, especially those who live in environments of neglect.

3. It is crucial to collaboratively construct a classroom community grounded in active listening, respectful dialogue, and openness to individual expression—the mainstays of cultural competency and inclusion.

4. Providing opportunities for student participation is the last step. This provision should involve incorporating movement-based and multimodal teaching strategies that engage different learning styles if we are to afford access to inclusive participation in math tasks and reap the positive academic and health outcomes from moving our bodies throughout the school day (Lunkenheimer & Kuntz, 2022).

Strong, trusting relationships are the mainstays of student success, and you will continue to see us highlight their significance all throughout this book. Research and practice inform this approach; in our many years of providing professional development to educators across the country, not once have educators whom we've surveyed cited math *content* as a significant contributor to their prior negative experiences with mathematics, if at all. Rather, teachers have primarily (and almost exclusively) identified their previous negative experiences with mathematics as linked closely to a relationship (with a peer, a teacher, and/or a parent). Across our informal surveys and discussions with educators in primary, secondary, and higher education settings, we have also found that relationships are also cited (alongside math content) as the primary contributor to their previous positive math experiences. Stated differently, teachers themselves have identified that relationships are a powerful facet of experiencing mathematics that can yield positive or negative attitudes. If we are to take anything away from this insight, we must shift our attitudes (and the attitudes of our students) away from the belief that math content is in and of itself driving students away. Instead, the relationships we forge with others around mathematics and within the discipline are what truly matter to positive mathematics attitudes and an end to math anxiety.

## Growth-Oriented Beliefs and the Power to Reason

Just as teachers can pass on emotions to their students through their instruction, so too can they pass down particular ways of thinking about said instruction. Research suggests that school staff members' belief that students have the capacity for behavioral change can have a significant effect on student academic outcomes (Donohoo & Katz, 2017). The reasoning skills necessary to achieve academic success require, again, that students are regulated and able to lean on their relationship with you and their peers. Awareness of *what* kinds of beliefs about math reasoning our students hold, *how* our students go about rationalizing math problems, and *how* those beliefs affect others are a critical first step in making sure that all students feel supported and able to learn. Teachers with a Moving and Learning Mindset hold and promote beliefs that welcome growth, empower full participation, and celebrate inclusion in their facilitation of the math classroom.

When we ourselves embrace a growth mindset, we can expect our students to follow suit via our powers of emotional contagion and trust. Every student has the potential to grow, and our powers in concert with one another allow us to pass this belief on to them in ways that have lasting effects.

We will now move on to discuss our movement-based framework. But we must highlight again that the three powers provide a way to conceptualize *how* we as educators are able to support our students with Triple R interventions. The following framework provides a more concrete bridge linking research and practice around how physical activity (and movement-based learning more generally) *streamlines* these processes. In other words, prioritizing movement in our instructional beliefs and in our powers boosts students' math outcomes and improves math attitudes at a striking rate compared to traditional and sedentary instructional approaches.

## The Five Catalysts of Movement-Based Instruction

It's one thing to have power in a classroom but another thing entirely to use it effectively and fairly. We believe that physical activity and math instruction should not be separate entities. Rather, math and physical activity can coexist in a classroom setting and *should* coexist so every student can reap their holistic benefits, from enriched and engaging math experiences to healthy lifestyles and learning habits (Colella et al., 2019).

Our movement-based framework bridges the instructional divide between mathematics and physical education pedagogies and is inspired by a rich body of scholarship on play-based learning, elementary education, and brain science. Structurally speaking, we have adapted the theoretical framework of van Oers and Duijkers (2013) to scaffold our discussion of movement-based learning in the math classroom. According to van Oers and Duijkers, five impulses guide the productive play of students during the school day. These impulses, when embraced and nourished by educators during moments of play, help orient, deepen, broaden, build upon, and reinforce student learning. In other words, these impulses make guided play a worthwhile method of teaching and learning in a classroom setting.

It must be noted first that van Oers and Duijkers do not explicitly reference physical activity or movement in their discussion of guided play or their five impulses. Guided play (used synonymously with *exploration* for older students) fits under the umbrella of *pedagogical play*, which is the intentional use of play to improve learning outcomes (Edwards, 2017). Play in this context allows for illustration, exploration, demonstration, and meaning making in a variety of learning contexts. Playful environments encourage children to explore, learn, and feel comfortable enough to make mistakes. Teachers who play with their students foster emotional contagion to spread positive energy, which in turn directly supports and improves students' moods and creates a welcoming environment of trust, excitement, and growth. Children are incredibly perceptive, so fostering growth beliefs and taking steps to build strong connections inside and outside the classroom help students calm their own math anxieties and make the learning process more enjoyable.

Teacher-led play, therefore, benefits the academic growth of students and should be incorporated within early math curricula (Ginsburg, 2006; Fesseha & Pyle, 2016). However, if play is to directly benefit student learning in their math classroom, math content needs to be part of the game mechanics, the content needs to be essential for further learning, and the game needs to fit students' individual needs (Vogt et al., 2018). Traditionally speaking, PA is usually implied, but our approach prioritizes PA in math instruction. Such an approach positions movement as the framework upon which we can hang our math instruction; every moment of instruction can and should be viewed as an opportunity for students to get up out of their seats and move their bodies.

We have adapted van Oers and Duijkers's five impulses (which we call *catalysts* in how they spur particular actions among students in a classroom setting) to fit a broader definition of guided play that pertains to K–8 students as a necessary component to all classroom activity. We ask that you consider these catalysts (and our detailed discussion of them in the following chapters) as the rationale behind why we all should be moving more during school time. Practically speaking, we ask that you consider these catalysts (see Figure 1.5) as an actionable guide when you design your own movement-based math lessons. Here we will introduce these catalysts, but in the following chapters we will delve into each one's practical significance and provide specific movement-based activities that you can immediately bring into the classroom to support student engagement.

FIGURE 1.5

**The Five Catalysts of Movement-Based Instruction**

| **Engagement** | Movement stimulates student engagement during mathematical tasks by *motivating* participation in the learning process, strengthening focus, and orienting attention and (positive) attitudes toward the task at hand. |
|---|---|
| **Scaffolding** | Movement bolsters student learning when coupled with math *foundations* practice (fact fluency and concepts) and when presented collaboratively and creatively. |
| **Expansion** | Movement expands student learning in how it opens students' minds (and brains) up to *change*, how it encourages exploring and connecting ideas and concepts together, and how it brings abstract concepts into the real world. |
| **Enrichment** | Movement enriches student learning in how it minimizes math anxiety, cultivates environments of trust, and primes the development of life-long learning mindsets. |
| **Review** | Movement stimulates *reflection* and facilitates review in how it minimizes anxiety around mistake making, spurs questioning and exploration, and makes proofing (as a method of mathematical communication and language building) accessible and enjoyable. |

Movement engages and expands students' learning during math lessons when teachers give them the opportunity to share experiences and express their individualized perspectives. Movement-based activities help foster a space where opportunities to connect stories and experiences with math content are plentiful, where perspective is gained and common ground is easy to find, and where collaboration, camaraderie, and cultural competency fuel discussion and practice. You will see that students' expressed individuality and engagement naturally (and confidently) emerge during physical activities.

Movement scaffolds and enriches students' learning when teachers center collaboration and frame mathematical problem solving in ways that relate to everyone and that home in on strengths rather than deficits. Movement-based math activities help to position problem solving and collaboration as critical drivers for student growth both mathematically and socially. Students engaged in collaborative, movement-based math learn how to manage their emotions and build trust as they transition between leadership and follower roles and, in turn, adapt their choices and decisions based on the math problems at hand.

Movement also supports the review process in the math classroom in how it empowers self-reflection, during which students take initiative in correcting their own mistakes and confidently offer explanations for their mathematical reasoning. Movement-based math activities help build critical thinking and empathy skills as students actively work with one another to solve problems and make discoveries with a shared arsenal of multimodal learning strategies. In a math class setting, the most observable indicators of these activities' success during and after their implementation include student excitement, collective vocalizations of joy and motivation to keep practicing, and more confident (and accurate) responses to activity-related math questions. This is what we call the Active Math Effect (see Figure 1.6). We should state here that these catalysts and your response to their emergence are an anticipatory effort; each catalyst and its related outcomes manifest and reinforce one another in no particular order or at any one particular time when students are participating in physically active mathematics. For this reason, we urge that you anticipate, celebrate, and provide space for each catalyst as they arise during active instruction.

## Wrapping Up

Let's return to Sarah's story:

> Looking back now, especially with what we know from brain research, I understand why movement worked so well. Fluency creates neural pathways, and those pathways are strengthened through repetition. That combination of movement and repetition gave me something I hadn't had before: math confidence.
>
> Now, I'll be honest—my math journey didn't stay movement-based after the mats were introduced. I wish it had. Once the movement stopped, the struggle started to creep back in. But then came 6th grade. Another breakthrough. My teacher introduced the

Cartesian coordinate system, and instead of just drawing it on the board, she mapped it out on the floor. We used our own bodies to graph points, literally standing on the $x$- and $y$-axes. We walked out lines, visualized slopes, and suddenly—it clicked. I saw math from a whole new angle that day (pun intended), and I aced that test.

Getting from there to where I am now—an engineering student in Germany—hasn't been easy. I've fought off feelings of mathematical inadequacy more times than I can count. But there's still a part of me that remembers what it felt like to get it. And every time I remember that feeling, it reminds me that I can get it again.

So here I am now—someone who once cried into her math boxes and now solves calculus problems in German. What changed? It wasn't just that I got smarter. It was that someone finally taught me in a way that my brain could absorb information. Movement, repetition, visual learning—those tools gave me access to something I thought I wasn't meant for. And if it could work for me, it can work for so many others.

The truth is that kids don't need to be labeled "bad at math." Nor do they need to be labeled "good at math." We need to do away with the good/bad labeling dichotomy. Kids need to be taught differently—with energy, with flexibility, with an asset-based mindset, with movement. Because, when kids get the chance to feel math—to jump, shout, laugh, and learn—the possibilities aren't just academic. They're life changing.

As educators, we have the remarkable capacity to influence the learning and life trajectories of those whom we teach. Our informed, curious, supportive, and playful approaches to math instruction and the steps we take to foreground movement in our math activities—like BDNF itself—*stimulates* and *strengthens* the connections necessary to not only succeed in mathematics but also foster a positive mathematics identity in our students. In the case of Sarah, her trajectory as a math learner, STEM advocate, and engineer-in-the-making was solidified—empowered, really—by including physical activity opportunities in the mathematics classroom. If her teachers had not employed this type of instructional approach, Sarah may very well have fallen out of love with STEM.

The Moving and Learning Mindset—a mindset grounded in trauma-informed instruction and supported by brain science—is the lens through which we approach every instructional instance. It is also the soapbox upon which we will unflinchingly advocate for the need for movement-based mathematics in today's educational landscape of rigid standards, incessant stress, and status quo.

In the remaining chapters, we will continue to provide evidence for why movement matters in the math classroom as well as supplement these perspectives with specific movement-based activities that we feel have significant value for K–8 math classrooms. We hope that this approach will provide you with clarity around the "why" behind what we do and actionable steps around how we as a community of moving and learning educators can activate math education for all, simply by starting with our own classroom.

With that said, let's get moving!

FIGURE 1.6
**The Active Math Effect**

# Movement *Engages* Math Learners

Picture your students returning from lunch. Their math block is scheduled immediately after this period. They have just eaten and socialized and are perhaps groggy at the thought of spending a few more hours in school before they can go home. Others, however, might be loathing their inevitable return to home and are spending their time socializing with friends while they can. Regardless, talking doesn't cease as your students filter into the classroom, with some dragging their feet into their seats and others milling around. Everyone is moving slowly—*thinking* slowly. Collective sighs are audible as the clock on the wall ticks closer to the start of class. What now?

Every teacher has struggled with this common experience: the glazed-over eyes of students who are not engaged with what rests before them. What many of us educators do initially is attempt to lift everyone's spirits with humor, inspirational words, or some activity to boost focus. More often than not, this activity attempts to foster discussion, which in turn amplifies engagement. Yet, such an activity by itself fails to get at the *core* of disengagement—the *physiological* disengagement of students' brains from sitting and eating during lunchtime and from out-of-school concerns or worries.

The purpose of this chapter is to kick off what will become the underlying thread of the following five chapters—namely, how teachers can couple their powers with movement-based teaching strategies to boost students' mathematics fluency and attitudes. For this particular chapter, we will begin with the first capacity of movement-based instruction: *engagement*. As you will see, physical activity increases students' engagement with academic content through its impact on the brain and on motivation.

Let's again start with a story to situate our discussion within the very real context of students' demands for *something better*. I had the distinct pleasure of working with a student named Jerry during my time in Florida. Jerry is a kind, compassionate, and spirited 3rd grader. Jerry also functions with a high dosage of childhood adversity. The occasional over-the-top outburst of anger was expected of him from time to time by peers and instructors, but when I arrived at his school, his teachers shared that they were becoming more and more frequent. I was informed that Jerry spent his 3rd grade year "unfocused" and "in hiding," striving to remain unnoticed while in class. In those relatively rare moments when he was focused, his teachers would notice him peeking out from his hands as he tried his best to cover the page from others' curious eyes.

Jerry attended a Title I school and studied alongside peers who, much like him, also lived in adversity, and the classes' test scores and collective behaviors were indicative of their struggles—their collective demand for *regulation*. Just before state examinations, Jerry's entire class began a two-week intensive movement-based learning intervention, which I had the pleasure of leading. The intervention entailed me working with the entire class of 3rd graders for 90 minutes in the morning as a part of their regular math block and 45 minutes in the afternoon. The morning session included pretesting, an introduction to a new multiple and another math concept, physical activity involving cross-body movements and jumping on floor mats, and opportunities for group work. The afternoon session followed up on activities from the morning session, offered additional practice time, and concluded with a post-test.

On the first day of the intervention, Jerry found that his customary approach of hiding was more difficult than usual; the entire class was expected to stand and jump on a huge 100 number grid that was positioned in the middle of the classroom. When I asked the students to locate an odd number, all the students had to identify an odd number and move their bodies to physically stand on it. Jerry's classmates helped him locate the odd number 31, which was adjacent to his friend and as far away from me as was possible. When I asked the class to "add one" to their odd number, a class discussion ensued. Students talked among themselves where they should move their bodies. At first, Jerry added 10 and moved to 41, but after listening to the class discussion, he corrected himself and moved to 32. Although Jerry did not smile or raise his hand to give an answer, I did notice that he was focused on the task at hand.

The second day we introduced multiplication by fours. Jerry scored a 2 out of 30 on the pretest in the morning. After verbal pretests were given, the students stood in a circle. We asked the entire class, "Let me hear you skip-count by 4s." A few students could skip-count to only about 16. Afterward, we engaged the students in rigorous, intentional physical exercise that included additional jumping, cross-body movements, and whisper-loud counting by 4s. Jerry stood in a corner of the room, as far from me as possible, but participated in the movements. Alongside his peers, he was entirely engaged. My years of experience as a professional interventionist and movement specialist prepared me for this moment, but I would be lying to myself if I said that this type of behavioral change—this growth—no longer affected me. The cross-body component of the math movement warmed up the students' brain and prepared them to absorb new information. I could see this happening to Jerry. In the afternoon, he solved all 30 questions correctly on the post test.

I want to pause the story here, as it goes without saying—and is also quite obvious to *anyone* who's ever taught students—that nobody truly learns unless they're engaged in some way with the content. Regarding mathematics, the content has historically been viewed as disengaging and more "objective" compared to other "more real-world" subjects like science, language arts, and social studies, meaning that the answers to questions and *how* those answers are arrived at is considered a black-and-white phenomenon with little to no room for discussions of the gray. We can see Jerry's unfocused, disengaged behavior in the classroom as an embodiment of commonplace negative attitudes toward mathematics. His shyness was particularly evident, as the traditional learning environment allowed him to escape the notice of his peers. What had changed in the movement-based learning intervention was a new learning environment in which he could build his confidence and proficiency while being totally and continually *engaged*—an environment that would quickly come to afford continuous opportunities to receive emotional support, build strong instructional relationships with peers and the instructor, and strengthen positive, motivated math attitudes through every activity we engaged in together. We will return to this story later.

## Emotional Motivation in the Math Classroom

Demir-Lira and colleagues (2020) analyzed brain scans of students completing multiplication tasks and found that *attitudes* toward math can predict math achievement. More specifically, those with positive attitudes were associated with exerting more effort on math tasks and, in turn, achieving higher math scores. This was due to the increased engagement of the learning memory systems of the brain. However, it's not just students' attitudes that we should be aware of. We should also be mindful of parents' math attitudes and teachers' math attitudes, both of which are significant contributors to the math attitudes and identities that students develop over time when engaging with math content (Bragg, 2007; Mazana et al., 2019; Peterman & Ewing, 2019; Hwang & Son, 2021). Just like our students' attitudes, our attitudes toward math comprise three dimensions: enjoyment, self-confidence, and value, all of which have the potential to greatly influence our motivation to engage with mathematics (Linder et al., 2015).

Math anxiety—which is often defined as any feeling of apprehension or fear toward math-related activities—appears to be more closely linked to motivation and general engagement than the other two dimensions of math attitudes due to how math anxiety contributes to total avoidance of math-related tasks (Li et al., 2021). Math anxiety has both cognitive and affective components, which include worry, nervousness, tenseness, and dread, all of which can erode student engagement with mathematics. The correlation between math anxiety and decreased motivation, in fact, is so strong that some researchers believe that this relationship is potentially *universal*, meaning that the impact of math anxiety on motivation is neither culturally nor developmentally situated. In other words, math anxiety's effect on student motivation could exist and extend across all cultural contexts and developmental stages (Li et al., 2021).

It must be said that the link between emotions and learning is complex and susceptible to numerous internal and external variables. This means that positive emotions may not always facilitate better learning, and negative emotions may not always lead to poorer learning. For example, imagine being so excited to hang out with your friends after school that math class and the day's lesson become an afterthought. Instead, better learning is facilitated through 1) an intrinsic desire to learn and 2) an interest in or passion for the material itself. Fortunately, both of these things can be linked to a positive emotional experience. The feeling of enjoyment is positively correlated with higher intrinsic motivation to learn, and it has been found to correlate with academic success on subsequent learning measures (Froiland & Oros, 2014). Experts thus recommend that schools should offer interventions—including physical activity—that increase enjoyment and, in turn, intrinsic motivation to enhance not only positive attitudes toward mathematics but also motivation to continue practicing math concepts. Our activity Zero Heroes (Appendix A.1) provides an opportunity for students to engage playfully and collaboratively with positive and negative numbers while building confidence around adding and subtracting, thus supporting the positive development of math attitudes.

Movement and play in the classroom have been associated with prevalent feelings of positive emotion, in turn, resulting in neural, emotional, and sociocognitive benefits. In the simplest terms, *moving is enjoyable*, and when one has fun, one experiences positive emotion! Children who are playing display more positive affect than children not playing, which doesn't come as a surprise when observing them. In one study, even adults described "active leisure" (otherwise known as play) as one of the things they kept pursuing in order to experience happiness (Moore & Russ, 2008). In another study related to movement-based reading strategies, 83 percent of kindergarten and 1st grade students preferred story time that incorporated physical movement to story time that required them to sit quietly. In the interviews after the intervention, students recalled significant feelings of positive attitudes and enjoyment toward active storytelling time versus inactive story time (Hammett, 2009).

Increased physical activity is beneficial to the health and development of all of us—young and old—and our persistence in physical activity is closely linked to important motivation constructs—namely competence, autonomy, and positive affect (Whitehead, 1993). In other words, if we can get our students to develop a habit of physical activity, we can set the foundation for hefty motivational attitudes.

How do we get our students to develop this habit? We need to first make sure that the activities they're doing are *fun*. According to Whitehead (1993), "fun" as it relates to physical activity is the product of a combination of three factors: skill improvement opportunities, personal accomplishment, and excitement. If students have opportunities to increase their motor skills and demonstrate movement patterns, if they have a chance to feel accomplishment, and if the activity that they're engaging in is enjoyable, they will have fun being physically active. Our Double Dutch Duos activity (Appendix A.2) comes from our training manual for physical educators and is aligned closely with state PE standards aimed to strengthen students' fine motor skills and coordination. Skill improvement is the name of the game here, and we've found high levels of engagement (via excitement) from students across grade levels who participate in this activity collaboratively.

We must also note that students' own *perceptions* of their math abilities related to the task have an effect on their motivation. If a student perceives themself as not competent, that student could have less motivation to continue practicing than another student who feels more competent in their skills. Motivation is highly situational, which makes it difficult as a teacher to make sure that *all* of our students are motivated at all times. Researchers, however, have identified cooperative physical activities that allow students some autonomy in their learning—combined with teachers who themselves have a positive outlook on mathematics and PA—to be effective in keeping students motivated in the task at hand (Whitehead, 1993; Meyer et al., 2021).

Of course, educators should not be expected to feign their emotions in front of their students. Not only would this be difficult to achieve and exhibit authentically, but our students know when we're not being genuine. Moreover, approaching or labeling certain emotions as "negative" or "unproductive" can be quite detrimental to students' psyches. Rather than hiding certain emotions like anger or sadness, experts suggest that the most appropriate strategy for educators is to practice *emotional regulation*, or the conscious control of emotions with the objective of fomenting emotional and intellectual growth (Rolston & Lloyd-Richardson, n.d.). Any emotion that is exhibited in class ought to be approached as a potential learning experience. As educators, we should work to instill emotional regulation in our students by approaching lessons confidently, optimistically, and with a lifelong learner mindset. When negative emotions arise or anxiety is expressed, those feelings ought to be approached as *opportunities* to explore and contextualize in order to maximize the growth of not just individual students but also the active learning community we aim to foster.

Positive emotions—or positive *affect*—greatly influence student motivation toward engagement with any learning task. This motivation is affected by a variety of factors, but *our own* positivity toward the subject at hand and consistently offering active math practice opportunities can help set our students up for success. Through increased physical activity, students will build their confidence while simultaneously boosting their math competence. Yet, the instructional relationship that you build with your students, which we will discuss further in this chapter, is more impactful on their academic outcomes than simply you being a conduit for positivity. The Mathematicians from Outer Space activity (Appendix A.3) offers a stellar opportunity for you to strengthen the instructional relationships within your classroom community and build communicative trust. The act of demonstrating math patterns *without speaking* also centers students' emotions and communicative creativity with a physical twist.

## The Focusing Potential of Strong Instructional Relationships

A trusting, personal relationship between teachers and students is indeed a powerful tool for focused engagement and, in turn, enhanced learning. From a motivational standpoint, a strong and caring relationship is closely tied to *beliefs*—that is, the beliefs of students and teachers that mathematics is positive and worth learning. In fact, researchers have found that there is a positive correlation between instructional technologies and elementary student motivation, which is quite dependent on their teacher's own beliefs about the instructional technology and the support they provide in the classroom (Linder et al., 2015; also check out Causton & Macleod's [2020] quick reference guide on building supportive classrooms). Teachers' beliefs are powerful, as they directly affect their students' learning in a variety of ways. From mastery to performance goals, from problem-solving strategies to providing a sense of independence and self-direction, teacher beliefs offer structure to learning environments that encourage substantive discourse.

Moreover, instructors who encourage their students to persist in mathematics 1) influence their students' perception of their teacher's teaching skills, 2) create positive atmosphere/environments within the math classroom, and 3) set the stage for engaging interpersonal relationships (Li et al., 2021), all of which create positive beliefs about mathematics more generally. Researchers Jensen and Sjaastad (2013) found that the instructors *themselves* were a strong influence on students' continued attendance in out-of-school STEM programs. Our Fantastic High-Fivers activity (Appendix A.4) supports students' development of positive attitudes toward mathematics through the intentional sharing and co-constructing of positive math beliefs.

Having positive beliefs about one's own math competence isn't just a morale boost for students; it has also been found to have positive longitudinal effects on math achievement (Pinxten et al., 2013). Positive emotions, such as enjoyment experienced by students and their teachers, help to mediate the processes that lead to perceptions of greater competency. One's perception about their own abilities has a stronger relationship with mathematics anxiety compared to actual math abilities (Li et al., 2021), meaning that what one thinks about their own competence matters more than their actual competency in terms of how math anxiety forms. With that said, in order to minimize math anxiety, all we need to do is focus on getting our students to *think* that they're competent and confident mathematicians—their actual success will quickly follow. Yet, convincing students that competency comes through practice and that math is *worth practicing* (i.e., building their confidence) becomes much easier to accomplish when they trust us—that is, when there's a strong relationship to lean on as they grow and challenge themselves. According to Li and colleagues (2021), through our strong instructional relationships we can support our students' perceived math competence by

- Providing learning tasks that are of moderate difficulty.
- Organizing math lessons that possess small goals.
- Encouraging students to put effort into their work and persist in solving problems.

Adding physical activity opportunities only strengthens the outcomes of these instructional strategies. The classroom study in which we got to work with Jerry in Sarasota, Florida, found that, after only 10 days of movement-based instruction, 3rd grade students saw on average an improvement of 89 percent in their multiplication test scores. Additionally, the performance gap between the highest- and lowest-achieving students in the class decreased from 53 percent to just 10 percent after 10 days of instruction (Math & Movement, 2024).

In practice, collaborative lessons or lessons that involve groups of students working together help boost individual student effort and perseverance. Additionally, when we break our lessons up into smaller tasks that students accomplish and can build off, we help our students develop a sense of self-confidence. The activities Who Wants to Be a 100 Millionaire? (Appendix A.5) and Ifs and Thens (Appendix A.6) aim to do just that—afford students an opportunity to work together and build from one another's mathematical discoveries and interpretations.

Negative attitudes are debilitating for student engagement and learning, which is doubly unfortunate because such attitudes are relatively common for children in the United States (Beilock & Willingham, 2014). Why negative attitudes are present in our student populations is not a question with a simple or straightforward answer. Poor instruction, the fear of failure, influence from parents and other teachers, historically low mathematical achievement, a general lack of enjoyment, and low confidence all contribute to this mindset (Marsh & Hau, 2004; Goodykoontz, 2008; Liew et al., 2014). The potentially *lifelong* effects of these negative attitudes are worthy of close concern, because researchers have found that, even though these negative attitudes and efficacy beliefs around mathematics often manifest in primary school, they have the potential to persist well into adulthood if not confronted and buffered by strong, trusting relationships with the math content, with peers, and with us (Ajzen, 1985; Beilock & Willingham, 2014; Körük, 2017).

# Orienting Effortful Math Attitudes

Out of all professions, teachers win the gold for having the one job that is as difficult as it is rewarding—rewarding not just personally but *societally*. Teachers are role models for our youth, and it is through teachers that our children learn to behave, socialize, play, and think in highly social settings both inside and outside the classroom. To achieve the lifelong learning goals that we hope to instill in our students requires fostering positive attitudes toward learning more generally. As we have discussed, positive attitudes yield greater motivation. How, then, can we orient our students' attitudes toward positivity in the math classroom?

Recent studies have come to the conclusion that in order for students to solve multiplication problems and foster the strategies to do so efficiently, teachers need to 1) provide them with a wide range of multiplication problems that test students' appropriate *use* of multiplication, 2) encourage students to trust their intuition and thought processes, and 3) flexibly provide a variety of multiplication representations (Watanabe, 2003; Vogt et al., 2018). In addition to intentionally supporting students' various learning styles, educators can reach more students and meet their different motivational needs when they themselves approach the teaching of multiplication differently and with a positive attitude (Mazana et al., 2019; Hwang & Son, 2021). Our Where's the Overlap? activity (Appendix A.7) builds students' confidence with multiplication through the hands-on manipulation of multiples (and classmates!) within a large Venn diagram.

Recent research findings can give us a more robust understanding of what we can do in the classroom to support students' motivation and efforts to acquire a positive math attitude. According to Linder and colleagues (2015), highly motivated students have been found to share common experiences with math instruction—namely, opportunities for self-direction, opportunities for peer collaboration, opportunities to see a clear link between math topics and future application, and positive interpersonal interactions with teachers. This tells us that we are able to set our students up to be more motivated in the math classroom by providing them the freedom to direct their own learning and the chance to work in groups. Additionally, if we can invest time in explicitly connecting what they're learning in class with what they can expect to encounter in the future—in addition to developing trusting relationships with individual students—we can help them see the value of mathematics beyond just problem solving. Researchers Li and colleagues (2021) identified four activity strategies that trigger and help maintain the math motivation of students, which align closely to the discoveries of Linder and colleagues (2015):

- Math activities must possess some *novelty.*
- Math activities must be perceived as *meaningful.*
- Math activities must be *hands-on* in nature.
- Math activities must involve *group work.*

Activities with these qualities allow students to explore and connect their mathematical knowledge to real-world situations in a distinctly social setting. Within this collaborative, meaningful environment, students come to see the real-world application of math and minimize their math-related anxieties. But what about physical activity? Of the two types of active play discussed in the introduction of this book, *pedagogical play,* which involves active participation on the part of the teacher, is the most common type of play used within a school setting and helps create a "richer world for students to experience" (Fesseha & Pyle, 2016; Edwards, 2017). Through the constant communication that play entails, the participating adult can give their children access to new cultural experiences that go ahead of the child's actual level of development (van Oers & Duijkers, 2013). Students of all ages benefit from our active involvement in the activities that we present to them in the classroom. Not only does our involvement inform our students that *we care* about the content (i.e., enjoy the activity), but it also creates a bridge of shared learning between us and our students. Deeper trust can form if *everyone* is held accountable for their individual and collective efforts to solve the problem at hand. This type of environment—in addition to the types of activities that we offer our class—can be extremely motivating for students to continue engaging in math tasks. Our Groovy Groupings activity (Appendix A.8) is a tried-and-true pedagogical play strategy to engage learners, strengthen communication and socialization skills, as well as engage educators in the creative play of their students.

Physical activity (PA) *itself* can be a source of intrinsic motivation for students that can influence their motivation for other, more academic subjects. Researchers have found that those who tend to be more absorbed in doing PA are those with greater intrinsic motivation (Isoard-Gautheur et al., 2019), and those with greater intrinsic motivation toward PA tend to experience less of the stress–burnout relationship of day-to-day non-PA activities. For adults, Isoard-Gautheur and colleagues (2019) found that physical activities can support one's mental health if the recovery experience is positive; their enjoyment of the physical activity nourished their mental health and mitigated their feelings of job burnout.

Increased PA leads to increased satisfaction in work and in life, as well as increased feelings of autonomy. In order to help increase the intrinsic motivation for PA to experience these outcomes, researchers Meyer and colleagues (2021) recommend the following supplements to physical activities:

- The promotion of process goals
- The provision of activity choice
- The provision of activity rationales
- An explanation of *why* a specific activity was selected

In the classroom, these supplements could take the form of us, as instructors, setting small PA goals for individual students as they participate in different active math activities, or we could give students a choice of what active math activity they would like to practice (as it relates to the context we're covering). We can boost students' motivation to continue engaging in PA (and in math learning) by also explaining to students (or allowing them to reflect on) *why* the chosen activity is important or matters to the subject at hand. Explanation and discussion about why we're doing what we're doing are beneficial to students of all ages and open up the opportunity for deeper reflection and extended investigations (this will be discussed further in Chapter 6). As a preview to our discussion and activities around engaging students in reflection and questioning, our Strategize, Gesture-ize! activity (Appendix A.9) helps students build those reflective, inquisitive habits around math content through gesturing and collaborative problem solving.

Orienting student effort could be considered a domain of classroom management. Many teachers have cited classroom management as a chief reason behind their hesitancy to engage their students in physical activities in the classroom. The saying usually goes "I worry that getting students up and moving around will interfere with effective classroom management practices." It is either implied or stated outright that their fear of movement comes from the idea of getting disruptive or misbehaving students out of their seats. If you want to actually support these students and increase their on-task classroom behaviors, you should be getting them moving *as much as possible*! According to Moon and colleagues (2022), "there is no reason to believe that MI [movement integration] in any way interferes with good classroom management practices in elementary general education classrooms" (p. 128). The researchers go one step further in their conclusions, stating that movement integration, effective instructional management, and proactive management strategies are actually *mutually supportive and reinforcing*. PA's positive impact on classroom behavior/cognition is well understood in how it supports

- Increased on-task behavior (attentiveness, alertness, focus) through moderate arousal.
- Increased attention span (serotonin, dopamine, norepinephrine, BDNF).
- Attenuated hyperactivity (boosted inhibitory control).

Teachers consistently report positive pupil outcomes and responses relative to classroom-based PA, including enhanced focus following activities, active engagement with classroom content, expressions of excitement and enjoyment, and transference of activities to contexts outside the classroom (Stylianou et al., 2016). A 2016 study conducted by Burns and colleagues found that on-task classroom behavior *significantly improved* during a movement-based intervention at both 6-week and 12-week time points. Nearly 1,500 students (ages 5–12) across 77 Title I classrooms participated in this study. What is particularly noteworthy about this movement-based intervention was how *little* time was allocated to PA to see such significant gains in students' on-task behavior; teachers were only expected to provide 10-minute activity breaks to their students only two to three times per day!

When supporting the positive attitudinal development of their students, teachers should have interdisciplinary knowledge of how to support their students physically, physiologically, and socially. Within trauma-informed education, this knowledge takes root in brain science, neurobiology, and mental health studies (Thomas et al., 2019). Every student experiences stress, and some stressors are more toxic than others. Sometimes this stress is invisible, and other times it is unmistakable through students' physicality or behaviors. We should be aware of the signs of stress and make the effort to help students *regulate* their brains by orienting their engagement via physical activities so that learning is possible. Physical movement is a powerful intervention for students who are functioning at the brain stem and midbrain levels. Stretching, swinging, yoga, rhythmic drumming and clapping, and even martial arts are wonderful ways to quickly regulate the brain stem, while walking, running, cross-body movements, dance, and most aerobic exercises greatly help to regulate the midbrain and, in turn, afford our students the ability to foster trusting relationships with others within our active classroom communities.

## Wrapping Up

Let's continue Jerry's story. During the 10-day movement-based intervention, we had a skip-counting floor mat to create a physical space where students could use their own bodies as manipulatives to practice skip-counting by 4s. Students lined up on both sides of the mat and chanted the multiples of 4 while one student in the class jumped on the mat. I remember Jerry positioning himself at the end of the line, farthest away from the starting point. When it was his turn to jump on the mat, he enthusiastically participated. As someone who has witnessed this time and time again, I was not surprised, but his teachers sure were. He was engaged not only while he hopped but also while his classmates took turns hopping. As the lesson progressed, Jerry continued to count and clap the multiple as he looked at the pictures on the mat. When it was Jerry's turn to jump on the mat, he followed the directions, jumped in rhythm, and appeared to be comfortable with the activity. Then came the smile.

This was the first time I saw Jerry smile, and I could also see the smiles of his instructors as he continued practicing. Our next task was to practice writing our answers down in the book. Jerry was quick to hold up his workbook and count in groups to answer the multiplication questions. I noticed that a few girls were goofy and tried to engage him by bumping him with their legs, but he only smiled and continued to focus on his work. He brought the book to me for correction. I found a few answers that needed fixing, but my corrections did not faze him in the slightest emotionally; with observable determination, he returned to his table to work and remained close enough to the mat so that he could use it as a tool. For 11 minutes he remained engaged with his work. He brought his book to another adult and requested corrections. She reviewed his work and asked that he prove his answers by hopping on the floor mat. After he hopped, he sat back down at his table, and one of his classmates sat next to him, sharing his chair. She attempted to get his attention, but still he continued to focus on his work.

After 25 full minutes of solid, attentive work, he brought his book to his teacher. After looking at all the problems on the page, his teacher handed the book back to him and said with a smile, "Nice job! Look at you!" Jerry's body language shifted. He turned back toward his desk with immense pride on his face in the form of a smile. He fist-pumped the air triumphantly, saying out loud, "Yessssss!" twice as he sat down. During the afternoon session, Jerry continued to practice his multiples of 4. In total, Jerry practiced for 90 minutes in the morning and 45 minutes in the afternoon. At the end of the afternoon session, the entire class was post-tested. Jerry scored 30 correct out of 30.

So, how did Jerry move from a 2 out of 30 on the pretest to 30 out of 30 on the post-test? Based on our observations and the copious evidence detailing the relationship between attitudes, math achievement, physical activity, and emotional regulation, three things set him up to ace the test:

1. Jerry was *engaged*, which encouraged him to practice his math. Repetition is key for infusing information into memory, but the traditional approach to the repetition of math facts is often boring for students and often inaccessible to students with different learning preferences. This is especially true for students who have faced adversity.

2. Jerry's teacher *believed* in him and was willing to vocalize his support and reinforce to Jerry that he could learn. When Jerry impressed his teacher, his enthusiasm overflowed.

3. Jerry's mindset *shifted* from "I need to hide. I don't want anyone to know that I don't know the answer" to "I can learn math. I am good at learning, and I am a successful learner."

Jerry felt genuine pride in himself and recognized that one can be successful and actually feel good when they put in the effort. If we can *engage* our students at the outset, then their math mindset becomes primed for positivity and motivated to practice. And when we start the day regulated and engaged, the rest of our time together becomes not only more productive but also more fun. In summary, our abilities to motivate student learning have the potential to make an incredible impact on student learning. Movement-based learning activities assist with this motivational force by increasing the enjoyment and self-confidence felt by students who move their bodies.

# Movement *Scaffolds* Mathematics Success

Now we have our students' attention. Physical activity has helped to motivate and orient our students toward what they *need* to know. Next, we need to continue the momentum of learning and pave the way for mathematics fluency; nothing is worse than squandering students' direct attention. You might have already guessed, but PA can drive the momentum forward and structure the learning to come. Movement's capacity to *support* student learning—as we have termed it—functions as a *scaffold* and thus allows the continuous building of math knowledge to continue safely and efficiently, by grounding students' understanding of abstract concepts (Williams et al., 2009; Slepian & Ambady, 2012).

The purpose of this chapter is to share how you can frame your math instruction with movement-based teaching strategies. You can compare adding movement to the curriculum to using *scaffolding* to build a house. Movement as scaffolding provides students with a dependable framework from which they can expand their conceptual foundations and enrich their learning using their own engaged voice. Math concepts build on one another constantly from elementary school to college, but we also assess student math achievement using cumulative state standards. The standards that we set for our students are rather rigid, but what we can do *within* the framework of expectations set by our state education departments can be flexible. We argue that PA brings flexibility and fun into this framework.

To showcase the power of movement-based instruction as a scaffold for continued learning, development, and constructive behavior, let's take a look at another classroom story, this time concerning a student named Bella. In Bella's home, there was one supreme ruler: Bella. I was informed that her parents' relationship was in conflict, and it often spilled over into her 8-year-old life. Each parent, striving to win her affection and loyalty, offered gifts and entitlement, which contributed to a lifestyle of little structure and little to no accountability. When she received homework, Bella chose not to do it because she didn't want to. Her teacher found that it made no difference what he said to her, how he pleaded with her, or how he tried to curb her behavior—homework was something that she just would not do. Bella's personal life coupled with her unfinished learning in prior grades and a weak foundation in math skills had direct ramifications for her behavior in the classroom. She did not try very hard, and she was hardly engaged. When it came to socializing, these factors manifested into bullying behavior. Her classroom of 3rd grade students knew to watch out for Bella. She was commonly identified as the class "mean girl," and only the boys she "liked" were safe from her bullying. Bella's bullying usually consisted of incessant, verbal abuse, which typically ricocheted to any student in the class who she felt was beneath her.

Soon after the beginning of the school year, one of her classroom teachers heard from the students and other teachers about her behavior. He knew that, in order to protect his students, her desk had to be placed within close proximity to his. He needed to be hyper-vigilant, but there were, of course, times that he couldn't keep an eye on her, such as during art class, recess, or physical education class. Bella was clever in hiding her behavior outside the classroom.

A soft-spoken, gentle, and shy girl named Kelly was a frequent target. Somehow, Bella had learned that Child Protective Services investigated a report related to Kelly's mom. Outside the classroom, during recess, in art class, or as they walked in the hallways, Bella would find opportunities to harass Kelly, whispering terrible things to her like "Your mom's a terrible mom. She's going to jail. She's a drug addict." One day, on the playground, Bella wouldn't let Kelly swing on the swings. Somehow, she enlisted the support of other girls to collectively bully Kelly. I was told that the girls laughed and pointed at Kelly, saying that "she smelled" and "her clothes smelled." Kelly ran to her teacher crying. One of Bella's accomplices, Molly, even used her social media prowess to help Bella locate a female classmate's phone number, call her up, and harass her.

Experts believe that bullies are born because of their own insecurities and that developing self-confidence reduces bullying behavior. This seemed to be the case for Bella. If students are to actually learn math (or *anything* in a classroom setting), such a feat demands a safe classroom environment, a dependable learning framework of compassion and collaboration, and a finishing touch of creativity. In Bella's case, it is quite evident how a lack of a strong and safe foundation in mathematics and in life can cause not only feelings of incompetence but also unwanted social behaviors. Physical activity adds support and structure to this analogous home throughout the entire construction process. We will return to Bella's story later.

## Environments of Safety and the Building Blocks of Math Fluency

A dependable, strong foundation, which allows students to learn what they need, requires a safe, warm, and welcoming classroom environment. Without such an environment, no learning can occur—a math classroom that students feel is unwelcoming or hostile can elicit feelings of anxiety and stress and promote unproductive behaviors.

Similarly, math fluency first requires mastery of the *fundamentals*. Let's take a look at the concept of multiplication and skip-counting, for example. Figure 3.1 shows a collection of concepts that—when built upon—demonstrate fluency in skip-counting, which is just *one* approach to building multiplication fluency.

Understanding the concepts at one level necessitates understanding the concepts in the level immediately below. Of course, a venture into each subdomain of skip-counting would require space far beyond what we are afforded in this chapter, but for our purposes, the activities in this chapter will pertain to the development of skip-counting fluency, which we believe is one of the most accessible and engaging approaches to building multiplication skills using physical activity. The activities in the three sections will involve practicing concepts at all levels of visualization.



**Conceptual Fluency of Multiplication Via the Skip-Counting Method**

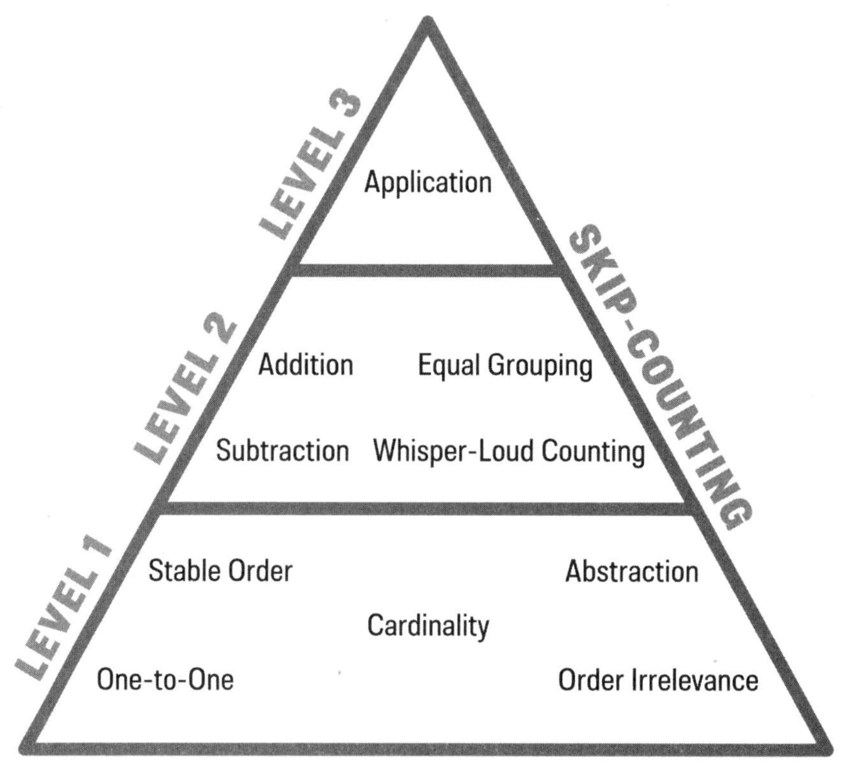


In the context of math achievement standards, a weak foundation in mathematics, particularly in fundamental concepts and operations like multiplication and division, causes deficiencies in the computational skills necessary for college study, job employment, and financial literacy (Lombardo & Drabman, 1985; Marsh & Hau, 2004; Williams & Williams, 2010; Vogt et al., 2018). Scholars and practitioners have found that repeated addition and equivalent grouping (the mainstays of skip-counting), if intentionally taught, enhance the automaticity of students' fact response. Repeated addition of equal sets is considered to be young students' intuitive model for understanding multiplication conceptually. Calculation strategies for this model typically involve "count-by" methods of rhythmic counting and skip-counting forward (Kinzer & Stanford, 2013; Smith & Smith, 2006; Wong & Evans, 2007). Repeated addition comes rather naturally to students, yet their recognition of appropriate equal-sized groups can cause difficulty. From our experience, intentional conceptual support from the teacher is required at this stage.

One way that we support students' internalization of multiplication concepts and provide such intentional support is through collectively performed, cross-body drills, which we call Active Math Movements. One such movement, which we've called Cat Scratch Fever! (Appendix A.10), breaks up the perceived monotony of class by engaging students in multisensory movements that increase their heart rate while simultaneously reinforcing the concept of skip-counting through a whisper-loud counting method. Our follow-up question for you is this: when during the school day (or during class) is there a time when students aren't actively doing something? Alternatively, how can those times (no matter how brief) be utilized to get students up out of their seats and engaged in mathematics? *Those* times (e.g., before class begins, after class ends, in between units, after quizzes, before/during assemblies, etc.) should be considered opportunities for students to build healthy PA habits by engaging in Active Math Movements.

A weak foundation is something that you would not want to build anything on. In the context of brain development and learning, as we discussed in Chapter 1, students are unable to build *anything* on a weak foundation. According to the National Child Traumatic Stress Network (NCTSN) (n.d.), around 40 percent of students in the United States have been exposed to some form of traumatic stress. This percentage, however, does not take into account the traumatic stress related to the COVID-19 pandemic. Without proper attention and support, the impact of ACEs can take a major toll on a child's ability to learn and thrive in the classroom. Our students, who often come into our classroom with trauma, stress, or having faced adversity, require a learning environment, a *foundation*, that meets them where they are and allows them to learn calmly and safely.

## A Physical Activity Framework

Educators play an important role in promoting resilience and creating a solid foundation of safety and math competency in the classroom, especially through their positive relationships with students and the inclusive teaching strategies they implement. One particularly powerful method of promoting safe learning environments is through physical activity (CDC, 2024). At the physiological level, movement and exercise can positively regulate a child's stress response system well into adulthood and help to reduce the presence of pro-inflammatory cytokines, which are cellular proteins associated with a wide range of diseases and disorders, including adolescent depression, childhood maltreatment, and impaired executive brain functioning (Peters et al., 2019).

What does this look like in practice? In our work, we have embraced the HOPE framework (Health Outcomes from Positive Experiences) as inspiration for the type of supportive math classrooms we want to foster at schools. The HOPE framework is a holistic approach to child healthcare that has been used as a guide for researchers to mitigate the effects of ACEs and foster resilience. According to Sege and Browne (2017), the HOPE framework has organized four broad categories of "positive childhood experiences" that promote resilience (p. S81):

1. Maintaining supportive relationships though
   - Secure attachments.
   - Physically and mentally healthy parent(s).
   - Trusting relationships with peers.
2. Learning in safe, stable, and inclusive environments that afford
   - Adequate nutrition.
   - Sufficient sleep.
   - Opportunities for play and physical activity.
3. Having opportunities to connect with others and, in turn,
   - Experience fun and joy in social activities.
   - Experience success and accomplishment.
4. Learning social and emotional competencies, including
   - Executive function skills.
   - Self-awareness.
   - Social cognition.

It's worth noting how physical activity opportunities play an important part in ensuring that these highly social experiences are positive. In previous chapters, we have written in detail about how PA supports positive relationships, learning environments that support *every* learner, peer-to-peer connections, and SEL. It should also be pointed out that the HOPE framework highlights "play and physical activity" not only as an example of a key positive childhood experience but also as experiences depending on one's living environment. Opportunities for physical activity and play are often dependent on *where* a child lives and learns, so it is crucial that we provide as many opportunities to play and be physically active as we can in school so that they can develop positive attitudes and resilience skills.

One activity that we have designed to be helpful in not only engaging students across grade levels but also building trust, class cohesion, and self-awareness is the Race to 100 (Appendix A.11). This activity can be presented competitively or noncompetitively, as an individualized activity or as a collective game. This particular activity has been historically quite popular among a variety of grade levels in the context of our family math engagement events (which we call Family Fun Nights) because of its simple rules and competitive nature. When presented in settings where multiple grade levels commingle, this activity has successfully brought students together to work toward a common goal: making it to 100!

## Spotlighting ADHD

A learning environment that truly supports *every* learner means that every student in that space has access to the tools and strategies necessary for academic success. This also means supporting the *spectrum* of student experience with an asset-based mindset about student abilities. Students labeled as having a learning disability often need different kinds of support than what they usually or historically receive in a traditional math classroom. A study conducted at a middle school in Tennessee found that providing students who have ADHD opportunities for physical movement is helpful in both decreasing ADHD-related behaviors and channeling those behaviors into different forms of stimulation (Dempsey, 2017). Students were able to channel their hyperactive behaviors during the unstructured movement time by using therapy balls and bouncy bands. Once the stimulation was provided in the form of movement, the amount of unproductive

ADHD-related behaviors decreased significantly, and students had more motivation and capacity to focus on what they needed to learn.

Keeping our students with ADHD engaged in the classroom is important not only for their academic development but also for their social development. Students diagnosed with ADHD often face more challenges socially, because they have more difficulties interacting with adults and responding appropriately to authority as well as maintaining friendships with peers (Stormont, 2001). Furthermore, slower reaction time and processing can cause gaps in conversations for some students with ADHD, which can lead to judgment and rejection by peers (Hoza, 2007; Licari & Larkin, 2008). We found a positive impact of movement-based teaching on these students through our own experience in the classroom. One 10-year-old boy, who was diagnosed as possessing ADHD, dyslexia, hearing/speech impairments, and ACEs, was of particular concern for an educator who asked us to provide movement-based programmatic support for her classroom. The student started the school year barely knowing any letters, not knowing any high-frequency words, and unable to write words other than his name. After being given the chance to express his learning via physical activity, it was as if a light switch had been turned on: his reading and spelling skills increased, and his use of these words in sentences demonstrated excellent retention. We found in an interview with him after the intervention that being physically active helped him feel more connected to his peers and teachers.

One activity we engaged in during this program—Kinesthetic Number Path (Appendix A.12)—was a favorite of this frustrated student; not only did it get all students out of their seats, but it required students to work *cooperatively* to identify the numbers, acquire the manipulatives, and build the path. We added an ELA component to the activity as a way to support the students in the class struggling with spelling and phonetics and had them practice writing in their journals the names and numbers of the items they acquired throughout the learning process.

In addition to supplying teachers with a practical and psychological framework to understand student behavior as well as tools to help regulate emotions and support learning differences, the primary goal of our Moving and Learning framework is to empower educators to establish a classroom environment where *all* students not only have access to engaging mathematics tasks and resources but also feel supported and respected (check out Place's [2021] quick reference guide on supporting emotional regulation in the classroom for some helpful strategies). Scholars, psychiatrists, and educators are recognizing that physical activities such as martial arts, yoga, acting, and sports can help stressed learners reduce hyperarousal, increase their focus, and (re)ignite a love of learning (MacNeill, 2019). Simple accommodations such as creating a safe space or calm corner in the classroom, creating sensory pathways in hallways, and giving students goal-directed tasks that involve physical activity can help them learn to recognize and regulate their emotions and, in turn, set strong foundations for continued learning.

As we discussed in Chapter 1, our brain grows and operates from the bottom up, but our brains get stressed from the *top down,* and students' anger and rage can highlight their brain's path down these steps (Eggleston et al., 2021). We must be cognizant of our students' behaviors and what potential stressors might exist in our learning environments that could be triggering. Relating to a child can occur only after they feel safe and regulated. By offering movement-based learning tools for support prior to (and even during) meltdowns, students themselves can begin to tolerate more and more stress. This is the physiological foundation for higher-order thinking that we need in the math classroom moving forward.

## A Collaborative Framework That Shapes Math Success

Once we have our foundation set, we can begin constructing the framework of our math fluency house. Like the foundation, it must also be strong and flexible enough to ensure that the house not only stays standing but also allows for growth and expansion. The framework of our math classroom contains the instructional processes that we implement to help our students learn the material. Without dependable and effective methods of teaching and learning, students will leave our classroom without a structured and lasting sense of what they learned and what is important to remember.

Your ability to build positive, instructional relationships is an asset here. However you plan on teaching a particular concept, the engagement of your students in the learning process relies heavily on *trust.* Trust is the necessary glue that holds educational frameworks together; trust strengthens your instruction and supports the learning framework that you implement in the classroom. Activities that afford opportunities for *teamwork* and *collaboration* help to build this trust. And movement-based activities can offer rich opportunities for collaboration to flourish. The collaborative Skip-Counting Parade activity (Appendix A.13) helps students build this trust by working together toward the common goal of designing and organizing a successful parade while also highlighting the uniqueness of individual students when they perform along the "parade route."

## The Power of Collaborative Activity

Teamwork and collaboration arise naturally in moments of physical activity and active play. This happens through students' direct observation of others' attitudes and the direct feedback that they receive from one another in a group setting. Structured and rigorous group work offers students the opportunity to build important empathy skills and practice positive behaviors (Akos, 2000). Slavin (2014, pp. 787–788) highlights four dimensions of learning that are the result of consistently engaging in group work:

- **Motivational**: The motivational rewards that are granted to groups based on individual learning goals support student learning.
- **Social cohesion**: Individuals' ability to identify with—and thus care about—the group enhances learning.
- **Cognitive**: Group work positively affects the cognitive development and demands of its members.
- **Developmental**: Individual members' modeling of positive, more advanced group behaviors aids in their own development.

In other words, working collectively to solve problems positively affects students' motivation, social connectedness, cognition, and overall development as learners. Slavin argues that these perspectives *in practice* are not separate but complementary. Researchers Jin and Kim (2018) have further delved into the cognitive effects of group work and discovered that metacognitive processes (i.e., the understanding of one's own thinking) occur at both the individual and collective (i.e., social) levels. At the social level, metacognitive *regulation* (which is the ability to monitor, evaluate, and control one's own learning process) strengthened students' scientific problem-solving skills, and this regulation was developed through collective activity. Students benefited greatly from group work because they were able to advance their thoughts and reflections with others, which they were unable to do alone.

Thinking and learning are distinctly *social* activities, and physical activity, by nature, affords additional complementary opportunities for students to work collaboratively. Recent interventions have shown that including movement-based strategies in the classroom can positively affect both teachers and students by increasing self-confidence, socialization skills, and content knowledge (Weight et al., 2018; Salciccioli et al., 2020). One activity that we have found recurring success with in supporting the motivational, social, cognitive, and developmental growth of students who need additional support is our Double It, Half It (Appendix A.14). This activity requires students to not only work together to solve problems but also solve problems within a specific time limit, which prioritizes group *efficiency* (which is also a requirement for building operational fluency). In this time-constrained context, and after intentional grouping of different skill levels by the educator, students are positioned in such a way where they must work together to identify the fastest strategy for solving the problem at hand.

But what about *us*? Should we as educators be participating in this teamwork too? You play a vital role in engaging students during these moments of interaction and learning. As teachers, we tend to prioritize students above ourselves, but positive teacher–student relationships that prioritize involvement, autonomy, structure, and compassion work both ways and benefit both parties. Research has shown that teachers who have strong, positive relationships with their students find greater fulfillment in their profession and are much less likely to develop or experience burnout (Spilt et al., 2011). This is crucial, considering the fact that between 25 percent and 40 percent of new teachers leave the field of education within five years of having entered it (García & Weiss, 2019). Teachers also recognize the value of collaboration and teamwork and often prioritize group work in their classroom activities. Yet, teachers do not tend to regularly participate *themselves* in the collaborative work of their students, much less with *other teachers*, despite the research out there that suggests that highly collaborative teaching environments lead to higher levels of trust, teacher satisfaction, and teacher improvement (Tichenor & Tichenor, 2019). We—along with scholars in the field of cooperative learning—believe that collaboration should be deliberate and meaningful to actually benefit all parties, both students and teachers.

But, as with any learning endeavor, practice makes perfect. The more you *yourself* participate actively in your students' learning, the easier it will be for you to plan for (and overcome) the inevitable learning obstacles that students face as they progress through the curriculum. In fact, our recent in-house study on the impact of physical activity on students' multiplication fluency found a statistically significant relationship between teachers' engagement in specific movement-focused activities and their math teaching competencies (NMF, 2023; see also Appendix A.20 for the specific activity). In other words, the more time that teachers spent teaching their students through physical activities, the more confident teachers felt in identifying and addressing their students' math deficits. Our Exploring Eights activity (Appendix A.15) helps illustrate how a teacher can be actively involved in students' collaborative math play and movement.

Unfortunately, even though physical education and physical activity are beneficial for learning and development, there is not always equal access. Students living in disadvantaged areas tend to have less access to recess breaks, a certified PE teacher, or after-school sports programs (Taverno Ross et al., 2020). Physical activity is a powerful equalizer because "children who spend more time on physical education, regardless of their socio-economic status, exhibit superior performance in academic subjects such as math and reading" (Hillman et al., 2008). Researchers Baumann and Boutellier (2011) are correct in their assertion that PA is "mainly caused by our environment" (p. 2)—that is, our immediate work environment affects our activity behavior at the individual and collective levels. We can, however, supplement our instruction with physical activities without needing any additional class time or change in environment. We can pepper opportunities for movement throughout the school day whenever there are times when students aren't actively doing something, which requires us as educators to *notice* when those times occur (e.g., as students shuffle into class, in between units/assessments, before leaving class, transitioning between classes). By creating a foundation of safety in our classrooms and by providing our students with physically active cooperative learning opportunities, high expectations, trust-fueled behavior, and math task engagement become the classroom norm.

# Fostering Creativity in the Math Classroom

So our "math fluency house" now has a strong, safe foundation and a movement-focused framework. As we continue to strengthen these frames through collaborative learning and activity, we can work on the finishing touches of our home and make it our own. An attractive house and its characteristic finishes should inspire both visitors and those who live in it. In the context of the math classroom, opportunities to express *creativity* provide our math classroom with its finishes; creativity empowers and inspires engagement in the learning process and, in turn, helps students maintain engagement and ownership over their learning.

## Play and Creativity

One of the first learning styles accessible to young learners is the kinesthetic/tactile modality. Considering that kindergarteners are constantly moving and touching everything, this really isn't that surprising. As children mature, however, they tend to shift toward preferring more visual modes of learning, but the hands-on approach never truly disappears (Keefe, 1987; Dunn & Dunn, 1993). In fact, it is quite beneficial as adults to maintain an openness to movement in all its forms, particularly play, which helps boost creativity, innovation, and subject mastery. Einstein famously came up with the theory of relativity after imagining himself riding in a kid's streetcar at the speed of light (Brown & Vaughan, 2009).

When we talk about *creativity*, we are talking about our ability to engage in both divergent and convergent thinking. Convergent thinking requires us to focus on identifying one well-defined solution to a problem, whereas divergent thinking involves exploration to identify multiple possible solutions and implies fluency, flexibility, and originality (Bollimbala et al., 2021). Creativity requires adeptness in both types of thinking. When developing activities and lessons that aim to foster creativity and curiosity in your math classroom, you should keep in mind these two points:

1. The learning environment should be playful.
2. The playful activities should be guided and purposeful.

Regarding the first point, according to Bergen (2009, citing Lynn Barnett), there are five different components of playfulness that foster creative adaptation to change:

- **Cognitive spontaneity**: one's ability to conceptualize the features of things in varied detail and imaginatively.
- **Physical spontaneity**: one's ability to manipulate/construct in various ways utilizing various strategies to do so.
- **Social spontaneity**: one's ability to engage (with) others in a variety of social contexts.
- **Manifest joy**: one's observable, undeniable expression of joy (usually perceived visually and/or audibly).
- **A sense of humor**: one's ability to make light of or see "bright spots" in the obstacles or hurdles set before oneself.

Teachers who make their classroom playful by adding spontaneity, joy, and humor to their lessons and activities directly support their students' development of critical thinking skills. The distinctly playful Let's Go Shopping activity (Appendix A.16) helps to reframe students' attitudes by giving them an opportunity to enjoy math through hands-on practice, by boosting their confidence though collaborative and individual activity, and by helping them see the value of math through the lens of personal finance.

The second point to developing activities and lessons that foster creativity and curiosity means making sure that play and movement-based activities are *purposefully framed*. Purposefully framed play is a combination of open-ended and modeled play opportunities. Modeled play (also called *pedagogical play*) is when the teacher models each activity, provides suggestions, and opens the floor up for continued discussion, which leads to more hands-on teacher–student engagement. This type of play requires engagement from the teacher. Purposefully framed activities allow for interaction, discussion, demonstration, observation, questioning, and connection with existing knowledge (Cutter-Mackenzie & Edwards, 2013). Edwards (2017) argues that teacher participation in play/movement directly enriches the learning "reality" and creative imaginations that the student experiences (p. 9; see also Fesseha & Pyle, 2016). A meta-analysis conducted by Bubikova-Moan and colleagues (2019) shows that modeled play is by far the most common role teachers report to actually adopt, which is not that surprising when looking at the research. The Skip-Counting Zookeeper activity (Appendix A.17) can function as an access point for teachers to actively participate in their students' play while facilitating intentional math practice related to skip-counting and multiplication.

## Regulating the Brain for Creativity

ACEs, toxic stress, and trauma are obstacles to creative thinking and learning. Trauma, if left unchecked, has the potential to follow someone throughout their life; over time this trauma can remanifest itself as different symptoms, which can affect adults in different ways than it affected them as children. For example, an ACE that could initially manifest as a lack of the capacity for creative play (which is one of the ways children learn how to cope with the problems of everyday life) could potentially lead to the inability to form and maintain healthy peer relationships in adulthood. Again, a key step in creating a Moving and Learning classroom is to establish a safe learning environment of playfulness where the students feel free to learn, explore, and make mistakes.

Movement-based learning strategies are extremely engaging for most students (young or old), especially for those who have faced adversity or live with trauma. The simplicity and intuitive nature of applying movement-based exercises to classroom activities allow many opportunities for students to confidently showcase their creativity and individuality while regulating their brains. Scholars identified not only that physical fitness is positively correlated with creativity but also that fluid bodily movements enhance creative generation, flexible thinking, and the ability to connect remotely associated concepts (Piya-amornphan et al., 2020; Slepian & Ambady, 2012). Physical activity influences creativity and, by extension, *innovation* due to how PA positively benefits students' cognitive performance, social competence, mood, and motivation (Baumann & Boutellier, 2011).

A study by Bollimbala and colleagues (2021) found that enjoyable physical activity (in this case, dance) improved cognitive processes, particularly in divergent thinking and convergent thinking. Positive effects were found immediately after the intervention period, which was only 15 minutes long. Furthermore, students retained these creative juices until the end of the day. Just think of all that our students can accomplish—especially those who struggle with stress—if given the chance to move their bodies. The Talent Show activity (Appendix A.18) is a fun, creative way for students to build self-confidence while crossing their midline and, in turn, regulating their brains. In a classroom setting, this activity can function as practice for students in designing their own Active Math Movements, but it can also be framed as the culmination of active math practice throughout your multiplication unit; in other words, your students can work toward this Talent Show event after becoming familiar with their multiples.

Movement-based learning strategies in the form of active play have been shown to positively facilitate learning and comprehension and, in turn, furnish our learning foundation and framework with numerous opportunities to boost student creativity. Novak (2017) demonstrated that incorporating movement into 8th graders' learning of linear algebra equations helped them transition from a mere surface-level understanding of the material to a deep comprehension of it. The integration of physical activity also aided in students' ability to comfortably use, recall, and articulate the correct mathematical vocabulary to their peers and teachers. Similarly, in a study by Bonny and colleagues (2017), students with a deep understanding of hip-hop (music, dance, and history) were more skilled at tasks employing mental rotation (a skill linked to higher performance in STEM disciplines) and were also more skilled at identifying positive emotions in others. In turn, the development of sociocognitive skills at the prefrontal cortex level reinforces a positive feedback loop that supports academic achievement and creativity (Blair & Razza, 2007; Piya-amornphan et al., 2020; see also the scholarship review by Vander Elst et al. [2023] about the learning benefits of dance more generally).

At the individual level, movement-based learning allows students to exercise their creativity, develop their imaginations, and make meaningful connections between themselves and the subject of play they're engaging in (Ginsburg, 2007). At the physical level, movement helps us develop dexterity, coordination, spatial awareness, and muscle mass. At the interpersonal level, cooperative and active play aids in developing social skills such as friendship, coordination, collaboration, and empathy. Active play even contributes to our sense of accomplishment and competence, giving us feelings of pride, joy, and a growing sense of individuality and identity—all of which help foster curiosity and proactive learning mindsets.

## Wrapping Up

During the last two weeks of Bella's 3rd grade, her class participated in an intensive movement-focused math intervention. And then, almost as if a light switch was turned on, Bella's bullying ceased. Bella's teachers believed that, before the intervention, Bella acted out because of the learning gap in her skills. Bella was well aware of her unfinished learning, which caused immense frustration when it was brought up by her teachers or peers. Yet, Bella was cognizant enough to know that she was lacking in basic skills and that others had mastered them. She was embarrassed.

Once her class began the intervention, the pace at which she learned skyrocketed. From knowing just a minimal amount of math facts, she made quick and solid progress with learning multiplication both factually and conceptually. She collaborated with students to check their work, and she found that she was able to locate errors in the work of the "smart kids" (her words). This discovery, though, did not lead to any harassment or judgment toward the "smart kids" whatsoever—instead, it motivated Bella to work even harder. She loved to come in, plop her book down at the table with the students she considered smart, and complete her multiplication work at an impressive pace.

Being a part of the students considered to be the overachievers of class, working next to them, and completing her work (and correctly) generated immense pride—a pride that manifested not as narcissism but as self-confidence. This self-confidence was genuine, which was not previously seen in Bella. Bella's curiosity in math blossomed. She inquired about solving higher multiplication problems such as 6 × 18. She learned how to decompose 6 × 12 to solve these problems and now wondered if similar strategies could be used to solve 6 × 18! After the intervention, we were informed that

Bella stopped "messing" with Kelly and that the classroom overall now emits an aura of cooperation, safety, and support.

The "house" within which Bella was initially positioned did not do her—or her teachers or peers—any favors. What was initially a foundation of little accountability or structure was turned upside down when she engaged in the movement-based learning environment. Her motivation, confidence, and learning soared. With this solid foundation and a new framework upon which Bella could alleviate her anxieties, she began to develop a new math identity that positioned her as equal to her overachieving peers, which only further motivated her to practice and succeed. What made the math classroom Bella's new "home" was her reinvigorated sense of curiosity, which manifested from intentional active math instruction.

# Movement *Expands* Mathematics Horizons

So we have our house plan—a blueprint, so to speak, for *how* we can approach supporting our students' math knowledge using movement as scaffolding in a classroom setting. However, we know that mathematics as a discipline does not exist in isolation; we see and utilize math all throughout our lives in a variety of situations and contexts. In our efforts to prepare our students to be able to apply their math knowledge to these contexts, teachers should focus equally on *breadth* of application as they should on depth. Seeing math in different contexts across the discipline (and across other disciplines) can provide students with richer perspectives and stories of mathematics' successful application in the "real world." Our own understanding of mathematics is informed by (and informs) other understandings of mathematics and how it is taught. It's a primary goal of math instructors to teach students what they need to know in order to succeed, which should entail providing your classroom with access to multiple approaches to solving problems.

In the previous chapter, we spent our time developing our students' foundational math skills using movement as a support structure. Now we will talk about the *horizontal motion* of learning, specifically how we can expand math learning within and beyond the math classroom using movement-based teaching strategies. When we discuss *expansion* here, we are talking about *breadth*—or the knowledge or awareness of the full span of a particular topic. Regarding multiplication, for example, breadth of knowledge can be achieved by providing students with multiple contexts in which to view and practice the concept of multiplication. How students actually acquire expansive knowledge is multidimensional, but if we are to get students to see the value in math as a worthwhile discipline to engage with, instruction should provide ample opportunities for (1) divergent thinking, (2) socialization and interdisciplinary collaboration, and (3) "real-world" math practice.

We couldn't think of a better story to illustrate this breadth of knowledge and opportunity via movement-based learning than that of Ronnie. A while back we interviewed a teacher named Kimberly about her experience using movement to expand her students' knowledge, and she opened the discussion with the following story:

> I have worked in the field of education for more than 25 years and have served as an elementary teacher, principal, and superintendent. I returned to the classroom three years ago, bringing with me all of the knowledge and experience of a seasoned professional. Teaching in the year 2023 is much different than teaching was when I began my career in 1990. We have always recognized the importance of connecting with students and the idea that students learn better through play and movement, but today's students, more than ever, learn differently.
>
> Ronnie was a student in my 3rd grade class for two years in a row. Ronnie started 3rd grade withdrawn, depressed, and unable to focus or remain still for more than a few minutes at a time. He rarely ate and often climbed on and jumped off of whatever he could in the classroom. He also had a very difficult time regulating his emotions. When he was stressed or overwhelmed, he often shut down completely and hid in his cubby with his hood over his head. Ronnie had ACEs—many ACEs—which included a neglectful stepmother and a mom who he was able to see only on rare occasions. His valid fears and resulting depression kept him from connecting with his

peers, his teachers, and the content of our lessons; his toxic stress and the negative emotions from home were prohibiting him from being able to learn and grow academically.

Each morning, my students had a Zones of Regulation chart on their desk, which helped to orient their feelings and allow for clear discussion about them with me and others. They were asked to mark how they were feeling as they entered the classroom, but they could change their charts throughout the day to align with how they were feeling. As their teacher, I wanted to be able to connect personally with each of my students and provide a space where they could express their emotions (both positive and negative) and have those feelings acknowledged by me and their friends. For Ronnie, this chart was an opportunity to express his voice and have that voice and his feelings validated. Ronnie and I developed a check-in/check-out protocol throughout the school day, and we were able to set him up with a counselor to address his anxieties and depression. Ronnie and I also worked together to set up times for him to be able to visit the sensory room or take his computer to the office for a 10-minute break.

Ronnie was two years below grade level when he entered 3rd grade. As his relationship blossomed with the special education teacher and myself, it became evident that Ronnie was much more capable academically than had previously been communicated to me. He was a hands-on learner. He enjoyed music, and he often stated that he planned to be a police officer when he grows up, once saying, "I want to be able to help everyone stay safe. To protect them and to help them."

The connection was made, and there was a relationship of trust and care that we were able to foster together. His counselor and I were then able to focus more on Ronnie's emotional regulation needs. A stand-up desk was brought into the classroom, and noise canceling headphones were available at all times when he was working independently. Ronnie slowly started using our Peace Corner to take breaks instead of his cubby. He would ask to speak with me privately when he was upset or anxious, and the more comfortable

Ronnie became, the more he realized that our classroom was a comfortable, respectful space where he would always be listened to.

Once his emotional needs were met, we were then able to focus more on Ronnie's learning style. In reality, Ronnie was not much different than most of my 3rd grade students who preferred standing up while learning, using fidgets to help them focus on lessons, and wearing noise-canceling headphones when it was time to work individually. All of these tools were available for Ronnie, who now had the regulatory capacity to use them consistently. To be successful, he—like so many other students—required a multisensory approach to learning.

Ronnie's motivation and growth started to unfold in the classroom as we used letter tiles, shaving cream, cross-body active movements, and tapping to practice sight words, vocabulary, and mathematics. I was aware of Ronnie's love of music, so I made sure to also integrate his passion into rhythmic reading and math lessons. Needless to say, his engagement increased, and he grew a full year academically between January and June.

Now a decision had to be made. Despite his incredible gains in his math and reading abilities, he was still a year below grade level in reading and writing and a year and a half below in math. His parents and I began to discuss options. Ronnie had vocalized to his parents how much he loved my class and how I believed in him, so we debated what could happen if Ronnie had another year with me. There was an understandable back and forth, but in the end, we decided to ask Ronnie himself how he was feeling about school and what he felt was best for him next year. The choice was ultimately his—a choice that many students would find debilitating, but a choice that would empower Ronnie for the next stage of his schooling.

Incorporating movement can assist in empowering students' value of mathematics and self-confidence by bridging math knowledge to other domains of life and of school, as it did with Ronnie. Movement, such as simply being given the chance to stand up during class, can help students experience the *expansiveness* of math opportunities around them and in turn support their divergent thinking, socialization, and mathematical modeling skills through the positive emotions, shared discourse, and practical utility PA evokes during math class. In other words, movement makes it easier for students to embrace new perspectives, and it's this perspective-taking ability that allows us to see the value of mathematics. We will return to Ronnie's story later.

## Positive Emotion, Adaptability, Divergent Thinking, and Math Attitude Expansion

Change is a good thing. It is inevitable, and it is embodied by our own students, whose own bodies, minds, attitudes, and outlooks are in a constant state of flux. This is the norm for young people, and we believe that math instruction should reflect this state—instruction that's flexible and adaptive to both their individual and collective needs. A variety of perspectives presented in a variety of ways can help inform and enrich what we already know. This is a two-way street. Through reflection on the similarities and differences between our approaches to solving problems, we set the stage for productive discussion and enhanced learning that is distinctly collaborative and task-oriented. We can make math fit in this framework. How, though, do we get our students to feel comfortable approaching and engaging mathematics in divergent and creative ways? Based on the research of mathematics attitudes, such reframing starts with a positive emotional outlook on the process itself.

### The Impact of Positivity

Teachers have the ability to make just as much, if not more, of an impact on their students' mindsets and achievement when they approach teaching with *positivity*. Teachers' own engagement, optimism, and even their joyful expression toward classroom material has been proven to increase student excitement, creativity, classroom participation, and satisfactory classroom discipline (Kimura, 2010). Positive emotions have also been linked to the development of thought-processing and resilience skills in how positive emotions uniquely "open us up" for broader thinking (Cohn & Fredrickson, 2006). When teachers display positive emotions like joy and excitement, middle schoolers have been found to become more "mastery-oriented" and are less likely to use self-handicapping strategies or task avoidance behaviors (Sutton, 2005). Positive emotions don't simply act as markers or signals of well-being and health but actually work to produce well-being and health (Tugade et al., 2004; Cohn et al., 2009).

At the physiological level, increased physical activity supports positive emotional expression and development through the chemicals that our brain secretes when we move our bodies (such as BDNF and dopamine). Aside from these chemicals, most kids naturally like to move around, especially with others. When students participate in movement-based activities collectively, they tend to be more engaged than when simply sitting, and this engagement regulates anxiety, boosts positive attitudes, and prepares the body for learning at the deepest physiological level. The Math Positive Affirmations activity (Appendix A.19) can function as making this positive thinking (and cross-body movement) a habit in your classroom.

## Self-Confidence and Embracing Change

Positive emotion supports perspective taking in how it mediates math attitudes and strengthens self-confidence. Students' self-confidence was first prioritized in 1989 by the National Council of Teachers of Mathematics as a result of their findings that self-confidence has a significant effect on both mathematics perceptions and attitudes. Self-confidence is intricately connected to one's perceived value of, confidence in, and engagement with math (Sheldrake et al., 2015). Those with low math self-confidence can be expected to be more disengaged in math tasks and lacking a certain *persistence* in problem-solving strategies, whereas students with high math self-confidence tend to enjoy their math tasks, are confident in their ability to solve math problems, and see the real-world usefulness of those problems. Of course, one's self-confidence can change over time with different experiences, but the level of self-confidence that students possess at any given time is an important predictor of future academic achievement (Morony et al., 2013).

Student self-confidence can be limited, however, if their perspective or experience with math is also limited. One student might find one problem-solving strategy understandable, while another might not. If one strategy is prioritized in the classroom, and this frustration continues without being addressed, gaps in self-confidence will widen. By providing students multiple learning resources and strategies, we can better guarantee that our students "get" what we're talking about. On the flipside, students who *do* understand a particular strategy taught to them in class could also be limited academically if that is the only strategy they are expected to follow. Learning multiple strategies could help that student discover an easier or more efficient way of doing things. On a more general level, multiple strategies increase students' awareness of the valuable breadth of mathematics.

Let's use multiplication as a conceptual example here. Traditionally speaking, memorizing facts to build fluency, usually by strategically incorporating drills, worksheets, and flash cards, has dominated the implementation toolbox of practitioners for decades (Smith & Smith, 2006; Kinzer & Stanford, 2013; Skarr et al., 2014). The goal of fluency building—and the reason for memorizing facts *in this way*—is to have a higher rate of correct responding. Yet, in order to find success in mathematics (that is, to increase *mathematics achievement*), these traditional methods that prioritize memorization and memorization *alone* are not enough (Van de Walle et al., 2022). From a practical perspective, to have one's multiples memorized does not necessarily entail knowing when or how to appropriately use multiplication in a given situation. A mathematical modeling approach—another instructional strategy—helps students overcome this hurdle by giving them hands-on application and language practice, usually in the form of creating word problems and math situations that students can relate to. Most math educators agree that a *combination* of these approaches helps students achieve competency and more positive math attitudes. Our Multiplication Moles activity (Appendix A.20) is inspired by the classic board game Battleship but instead offers students a chance to manipulate numbers on a large multiplication grid to build multiplication competency and strengthen positive mathematics attitudes.

## Divergent Thinking in the Math Classroom

How math problems are formulated and how they're presented can matter greatly in our attempts to get students excited about math. Closely connected to positive emotions and self-confidence is the cognitive ability to think divergently—or with multiple potential solutions in mind. *Divergent thinking* (DT) is the act of pursuing variety in solving a given problem without a single fixed answer (Kwon et al., 2006), or, more generally, thinking with different perspectives (Pásztor et al., 2015). Most researchers agree that DT is a combination of three dimensions:

- **Fluency**: being able to freely put forward many ideas.
- **Flexibility**: being able to devise new strategies upon discovering the limitations of old ones.
- **Originality**: being able to think up unexpected ideas.

DT is mediated by a number of different factors, such as general creativity skills, personality traits, cognitive processes, teaching approaches, and individual math tasks (Bingölbali & Bingölbali, 2020), but it has been found to predict math achievement with comparable magnitudes across all three of its dimensions (Pásztor et al., 2015).

The mediating impact of *math tasks* and *instructional approaches* is particularly relevant here in our discussion of expanding students' math knowledge. We can actually strengthen our students' DT skills by providing math tasks that have DT features. According to Bingölbali and Bingölbali (2020), tasks with DT features afford opportunities for problem solving, problem posing, and redefinition (p. 243). In other words, students can strengthen their DT skills by participating in math tasks that get them to interact with a math situation from a number of different angles. For younger students, researchers have highlighted how *active play* fosters DT due to its cognitive and affective demands (Wallace & Russ, 2015). When playing, students define their own problems, solve said problems, and revisit and rethink about these problems, oftentimes with others. Wallace and Russ (2015) discovered that students who expressed more affect (or emotional variety) in their active engagement in this play cycle were better divergent thinkers, which predicted math achievement longitudinally.

For older students, researchers have discovered the positive impact of open-ended math problems on DT skills, particularly original thinking (Kwon et al., 2006). Open-ended math problems have a clear starting point but are open to multiple different solutions. Truly open-ended problems allow students to choose their own approach and to explain why they chose that particular path. The advantages of open-ended problems are many:

- Students have more opportunities to use their math skills and their knowledge more widely.
- Students have more freedom in expressing their ideas and actively participating in class.
- Students can find greater authenticity in math by having the autonomy to answer in ways that they find meaningful.
- Students have the opportunity to feel accomplishment through discovery and feedback from peers.

Our Change for $100 activity (Appendix A.21) spotlights the significance of open-ended problems in how students can work collaboratively to identify different ways to make sense of money. Money, again, provides a wonderful lens through which students can relate to and see the value in knowing mathematics.

Divergent thinking sets the cognitive groundwork for one's ability to adapt their strategies and grapple with the stress of failure when learning something new. It affords comfort with change and competence in task switching. When students approach math with emotional positivity, they are able to shift perspectives and are open to new ways of thinking, and they become that much more prepared to learn *how* and *when* particular math concepts should be utilized. DT sets the groundwork—and provides ongoing cognitive support—for the expansion of knowledge. Movement-based instruction supports this expansion.

## Interdisciplinary Collaboration Puts Mathematics into Context

The expansion of math skills, math confidence, and math utility often occurs when disciplines collide or overlap. For example, a teacher might introduce mathematics concepts using baking as an instance of real-world application of fractions and measurements, or they might frame certain activities like knitting as mathematical (Chapman, 2022). In reality, math is all around us and not limited to its own isolated domain. Our ability as math educators to get our students to reflect on their own understanding of mathematics and how we use it on a day-to-day basis beyond the math classroom proper helps them to recognize this fact. Physical activity can help ease this shift in mindset.

## Mathematics as an Interdisciplinary Discipline

When multiple disciplines interact, we call them *interdisciplinary.* Without getting into the nitty-gritty of the definition, *discipline* specifies the organized ways in which people go about their work such that they can be identified in terms of specific practices (Williams & Roth, 2019). Mathematicians, for example, identify with the discipline of math and carry out a number of specific activities using specific tools (e.g., equations, formulas, operations) and specific terms (e.g., attributes, dividends, frequencies) to solve problems. Our students, on the other hand, tend to not have a strong attachment to individual disciplines but instead find importance in their *utility,* or how they connect to real-world practice (p. 29). According to Williams and Roth (2019), "interdisciplinary math" involves connecting mathematics with other knowledge in problem solving and inquiry. Because any form of work involves some amount of collaborative labor, providing students with interdisciplinary skill practice is a worthwhile endeavor!

We might not be able to get our students to self-identify as mathematicians or subscribe fully to the discipline, but we don't need them to do this in order for them to reap math's academic benefits. Researchers have argued that, through exposure to a variety of math practice strategies during school, students begin to internalize the discipline and how to speak about it. As this *way of talking about math* is reinforced through the tools they use, the activities they participate in, and the relationships they build through such participation, students begin to do math *without thinking about the discipline.*

When we become aware of how other disciplines and discourse influence our math work, it then becomes possible to say when math is and isn't relevant to the problem at hand. Becoming aware of these other disciplines while in this state requires *reflection*—that is, explicit discussion (either individually or collectively) around why we use the problem-solving strategies that we do. In short, if we are to get our students to understand the utility and breadth that math has to offer (and, in turn, increase their engagement and achievement), we need to offer our students opportunities to step back and reflect on what they're doing and why they're doing it. Our

Math Investigators activity (Appendix A.22) gives students an opportunity to ask questions, connect mathematics to other disciplines, and describe systems using acquired math language from the engaging perspective of a private investigator as well as participate in active reflection with others on the significance of their mathematical discoveries.

## The Importance of Reflection

Reflection is key to achieving interdisciplinary math skills. Without interference via reflection, our unconscious knowledge about math remains unchallenged, and we continue to internalize our particularly situated conceptualization of math, which (for our students) could diminish their appreciation for the utility of math and, in turn, contribute to negative attitudes toward it. If, for example, a student is expected to practice math solely using worksheets and is expected to apply their memorized formulas to solve problems on said worksheets, that student might find mathematics to be abstract and thus not useful in the real world. High school students tend to throw their hands up impatiently in their math classrooms and shout, "When am I going to use this?!" Of course, the quality of the practice materials, teaching style, and learning environment can affect this frame of mind. For most students, math is viewed as not applicable to real life or is seen as a discipline that one needs to only "survive" as they progress through school. How, then, can we get our students to see the utility of math and expand their knowledge and appreciation of the subject?

To be able to talk about and apply math in the real world *requires enough* knowledge of math in relation to other pertinent disciplines. This knowledge can only be acquired through intentional reflection on the taken-for-granted problem-solving strategies of mathematics. From an implementation standpoint, if we want our students to successfully apply their math knowledge to solve a variety of problems (which is one of the primary goals of standardized math curricula), we need to provide a variety of learning strategies as well as facilitate intentional reflection about math and its relationship to other disciplines. This ability to pivot application strategies to different contexts demonstrates *breadth* of mathematical knowledge.

In practice, this approach might seem more appropriate for higher-level or older students, but that is not the case. In fact, *all* students regardless of age or support needs can benefit academically from multidisciplinary reflection (Benson-O'Connor et al., 2019). We can adapt our math curriculum to support this reflection regardless of grade level or math ability by providing opportunities for collaborative practice and by providing students with authentic, real-world math problems and examples. Collaboration allows for *different perspectives* to arise that challenge the status quo of what problem-solving strategies are appropriate in which contexts. Real-world math problems (which we will discuss further in the next section) allow for *different opportunities* for contextualizing math. Math can take many forms and can be useful in solving many different problems, so for students to be able to know when and how to solve these problems, they need to have exposure to a variety of math problems that they can relate to and that reflect its multidisciplinary nature. Movement can help positively frame these problems as enjoyable and social. The Timekeepers activity (Appendix A.23) provides students an opportunity to reflect on the various ways in which we can use a tool (in this case, a circle) to assist us in solving math problems that cover *multiple* concepts, all while being up and out of their seats and actively engaged.

## Self-Confidence, PA, and Interdisciplinary Math

Self-esteem and self-efficacy contribute rather significantly to interdisciplinary learning in how students engage with their own learning and others' learning. If we're to set students up to engage with others and reap the benefits of collaborative math, we need to make sure that they're confident in their own math abilities and have the self-esteem to collaborate with others. Physical activity strengthens our brain's neuroplasticity, which in turn primes the brain for self-efficacious beliefs and achievement (Baumeister et al., 2003; Ciarrochi et al., 2007; Bachman et al., 2011; Supekar et al., 2015). Movement also functions as a multimodal mechanism for students to practice and demonstrate a variety of math concepts, thus giving students the confidence to tackle variable math challenges (Gardner, 2012; Tate, 2009; Peterman & Ewing, 2019).

In addition to intentionally supporting students' various learning styles, we can reach more students and meet their different needs when we approach teaching math with positivity and inclusivity (Watanabe, 2003; Vogt et al., 2018). Physical activity is an immediately and sustainably engaging way teachers can enrich this approach. The Clipboard Math activity

(Appendix A.24) is a mainstay activity in all of our movement-based programming; it's an opportunity for students to pull together all of the strategies and tools accessible to them in order to complete multiplication and division problems. In this context, students utilize the movement-enhanced tools/spaces as a resource to aid in review and proofing.

Unfortunately, traditional math curricula do not help students obtain this interdisciplinary "know-how" very well, mainly due to school math not consistently affording opportunities for reflection and authentic collaborative problem solving, but also due to how schools are built, which do not afford easy communication between classes/disciplines. As a consequence, our students may learn that math is pretty isolated and useless. This is not good. Interdisciplinary collaboration helps students see the practical utility of mathematics through the discussions and dialogue they engage in. Students start to see how math takes shape and how it functions in disciplines beyond just math when they engage with real-world problems and with other learners across different disciplines. Movement helps students witness and enjoy this utility in action.

## Real-World Math Helps Students Discover That Math Is All Around Us

Despite the differences that each of us hold individually toward the discipline of mathematics, at the end of the day we all share a common experience—*doing math on a daily basis*, whether we know it or not. Until now, we have discussed how we as learners should be constantly surrounded by multiple perspectives and approaches to solving math problems. These differing perspectives, however, do not change the fact that math is all around us. Simple reflection on this fact, as we will discuss, helps us (and our students) become better equipped to know *when* and *how* to appropriately apply specific math strategies to specific situations. Beyond reflection alone, engaging with these different perspectives through practical math examples and collaborative dialogue helps students see math's value. By focusing our math instruction on the real-world applications of mathematical concepts, we can highlight the practical utility of mathematics and in turn enhance student math attitudes and the expansion of their math knowledge.

## Effective, Real-World Math Problems

Mathematicians and math educators alike often consider math to be a *tool*—a tool that helps describe aspects of the real world as well as analyze abstract structures. We know the benefits of approaching math with aims to solve real-world problems and how understanding its practical nature can contribute to informed citizenship (De Corte et al., 2000), yet our math curricula are not designed in a way to achieve this goal. Due to how math has been traditionally taught—that is, as an abstract collection of operations and artificial formulas—students don't find their real-world experiences and knowledge compatible with the discipline (Colvin, 1999). This has led to a vicious cycle in which students refuse to bring their lived knowledge into the classroom to make sense of math. The math classroom has become the domain of operations; unfortunately, the implicit and sometimes explicit "rules" of the math classroom paint real-world knowledge and experience as irrelevant to "understanding math" (De Corte, 2000).

How do we break this cycle? What can we do in our math classrooms to highlight the utility of math and prep our students for further engagement in the discipline? Many researchers agree that the *type* of math problems we present to our students can make a significant difference in helping students know when and how to apply math in a variety of situations. Effective real-world math problems (1) have a verbal and written component to them, (2) include content that is authentic to student experiences and grounded in a collaborative classroom culture, and (3) involves mathematical modeling (De Corte, 2000; Larina, 2016). Additionally, Larina (2016) argues that *teacher attitudes* affect not only the characteristics of practical math problems but also the impact that real-world math has on student understanding. In other words, *your* attitude toward practical math will influence your students' success. Students will look to you for affirmation that it is OK to bring the real world into the math classroom and that *you* will provide the proper parameters/criteria for evaluating their performance. Researchers have found that, when teachers give students the freedom to create their own word problems or apply their real-world knowledge and interests to classroom problems (under proper parameters), their understanding of the problem-solving process flourishes (Benson-O'Connor et al., 2019). Our Math Is Everywhere! activity (Appendix A.25) is one way we can productively tie in students' interests and experiences into mathematics, which provides an additional benefit of inspiring students to conduct further research into potential career pathways both within and outside mathematics.

## Practical Math and Authenticity

Practical math also leads to greater *breadth* of math knowledge. Colvin (1999) found that students in a reform-oriented integrated math course (that is, a course that focuses on grounding all interaction with mathematics in real-world, relatable situations) gained exposure to a wider range of mathematical concepts, which ultimately led to greater levels of engagement and achievement. Students need instructional support, and they need opportunities to discuss their concerns and thought processes with others if they are to understand the wonderful utility of math. Benson-O'Connor and colleagues (2019) accomplished this by supplementing math practice with *writing* and *journaling* activities. The researchers found that, by writing, students became more familiar with and confident in their use of math vocabulary, strategy methods, and assessing their own understanding of the content (p. 17). There were higher levels of self-awareness among the "journalists" who were able to connect what they were doing in class with how they felt and what they thought was important to know—math became "real" to these students. Moreover, the researchers found that even kindergarteners benefited from writing time during math class.

Adding a writing or oral component to your math lessons could make all the difference in student engagement and exposure to different math concepts. Any opportunity where students have dedicated time to reflect by themselves and (ideally) with others on what they're learning assists with engagement and comprehension. Physical activity is an effective supplement to such opportunities for reflection (which we will discuss further in Chapter 6) and can help students see the real-world nature of mathematics, especially when their own bodies become manipulatives in solving math problems. The Travel Agents activity (Appendix A.26) puts students in the shoes of travel agents who are tasked with budgeting and planning vacations for clients; in this context, students get to share their interests and experiences traveling and preparing for trips while simultaneously honing their addition and subtraction skills and reflecting on their decisions in a journal, which is ultimately presented to their client (you).

### A Contextualized Look at Mathematical Modeling

Real-world math is often conceptualized as carrying out "mathematical modeling" practices. Mathematical modeling involves identifying the relations between objects in a problem. As such, mathematical modeling is a complex process that involves

1. Understanding the situation.
2. Creating a relevant model that accurately reflects the situation.
3. Implementing the model.
4. Interpreting the outcomes of implementation.
5. Arriving at a solution to the problem at hand.
6. Evaluating the outcome in relation to the original situation.
7. Communicating findings.

It should be obvious that productive engagement in this process would require and benefit from the application of *many perspectives* and the presence of a *collaborative* environment in which to solve the problem. Moreover, mathematical modeling is *cyclical* in that the "givens and goals" do not follow a linear progression but instead inform and are informed by one another until a solution (or many solutions) is found (De Corte et al., 2000). The cyclical nature of mathematical modeling fits nicely within our cyclical "capacities of movement-based instruction" framework, but more important for our present purposes, it supports the acquisition of divergent thinking skills through collaboration, which ultimately helps students realize the utility of mathematics. Our Math Buddies activity (Appendix A.27) provides students with the opportunity to work with partners to physically solve word problems, following the mathematical modeling process listed in this chapter.

# Wrapping Up

Let's finish this chapter with the conclusion of Ronnie's story:

> We brought Ronnie into the conversation and asked him what he felt was best for him next year: either stay in my 3rd grade class to catch up on his learning or move forward to 4th grade with his peers. Ronnie immediately said that he wanted to stay in 3rd grade.

Ronnie said he wanted to stay with me and that he would do better in 4th grade if he learned more of the 3rd grade reading and math. Not just that, but he was happy to let his peers know that he was choosing to spend another year with me because it was what he needed and wanted to do. What a brave young man. He was still in counseling, learning to address his anxieties and bouts of depression, but he had fewer moments of shut-down and enjoyed knowing the ins and outs of the classroom environment and expectations we had set for him. He developed friendships and worked well with his peers and was at a point of maturity in his social development that he felt comfortable informing them of his decision.

Most exciting for Ronnie and me were the accomplishments he made that second year. Ronnie ultimately went into 4th grade performing on grade level in math, reading, and writing. He also went onward with a "toolbox" of skills and resources for coping with his anxiety and a plan for helping regulate his emotions. As is common with many students that are classified as A-Typical, the key to making academic progress was to first develop a relationship of trust and care in order to foster a positive classroom environment that focuses on a growth mindset. The second step was to implement a multisensory, inclusive approach to math and reading instruction, which made learning physically and intellectually engaging. Together, these are the keys that unlocked Ronnie's potential.

Ronnie's multisensory learning style is not unusual in today's classrooms. Students are accustomed to a very fast-paced yet sedentary world where television and video games entertain them from toddlerhood onward. Traditional classroom instruction and practices that focus on sitting still and listening to lectures no longer motivate and engage the majority of our students, nor do they lead to mastery learning for the largest percentage of our children.

Ronnie told me that he loved me at the end of 3rd grade. He asked if he could stay another year. I assured him that he was ready for 4th grade and that I would always be here for him. Ronnie's classroom was three doors down, and I saw him daily at lunch and recess. To this day, he hugs me and says, "Love you." I know that

I have forever made a difference in this young man's life. I am so happy for Ronnie, as he has a 4th grade teacher who also puts relationships and connections first. His daily check-ins and lessons are continuing to help propel him forward, and when we see each other, he always has a smile and a hug for me.

Ronnie's success here wasn't the result of just one change but the cumulative result of ongoing support from his teacher, his growing group of friends, and the inclusive, active resources made accessible to him that were utilized consistently in a distinctly safe and welcoming classroom environment. Anxiety turned into curiosity, and avoidance turned into confidence as his voice grew to shine bright as a fellow participant in the learning community that his teacher facilitated. As educators, we can help our students acquire a breadth of math knowledge and empower their voice within our classrooms by providing opportunities for students to foster divergent thinking skills, to engage in interdisciplinary group work, and to practice real-world math. Movement-based learning strategies assist with this expansion by increasing student enjoyment, engagement, and social cohesion.

# Movement *Enriches* Mathematics Curricula

So your students have proven that they know and can apply the material in front of them. Awesome! What next? How can we go *deeper* to make sure that their transition to the next topic goes as smoothly as possible and builds on their recently acquired knowledge and skills? *Enrichment*, by definition, is the action of improving the quality of something. When we discuss enrichment here, we are talking about *depth*, which implies vertical motion in the learning process where students either dive "deeper" into their understanding of a particular topic or gain a "higher" level understanding of it. In the context of mathematics education, enrichment has purpose, and it pertains to the act of *going beyond* what is in front of us on the math worksheet. Enriched mathematics entails a deeper understanding of mathematics, a fluency, wherein students can accurately answer questions, efficiently apply correct strategies to solve problems, and flexibly adapt known strategies to novel situations (Bay-Williams & Kling, 2019). How, then, can we provide this enrichment? And furthermore, how can physical activity support the enrichment process in the math classroom?

Again, a story, we feel, sets a better stage for discussion than any single study ever could. Let's hear from Sean—a true Moving and Learning teacher—who at the time of writing this book was an enrichment instructor with Peaceful Schools in Syracuse, New York. Peaceful Schools provides comprehensive education and conflict resolution products and services to schools across the state of New York with the goal of fostering calm classrooms. The following story illustrates Sean's experience with one of his students—a student whose learning he was able to fully enrich through an active approach to instruction. In his words:

> I work with students who learn differently. The students in this class display a beautiful array of intelligences. Each one of them has their interests, their gifts, and even their self-doubts. As an empathetic human, I work to encourage in people the further development of the self, of ambitions, dreams, talents, and overall well-being. As an SEL Enrichment instructor, I embrace my responsibility of teaching the students to see the power they all hold, how to tap into it, and how to share it with others.
>
> As in all classes, good teaching in a special education setting starts with building strong relationships with my students. One particular student in this class, a 12-year-old girl named Sha'kaysia, has a drive to learn how to draw better. On the first day of school, Sha'kaysia learned that I am an artist. Quietly, she showed me a drawing of her own and hesitantly asked me what I like to draw. In her timid question, I saw a spark. I knew this was an incredible opportunity to open up a dialogue with my student. Responding to her interest, I found a safe avenue for her to travel in the form of communication, relationships, and expression.
>
> In all of my Enrichment classes, we start the day with a check-in. I enter the classroom, wait until the students are settled, and ask some version of "How are you doing today?" As students respond, and even as some students choose to pass, I take notice. I look for cues to how I should approach the day's lesson. Students' inner worlds mix with their school life, bringing the two together like a dance. Little by little, this dance begins to move. The best instructors learn to adjust their steps to meet the needs of the relationship. In each day's interaction, I pause to reflect on one fundamental question of this dance: "How do I, as the teacher, make

progress developing relationships with each student and their diverse needs?"

Our students are consistently looking for support and validation. Validation for things like abilities, qualities, and social skills. They are changing every day right before our eyes and need constant support for that change. Each time I saw Sha'kaysia in class, I purposefully found something in her art to praise. Sha'kaysia absorbed these appreciations and encouragements like a sponge. Throughout the year, I nurtured my relationship with Sha'kaysia through our art connection. Relationships are not easily defined; they are wholly specific to each person they are built upon. They are fluid, changing daily and in need of continuous checks and balances. By recognizing her drawings, complimenting her work, and listening to her thoughts about how she views her work, the soil was laid with encouragement. From there, I found ways to weave in calming lessons with artistic flair to assist in her growth. Many of the students in the class were interested in and enjoyed drawing, so I implemented drawing days into my lesson plans.

During these drawing days, I led a quick drawing exercise, or we followed along with a video tutorial. To build in opportunities for social-emotional learning, I often paused the instruction to check in with students, asking if they needed any help. I tried to spark a little conversation about whatever creative act has sparked in them. Modeling how to be an empathetic listener, I prompted students to respond to each other and reflect on their drawing to help them build communication skills and empathy for each other. As we continued the tutorial, I walked around the room to magnify the great things I saw in their drawings. I gave positive encouragement to feed their passion and process.

This hands-on, artistic initiative opened up more opportunities for Sean to spread positivity, enhance growth, and foster positive relationships with his students. While being exposed to different learning styles, teachers are able to try the approach similar to Sean's with little to no instructional barriers present. As we work toward an answer to Sean's question about how we can build relationships with our students, we are preparing ourselves to meet the different needs of our students both inside and outside the math classroom. When considering the individual barriers to student learning, it is important to keep in mind that as teachers we must adapt our teaching methods to meet each student at their own unique level. This attentiveness brings fairness and agency to the forefront of our instructional interactions. By starting with regulation and inclusivity, we can then build from and enrich the learning that naturally arises in such an environment. We as active teachers can enrich student learning through our capacity to quell math anxiety, build trust, and instill lifelong learner values in our classrooms. We will return to Sean's story later, but first, let's discuss how movement amplifies each of these capacities and provide a number of pertinent movement-focused activities that you can start applying to enrich your math curriculum.

## Revisiting Math Anxiety, the Enemy of Enrichment

In an educational context, *anxiety* is generally defined as an unpleasant, affective response to the idea of learning or being tested on particular educational concepts. Anxiety as it relates to school has been proven to hinder student learning, diminish positive feelings toward complex topics, negate feelings of calm, and harm individual performance, all of which enrichment initiatives aim to strengthen (Akin & Kurbanoglu, 2011). *Math anxiety* in particular is experienced by more than 50 percent of Americans, and research has shown that it affects female students and teachers more often than male (Picha, 2018; Goetz et al., 2013). Students, especially girls, who learn from math-anxious teachers are significantly more likely to develop math anxiety themselves, and math achievement for math-anxious individuals is lower overall (Beilock et al., 2010; Ganley & Vasilyeva, 2014). This is significant considering that women make up around 90 percent of elementary school math teachers (Bekdemir, 2010; Bergen, 2009). This anxiety emerges from the fear of making mistakes, feeling foolish when getting a problem wrong, and having little to no confidence in one's ability to teach math (Harper & Daane, 1998).

Math anxiety can trickle down to the classroom environment and influence students' mindsets in often subtle ways, which can negatively impact achievement scores (Ramirez et al., 2013). As discussed in Chapter 1, the phenomenon of emotional contagion is a double-edged sword; anxious teachers may pass their anxiety down to their students by subconsciously modeling behaviors that relay their discomfort (Beilock et al., 2010). Emotions, mindsets, and relationships are closely connected in school settings and can directly affect school achievement; a study on 167 pre-service elementary school teachers showed that many of them attributed their current math anxiety to a past negative experience or *relationship* with a math teacher (Bekdemir, 2010; Bergen, 2009; Kumaş & Ergül, 2021). Young students are especially prone to modeling this type of effect toward math; a study by Jackson and Leffingwell (1999) found that 16 percent of the students they surveyed had their first negative experience with math as early as 3rd grade. Such an early experience, however, can influence students' perceptions of their own abilities later in their education (Zakaria & Nordin, 2008; Vogt et al., 2018). From the angle of brain science, math anxiety in particular can directly affect students' higher-level mathematical thinking through its influence on working memory and self-efficacy (Newcombe, 2010). It is thus important to prioritize self-efficacy support in an elementary setting for both students *and* teachers (Allen-Lyall, 2018; Demir-Lira et al., 2020).

What, then, can we as educators do to squash math anxiety? How can we support students' working memory and self-efficacy as they learn? Let's consider physical activity again as the vehicle toward a solution. Aerobic exercise, which is usually associated with more rigorous movement and play, has been proven to not only fend off anxiety through the relaxation of muscles and boosting serotonin levels but also treat the *trait* of anxiety by producing the chemical growth factor BDNF (Broman-Fulks et al., 2004). According to Ratey and Hagerman (2013), "BDNF directs traffic and engineers the [brain's] roads.... It improves the function of neurons, encourages their growth, and strengthens and protects them against the natural process of cell death" (p. 40). BDNF helps to rewire positive memories in the brain around and away from the fearful ones that usually kickstart anxiety attacks. A study by Ströhle and colleagues (2005) showed that running on a treadmill for 30 minutes compared to simply resting reduced panic attacks by a ratio of two to one. These researchers argue that exercise and rigorous play helps students who struggle with learning anxiety by providing them needed distraction, reducing muscle tension, boosting serotonin, rerouting brain circuitry, and strengthening resilience. Of course, you probably don't have 30 spare minutes to get your kids on a treadmill. But fortunately, there are strategies that you can implement in your classroom during or around instructional time to get their heart rate up. One of our favorite activities that does the job here is the Nines Twist (Appendix A.28).

All in all, not only do movement-based learning strategies aid students in better understanding and comprehending the material at hand and developing the mental skills necessary for higher-level learning (like mental rotation), but these strategies also support healthy social and emotional functioning, whether it be via direct effects on the brain's functioning at the neural level or through indirect effects on a student's experience of positive emotion, fulfillment, or confidence (see the findings of Goh et al., 2022). This is especially true for students whose cognitive, social, and emotional systems have been negatively affected by trauma, ACEs, and/or toxic stress. Movement-based teaching and learning strategies are an invaluable tool for educators seeking to support students with trauma and to create more inclusive classroom environments in general. Creating a PA-encouraged classroom environment benefits all students but *especially* those who have experienced adversity. Affirming Journalists (Appendix A.29) is a helpful positive-affirmation activity that supports students developing their sense of self and their mathematics identity.

The benefits of PA-focused learning for children are immense. However, the enriching benefits of moving and multimodal instruction need not stop once students graduate primary school. Despite the more advanced learning objectives older students face, movement-based learning strategies can still be incredibly useful in a classroom setting so long as they are tailored to the student's skill level and the subject material. Educators have come up with creative ways to implement movement-based learning strategies in their middle and high school classrooms to capitalize on the benefits of physical activity. Kirin Sinha (2014), the founder of SHINE for Girls, for example, details the experience of a teacher who sought to help her female students overcome their math anxiety by building their math confidence without them even realizing it:

Using kinesthetic learning, girls can learn math in an environment when their mental barriers are not up. For example, algebra can be introduced through choreography. Girls can create a simple dance of three twirls followed by a jump and will write it down as $3x + y$, where $x$ = twirl and $y$ = jump. Through dancing, these students ultimately came to realize that $3(x + y) = 3x + y + 2y$. Before they can say, "I can't do algebra," they already have! This begins the positive feedback loop of girls believing in themselves, and their confidence stems from knowing they have the ability to succeed. (para. 6)

This teacher observed the efficacy of movement-based learning strategies in a classroom setting, which facilitated the elimination of math deficits through a positive feedback loop. When teachers integrate physical activity into their lessons, the classroom as a whole becomes a space where learning takes place *without barriers*; movement—because it is fun and all students can relate to it—helps students believe in themselves as able to succeed, which in turn strengthens resilience and sets the stage for internalizing the material. The Algebra Dance (Appendix A.30) is modeled after Sinha's stellar activity and aims to support this positive feedback loop through positive collaboration and creative expression while engaging in algebraic content.

The observable connection between movement-based learning and decreases in (math) anxiety are also evident in neuroscience research. Lyons and Beilock (2012) demonstrated that, when individuals experience high math anxiety prior to taking a math test, going to math class, or even thinking about an upcoming math task, the activated brain regions overlapped significantly with the prefrontal cortex. The prefrontal cortex is associated with threat detection and the sensation of physical pain. In other words, depending on the amount of anxiety that students have toward math, simply thinking about performing well on a math test can actually cause sensations of physical pain. Luckily, the implementation of physically active learning strategies (strategies as simple and as quick as having students stretch or do jumping jacks before a test) has been shown to increase student motivation and, at the neural level, serves as a buffer to math anxiety.

## Building Trust for Deeper Dives

One of the strongest protections for children against toxic stress, anxiety, and ACEs is having a positive relationship with a supportive, caring adult who they can *trust* to meet their needs (Sege & Browne, 2017). A teacher can be—and often is—one of these adults. They might even be one of few adults that kids who live with toxic stress can actually trust. Students who struggle with adversity and who perceive their teachers as projecting emotions like joy and curiosity are much less likely to misbehave in the classroom and engage in at-risk behaviors. More specifically, teachers who teach with enthusiasm have been shown to (1) increase their students' motivation to learn, (2) promote positive relationships with adults, and (3) encourage goal achievement (Sutton & Wheatley, 2003; see also Zacarian & Alvarez-Ortiz's [2020] quick reference guide for teaching and supporting students living with adversity for some helpful trust-building strategies).

Researchers have found that teacher–student closeness—which supports the development of trust—can predict gains in both reading achievement and social development, while teacher–student conflict predicts lower levels of each (O'Connor et al., 2011; McCormick et al., 2013). How teachers view their students and, in turn, respond to those students in the context of instructional support can also affect engagement levels—levels that influence students' willingness and confidence to take deeper dives in subjects that they might already be familiar with. Higher-quality instructional support (that is, a teacher's encouragement of higher-order thinking when new topics are discussed) has been directly linked to higher test scores in mathematics and reading (Curby et al., 2009).

The power of the student–teacher relationship and trust building actually extends beyond age groups. In a 1997 study by researchers Birch and Ladd, kindergarteners reported liking school more and feeling less lonely when they had a close relationship with their teacher. These students also performed better on tests of early academic skill. Fifth graders whose math teachers provided higher levels of emotional support were more engaged, enjoyed thinking through the problems, and they even helped other students learn the material (Rimm-Kaufman et al., 2014). *Trust affords opportunities for enrichment*; a strong instructional relationship between student and teacher allows for the amplification of academic exploration. If a student trusts their teacher and knows that they have their best interest at heart, they will be more comfortable taking academic risks and taking their learning one step further. Within the mathematics classroom, this phenomenon is usually observable in how trusted teachers can get their students to challenge themselves once they've become comfortable with the subject at hand.

How can PA assist in trust building and, in turn, enrich students' desires to deepen their math learning? By strengthening resilience. Resilience, or the ability to "bounce back" in the face of adversity, is also enhanced by trust and high-quality instructional support. According to Eggleston and colleagues (2021), building resilience "is as much biological as it is sociological" (p. 33), meaning that we can strengthen our students' resilience by providing them with opportunities to build their brains and form trusting relationships. Exercise (which in turn increases BDNF), as we discussed previously, is one way that students can *biologically* empower their resilience. Moreover, because moving and playing is fun for students, the intentional incorporation of movement into the curriculum helps to strengthen more productive and enjoyable relationships between students and their teachers.

As discussed in this chapter, movement eradicates anxiety. Fear drives anxiety, which, in turn, drives unwanted behaviors, particularly those of students with trauma. When we are proactive about infusing PA into disciplinary (i.e., regulatory) practices, we are more able to successfully de-escalate unwanted behaviors and progress through our lessons without distraction. Providing students frequent opportunities for physical exercise and brain breaks are tried-and-true, proactive de-escalation measures that get students to both *regulate* and *relate* their brains, which sets the stage for trust-building exercises (Forbes, 2012; Eggleston et al., 2021). The Bean Pole Method (Appendix A.31) is a wonderfully simple regulatory exercise that we've found significant success in focusing students' attention and preparing a classroom for more rigorous content-based movement activities.

In order to both foster and maintain trusting relationships in school, educators and administrators need to approach discipline with brain science, inclusivity, and physical activity in mind. Recent studies have shown that exclusionary practices (such as out-of-school suspensions) and a punitive approach to correcting behaviors are rarely successful (Rafa, 2019; Eggleston et al., 2021). The work of Eggleston and colleagues (2021) provides teachers with a clear, well-informed structure to help redefine school discipline that focuses on training or developing students' ability to exercise self-control. This approach redefines and reorients our perceptions of discipline from a tool of punishment to "a process of instruction and a product of social and emotional health for all students" (pp. 2–3, 118). Punitive discipline—rather than instructional discipline—is *reactionary* at its core, and we know from trauma-informed practice that reactionary behavior and learning are incompatible. Teachers can engage in positive instructional discipline (and in turn develop trust in their math classroom and resilience among its members) by

1. Fine-tuning their instruction to be relationship-driven, relevant, and rigorous.
2. Modeling and teaching the restorative discipline skills that they want to see (see Eggleston et al., 2021, p. 105, for these specific skills).
3. Creating routines and procedures that students can trust and allow for choice.
4. Engaging students in cultural competence training.
5. Utilizing de-escalation techniques to emotionally regulate misbehavior.

Movement fits into this inclusive discipline framework quite snuggly. We have already discussed how PA helps students regulate their brains and relate with one another and their teachers, but PA also provides opportunities for students to practice conscious discipline skills: the structured, rigorous, and collaborative movements required of many of the activities listed in this book enrich students' skills in composure, encouragement, assertiveness, autonomy, empathy, positive intent, and accountability. Furthermore, by giving your students regular opportunities to move their bodies (e.g., starting off the class with an Active Math Movement [see example activities A.10 and A.28] or transitioning between units with a skip-counting exercise on the floor or in the hallway) creates a *fun* routine that your students can depend on to help them focus on the tasks at hand. It should also be noted that any physical activity that helps students release serotonin is helpful in de-escalating unwanted behavior; discipline, being a proactive rather than reactive measure, must include opportunities for frequent movement and brain breaks (Eggleston et al., 2021). Our activities The Five Rites (Appendix A.32) and The Five Animals (Appendix A.33) allow students to practice emotional regulation, conscious discipline skills, physical balance, and skip-counting by 5s and 10s through collective breathing and full-body stretching.

After we build trust through movement, we must make a continuous effort to sustain these connections through a clear, growth-focused mindset. These activities should assist you in fostering trust-fueled mathematics environments for your students. Trust is the bedrock of strong instructional relationships, and it functions as a foundation for higher levels of interaction and exploration of academic material; in other words, if students don't feel that they can trust their teachers or classmates, why would they ever *want* to try to solve a math problem, knowing that there's always a possibility of making a mistake? Again, by investing in the relationships of our classroom, which itself is made easier through the implementation of movement-based learning strategies, we can then take the necessary steps to foster opportunities for deeper reasoning and instill in our students lifelong learner values.

## The Lifelong Learner Objective of Enrichment

Most educators would agree that the ideal educational outcome for their students would be that they develop an enriched drive to continue learning beyond their formal schooling. All we can do, though, is hope that our students ultimately find purpose in their work and that what they learn under our wing sets them up for success in what life has to offer; we are in the business of creating *lifelong learners*. But what does that mean? And how can movement impact the competencies that form the foundation for lifelong learning? Let's start with the concept itself.

There have been multiple definitions of *lifelong learning* developed over the years, but scholars on the subject agree that it is an ongoing *process* of steps that an individual can take to improve their knowledge, skills, abilities, and competence across their lifespan (Laal & Salamati, 2012). This lifetime acquisition process, however, isn't carried out for the love of learning per se, but to a *practical end,* usually within the social or citizenship domains. In other words, lifelong learning is the continuous "putting into practice" of skills and knowledge acquired through the continuous process of learning.

There are a number of competencies that underlie lifelong learning—too much to go into detail here—but Sahin and colleagues (2010) identify *math* and *STEM* competencies in particular as necessary for building lifelong learning values. Math competency implies that an individual (1) can develop and accurately apply mathematical thinking to a variety of real-world situations, (2) can use logical reasoning to solve problems and do so with high self-efficacy, and (3) is willing to use mathematical tools (like formulas, models, and tables) to do so. From an employment standpoint, mathematical skills and competencies are important for most professions—up to 90 percent of professions, according to Kumaş and Ergül (2021). Our To Chance or Not to Chance activity (Appendix A.34) engages students in the competencies of this lifelong learning model.

Researchers have also identified—and tend to agree on—a slew of benefits from pursuing lifelong learning. For our present purposes, lifelong learning benefits the individual in how it enriches life experiences through the fulfillment of personal goals; the bolstering of self-confidence, communication, and interpersonal skills; and the opening of doors to better career opportunities (Laal & Salamati, 2012).

What, then, can *we* do to make our students lifelong learners? Scholars say that such an accomplishment requires effort from both teachers and their schools. First, teachers should themselves demonstrate to their students their own commitment and enthusiasm for lifelong learning (Day, 1999). Researchers Uzunboylu and Hürsen (2011) go a step further in their assertion that the training of lifelong learners can *only* be realized through teachers who are themselves lifelong learners. Teachers must be the ones to create classroom conditions that allow for growth in self-esteem, self-efficacy, motivation, and the commitment to continuous learning by stimulating critical attitudes and supporting learning styles that are, at their core, *active* (Day, 1999, citing Beernaert, 1994). Our Leaping Arrays! activity (Appendix A.35), which was featured in the National Math Foundation's

Mighty Multiplication Project, was found to have a statistically significant, positive effect on participating teachers' ability to support a variety of learning styles—a core requirement of fostering lifelong learning mindsets.

Schools, on the other hand, need to support their teachers as they spearhead this process. Schools need to invest in the lifelong learning of their teachers and foster a community that promotes 1) the achievement of every individual, 2) the development of a *broad* knowledge, and 3) societal inclusion (Day, 1999). According to Day (1999), lifelong learning requires teachers to be "emotionally intelligent" and provide their students with challenging work and unyielding support—a requirement that itself requires schools to support the self-esteem and self-efficacy of their own teachers (pp. 208–209).

Self-efficacy is a fundamental competency of lifelong learning and serves as a powerful predictor of performance and behavior in the math classroom (Bandura, 1982). Moreover, a lifelong learning mindset requires strong efficacy beliefs to actually function. Efficacy beliefs directly affect motivational, persistence, mastery, and resilience efforts when engaging in an activity, and the higher the perceived efficacy, the higher the likelihood that those individuals will persist in their efforts until they reach success (Bandura, 1995; Akin & Kurbanoglu, 2011). Low levels of self-efficacy can negatively affect achievement, and this is primarily due to the belief/behavior connection between efficacy and hesitancy; when tasks are perceived as difficult or personally threatening, people with low self-efficacy will tend to avoid them outright (Doménech-Betoret et al., 2017; Ramirez et al., 2013). Self-efficacy has a strong influence on self-confidence and, in turn, the willingness of students to pursue learning opportunities over the course of their life.

Physical activity and its capacity to enrich student learning supports the development of self-efficacious, lifelong learning mindsets (Carr et al., 2024). On a physiological level, physical activity sets the stage for a growth-focused, lifelong learner mindset. For a child whose brain and body have been negatively affected by toxic stress, movement and play can regulate the activity of an overactive amygdala, helping it better discern which situations are actually threatening (and thus warrant a productive initiation of the stress response system). These types of stimulation and activities may lead to some of the same symptoms of stress response (such as elevated heart rate) but are ultimately harmless and potentially enjoyable. Additionally, physical movement can lead to the release of the hormone adrenaline but not the hormone cortisol which, as previously discussed, creates much of the wear-and-tear effect of toxic stress on the stress response system when it remains elevated for long periods of time (Harris, 2019). Consistent physical activity makes it possible for children to begin developing the protective factors that will continue to help them become more resilient to toxic stressors *throughout their lives.* We all have the ability to foster lifelong learners in our classrooms and enrich our instruction with reflection, guidance, and an openness to change. PA makes this process unbelievably easy; our Fast Fact Workout activity (Appendix A.36) is a more aerobically rigorous activity that helps counter cortisol buildup in students' brains through the surplus creation of BDNF. As such, this activity is a perfect warm-up for students as they enter your classroom.

For students who have experienced trauma, adversity, or toxic stress, teachers who promote growth mindsets through their instruction are especially impactful (Hochanadel & Finamore, 2015). The brain is elastic, and one's stress response systems have the capacity to change and rewire themselves, which is achievable through positive support, continuous effort, and immersion into new experiences. The fundamental approach to the growth mindset (i.e., that our intelligence is capable of growing and changing over time) is methodologically congruent with the principles of lifelong learning as well as our current understanding of the elastic brain in childhood neurobiology (Demarin et al., 2014). Just as our ability to learn is nonfixed, the same goes for our neural connections. Like a muscle, these neural connections and learning frameworks can be strengthened or weakened depending on their use. It just so happens that increased PA greatly strengthens these frameworks at a physiological level.

The emotions of *just one* teacher has wide-ranging effects on both immediate and future mindsets of students and, in turn, whether they develop a lifelong learner mentality. We must remember that everyone is capable of learning math, but how we respond and react to it as educators can set students up for future challenges or success. Therefore, we must invest our effort in building students' confidence in *learning* in general—when a student and their teacher are confident in their own abilities, that confidence can be a source of internal motivation to teach and study any subject further (Doménech-Betoret et al., 2017).

# Wrapping Up

Let's return to Sean's story about his experience working with Sha'kaysia:

As the year progressed, Sha'kaysia became much more vocal about her enjoyment of drawing. Her family even gifted her a drawing book, which she loved, and dug into the process of improving her craft. Watching her grow as a confident artist and communicator inspired me. In April, Ska'kaysia came up to me and showed a drawing of an anime face she had been working on from her drawing book. Previously, she would show her drawings and point out flaws. This time, however, she talked about the technique she used and that she thought it looked really good. Her drawings were already very good in my eyes, but to see and hear her describe her work in a positive way was a blossoming moment. I saw how my intentional relationship building had helped Sha'kaysia find her voice.

By connecting with Sha'kaysia through art, I saw her more eagerly share her inner beauty with others. In June, my cat, Welkin, passed away. The students knew about Welkin because I always shared pictures and videos of him with them. My students did not know he was sick, and the day after his passing my smile quivered with sadness as I addressed the class. As I gathered my materials at the end of class, I heard a voice ask, "Mr. D, are you OK?" I looked up to see Sha'kaysia with a compassionate expression on her face. The question was all it took for my shell to crack, and I told her about Welkin. Soon it was not just Sha'kaysia grieving with me but the entire class. Student after student came up and gave their condolences. It was a comfort amid my loss that meant the world to me. When our students unlock their own peaceful power, we all reap the rewards.

It doesn't—or shouldn't—take someone like Sherlock Holmes to see what the turning point was in the success of Sean's students. In this case, the key to their success was that the teacher saw what his students needed and, in turn, employed the necessary resources to create a learning experience that ultimately enriched their curriculum and transformed their struggles into triumphs. Sean recognized his instructional powers and could therefore meet his students' needs by designing a hands-on, dynamic learning environment for his students. His inclusive presence, empathy, educated awareness, and passion for change made all the difference in building trust and instilling the necessary competencies for lifelong learning. Of course, what Sean did was not a single act but a *process* of enrichment that centered relationships above all else. This process requires continuous effort and adaptation to meet the needs of individual students. What seems at first glance to be an insurmountable challenge for teachers with multiple high-need students who lead classrooms with limited resources or time constraints is actually made manageable through informed, (pro)active teaching strategies that capitalize on our natural inclination to be active and explore the world around us.

# Movement Makes
# Math *Review* Count

In this book, we've covered numerous concepts and applications of how movement-focused instruction benefits students' mathematical learning and boosts engagement, structure, breadth of learning, and depth of learning. Now we will discuss the impact of movement-based instruction on students' review and reflection of math content. Again, emotional regulation, relationship building, and mindset framing are potent contributors to the efficacy of students' learning, and activities that get students out of their seats and moving their bodies only speed up and make the process of reflection that much more engaging. Movement can help students (1) learn from their mistakes in an enjoyable way, (2) develop the necessary question-asking skills to more deeply comprehend their math material, and (3) develop their proof-making and proof-reading skills, which strengthens their connection to—and perceived value of—the discipline of mathematics.

At the time we were writing this book, Maggie was in her 19th year as an educator in a suburban elementary school outside Charlotte, North Carolina. She's been using movement-based learning for more than 10 years in the classroom, believing physical activity to be critically important to healthy living and learning, particularly for learning fundamental mathematical concepts like multiplication and division. In her words:

Learning basic multiplication and division facts is a core math skill for 3rd grade students. They are expected to know these math facts fluently with factors up to 10 by the end of the year. Throughout my teaching career, I've noticed how students tend to struggle more with learning division facts, even though division is an inverse operation of multiplication. Most have fluent strategies to multiply and can apply this operation to other math concepts. However, applying division to other math tasks seems to be a more daunting process for children. I have observed how this can cause students to get frustrated, make more mistakes, and feel less confident as math students. They want to stop trying or will say, "I don't get it," or, "I need help." I have tried using flash cards, games, math sheets, math models, and other activities to support students to learn these division facts. However, for children who are not as proficient with number sense, patterns, and multiplication, these activities are quite difficult and somewhat competitive in nature. For this reason, I started to use movement-based activities for math fact practice.

I work with students to skip-count, write, and say equations, but I've come to focus our efforts on practice by using physical movement—movements such as hopping, tapping, and skipping. Time is built into our math schedule to practice each day. We use printed math floor mats, wall charts, and desktop hundred charts to practice skip-counting. These all allow students to see the skip-counting pattern they are working on. These scaffolding materials support their practice work. I have noticed how students are more engaged in this type of fact practice mostly because it's fun but also because it's unintimidating and not based on individual results. The added benefit here is that they are engaging in aerobic exercise as they learn! Many students often say, "This is fun. Can we do it again tomorrow?"

I've noticed how students are more eager to review their math facts when there is not a graded outcome (as with a game or worksheet), yet there remain high expectations for accuracy and camaraderie. They've vocalized that they feel comfortable practicing math and enjoy moving because they can "go at their own pace" and converse as they move. My students who tend to be more quiet have also shared with me that this approach to reviewing math minimizes feelings of judgment from other classmates who are simultaneously doing their own movement practice.

Eight- and nine-year-olds naturally want to move, talk, and take part in enjoyable events with their peers. It might seem obvious that this is the case, especially if you've spent any time around kids. Yet, with so much available information correlating the benefits of movement to learning, it is imperative to include physical activity as an essential component. We need to take advantage of our kids' natural inclinations and preferences for movement to help them be happy and involved learners. I've observed how the quality of our fact practice and review lessons has improved when we use physical movement in the classroom. Not only is student behavior more positive, but they are also more on-task, more enthusiastic, and more willing to help each other!

I have also noticed that as students become familiar with how to effectively practice their math facts by moving, discussing, and collaborating, they then begin to apply these strategies to their independent work outside the math classroom. They also ask to practice facts with movement if they have finished their other work. These movement activities have even carried over to the playground and at students' homes. Students create skip-counting hopscotch outside with chalk at recess, where they practice math facts using the same process as in the classroom. Several do the same at home on their driveway or inside with number cards. As a teacher, when I see students transfer and share what they have learned in the classroom to other areas of their lives, I can tell they are excited and actually want to do it. One year I had a boy named Chris in my class. Chris wanted to learn. He had attention deficit disorder and often needed reminders to pay attention. Chris was on an intervention plan in math due to his low-performing scores over the last two consecutive years. Additionally, Chris was afraid of making mistakes. Movement in the classroom, I felt, was exactly what Chris needed to help him stay focused, energized, and learn.

## Learning from Mistakes Can Actually Be Fun?!

It's never fun to make mistakes. Or, it never *feels* fun when you do it. When we and our students make mistakes, it's usually unpleasant. This feeling has two primary components: one that is affective and one that is cognitive (Heinze, 2005). We often *feel* unpleasantness from our mistakes in the form of either embarrassment or judgment toward our competence. This feeling, if strong enough, keeps us from making errors. Yet this feeling does not guarantee that we will never make another mistake again. To err is human.

However, researchers and educators for a long time (since the ancient Greeks, really) have found numerous ways to capitalize on our natural mistake-making tendencies, turning them into learning opportunities. In practice, we often think of mistakes metaphorically and tend to polarize our mindset toward them by framing them as either problems or resources (Alvidrez et al., 2022). Mistakes framed as problems are meant to be eradicated and/or corrected, whereas mistakes framed as resources are opportunities to get deeper into the subject matter at hand. How we think about mistakes matters greatly in how our students learn from them and, in turn, take risks in the classroom. As we've discussed throughout this book, our own mindset toward mistake making can have an impact on our students' attitudes and learning of mathematics.

Because play and movement-based learning often manifest in the typical classroom via practical application, experimentation, and learning-through-doing, a movement-focused approach to learning offers students the unique experience of making—and learning from—their own mistakes. Although it can be unpleasant, making mistakes in the classroom can be extremely beneficial for learning, especially if teachers' responses to mistakes are positively delivered and constructive in nature. Modern scholars of education—particularly those who follow the philosophical tradition of John Dewey—believe that we are compelled to think *only* when we actually face a problem; in other words, *all* learning begins when our comfortable ideas turn out to be inadequate, so it is imperative that our students experience environments where their ideas and perceptions are consistently challenged. It is thus our jobs as educators to help them realize their capacities as critical thinkers by creating these hands-on, experiential environments (Dewey, 1897; 1902). The realization that one has made a mistake involves a certain level of in-the-moment problem-solving and critical-thinking skills, cognitive awareness, and memory, all of which cannot fully develop in children unless they themselves make mistakes and the teacher addresses them consistently. Interestingly enough, research has shown that when people (not just kids) make mistakes before they come to the correct answer, they are more likely to remember the correct material than if they were originally correct, a phenomenon known as "productive struggle" (Terada, 2018).

Corrective feedback is crucial to experiencing the benefits of error making, and movement-based learning makes the correction step of the learning process even easier; *physically* showing students where they went wrong (and how to reflect on how they got there) engages the whole child (see Metcalfe et al., 2019). Aside from priming the developing brain to be resilient toward adversity and anxiety via elevated dopamine and BDNF, physical math activities increase class cohesion through collective engagement, which reframes mistake making and mistake correcting as a low-stakes, community-oriented, and dynamic process. Moreover, physical activities are easy to apply to academic content and can often take the form of games, which can help students review difficult concepts without sacrificing engagement or instilling anxiety. Overall, physical movement (inside or outside the classroom) helps students foster relationships, build capacity to make meaning, and support conceptual rigor (Ciullo & Fede, 2017; Goh et al., 2020). Our Shapeshifters activity (Appendix A.37) offers multiple opportunities for you to provide students with corrective feedback and, in turn, work toward creating an active math environment where mistakes are to be welcomed (and celebrated) rather than avoided.

When we reframe our metaphor of mindset about errors—as *resources* rather than as problems—we can then approach using them as productive tools for learning. Additionally, by taking on a strengths-based perspective toward student thinking, we can develop an appreciation for error making as an *asset* in the classroom. In order to productively use mistakes for learning purposes, we can follow a simple path (Heinze, 2005):

1. Recognize that a mistake was made.
2. Analyze the mistake to understand what went wrong in the problem-solving process.
3. Correct the mistake.
4. Develop a strategy to prevent future mistakes.

By following this process, we can support students' mathematical agency through a well-defined classroom-wide response to errors. Providing counterexamples is an important practical support strategy, because "knowing" involves an awareness of both correct and incorrect answers. Additionally, as teachers we should prioritize students' self-esteem and work to develop their adaptive reasoning skills in order to boost their own math confidence (Alvidrez et al., 2022).

Being explicit about the mistake-making process as a fundamental, inescapable part of mathematical problem solving is beneficial at all levels of the learning process; by framing mathematical problem solving as a *dynamic* phenomenon that necessitates review, analysis, and reflection, we can begin to incorporate mistakes productively into the day-to-day classroom curriculum (Swartz, 2016). This, however, requires us to be able to effectively *notice* teachable moments within our classroom; in the literature, the capacity of teachers to attend to, interpret, and respond to classroom events is called *teacher noticing*, and it can create more learning opportunities for students (Scheiner, 2023). According to Scheiner (2023), such noticing entails explicitly highlighting students' strengths—rather than their weaknesses—when solving math problems and deliberately focusing our attention to the *context* in which student thinking occurs. In practice, we can improve our noticing and enrich, extend, and build upon our students' thinking by asking probing questions and providing collaborative learning opportunities as part of math practice. Our Heads Up, Sevenths Up activity (Appendix A.38) requires both you and your students to work together to develop creative solutions to fraction-related problems using movement as a mediator.

The feeling of negativity, fear, or anxiety about making mistakes is not an invalid or surprising feeling when it comes to mathematics. We can, however, take specific steps to reframe our perspective about mistakes in our classroom to begin thinking positively about math errors. Not only will this help our students take more risks in their problem solving, but it also will help us more confidently approach our students' questions and answers when issues do arise. Swartz (2016) sums up five basic assumptions that we as learners have about mistakes:

1. Mistakes can be seen as an unavoidable and inevitable part of any human activity.
2. It is possible to be optimistic about mistakes because mistakes can be used to help people improve.
3. The discovery and elimination of mistakes can be seen as one way to get closer to the goals of trust and perfection.
4. It is possible to decide to search for unattainable goals such as truth and perfection.
5. People can make decisions and act in the world in spite of the fact that they are uncertain about whether their decisions or actions are true or perfect.

With these assumptions in mind, what can we do to *reframe* our mindset toward errors and incorporate the study of mistakes into our math programs? Swartz provides six suggestions:

1. We should encourage people to be clear about what problem a decision or action is related to.
2. We should try our best to control and choose the kind of mistakes we are willing to make in various situations.
3. We should be willing to expose our decisions, actions, and possible mistakes to others.
4. We should try to objectify our mistakes and view them impersonally.
5. We should concentrate our energies on avoiding future mistakes rather than on regretting past ones or fearing new ones.
6. We should allow problems to be studied historically so that mistakes can become a respectable part of the school curriculum.

Our Wait! That Doesn't Add Up! activity (Appendix A.39) embraces these suggestions put forward by Swartz. Mistakes, errors, contradictions, differing opinions, and confusion are inescapable aspects of learning mathematics. They're inextricably linked to the learning process and have the potential to be extremely beneficial to student understanding if we can intentionally turn mistake making into a productive *activity* while simultaneously fostering a learning environment where students are confident enough to take risks and ask questions. As these activities highlight, incorporating physical activity into your math lessons can inject fun and collaboration into the day-to-day exercises of your math classroom. When students are having fun and moving their bodies, their regulated brains and calm emotions open them up to new experiences, greater challenges, and higher-order thinking.

## Questions, Discourse, and Making Reflection a Habit in the Math Classroom

As we briefly mentioned earlier in this chapter, the activity of *asking questions* falls within the learning process and is critical to strategizing future error avoidance. Asking good questions is very much a skill that is learned and perfected over time. A productive and inclusive math classroom affords both teachers and students the opportunity to ask questions as members of a lifelong learning community. Questioning is a mechanism of critical thinking, and as such it should be our duty as facilitators of the classroom community to allow voices to engage in dialogue and problem solving through the vehicle of questioning. The more we practice asking questions, the better we get at both asking and identifying which questions are most beneficial to support learning. Some questions are better for learning than others; some questions (and how they're presented) help us get deeper into the content and further internalize important concepts. *Surface* (or reproductive) questions prompt students to imitate, recall, or apply information provided by the teacher, which is then mimicked by students; whereas *deeper* (or productive) questions provide opportunities to create, analyze, or evaluate the subject matter (Teodoro et al., 2011). Deeper questions are usually open-ended in nature or require a fair amount of divergent thinking to answer fully. Of course, if we want our students to actually *understand* the material we teach, we would want to focus our efforts on asking—and getting them to ask—productive, deeper questions.

Questions arise during moments of discourse or speaking during classroom time. We can help our students become more productive *talkers,* and in turn *askers,* by focusing on their precision and explicit references to specific material (Franke et al., 2009). In other words, when we talk in the classroom, we want to make sure that what we're talking about is pertinent to the subject matter and is spoken to an extent that students have a chance to build on or contend with what is said. In fact, researchers have found that, when students have the chance to both raise and refine their own questions in collaboration with others, their motivation to engage in problem-solving activities increases, and their deep processing of information strengthens dramatically (Reiser et al., 2017). We can create classroom environments where deep questioning is a habit by strategically asking our students probing follow-up questions as they raise them. This, of course, requires adept familiarity with the content material as well as the question-asking tendencies of individual students. Acquiring this skill takes time, but practice is the key to success (see McTighe's [2017] quick reference guide for *Designing and Using Essential Questions* for some helpful strategies). Not only do appropriate follow-up questions help teachers understand student thinking, but they also help our students clarify, solidify, and correct their own thinking and support students in connecting their own ideas to what their peers are asking/answering. With that said, students' own questions *must* play a role in establishing the classroom community. We shouldn't be the only ones to set the rules, establish the norms, and ask the important questions—our students must be involved partners and leaders in this process if they're to acquire lasting motivation or incentive to do well in the math classroom now and in the future (Reiser et al., 2017). Our Geometry Taboo activity (Appendix A.40) sets the stage for constructive communal conversation around math tasks and concepts in how students are expected to work together to identify, explain, and deliberate mathematical (geometry) vocabulary.

What, then, makes a good productive question? According to researchers Reiser and colleagues (2017), good questions that support deeper processing connect directly to the material/concepts at hand and, more important, get at the *how* and the *why* mechanisms. In other words, we need to get our students beyond *what* explanations and instead get them to explain the mechanisms underlying the concept that allow it to work the way it does. Additionally, good questions not only demand empirical evidence of a phenomenon happening the way it does but also require students to build models that can be applied to new situations. Our questions should be answered by students in ways that get students to understand the mechanism at play and *how it can take shape in different contexts.*

Asking questions is beneficial to student learning if students themselves are the ones asking as well as answering. According to researchers Good and Slavings (1988), student-initiated questions help students understand their assignments and communicate with teachers, but they also help motivate and engage students in their assigned work and in mathematics in general (see also Reiser et al., 2017). By asking questions, students collect the necessary information to make sense of the content and prescribe *value* to said content (Good & Slavings, 1988). This demonstrates self-regulation when students make math meaningful and useful by asking good questions. If we allow our students opportunities to take ownership of their own learning while consistently working in collaboration with their peers, we can develop our students' skills in asking good questions (Teodoro et al., 2011). The Guess Who, Place Value! activity (Appendix A.41) is a movement-based question-asking activity that helps students work toward the *best* possible questions to identify a particular number. This activity is helpful in getting students to think critically about best practices and the multitude of problem-solving approaches.

If questioning is to be an effective tool in the classroom, it must be done collaboratively between teachers and students. Through collaboration, students better understand their own math identities in the context of the math classroom and are better able to align their sense of self with that of the discipline of mathematics more generally (Darragh, 2014). This alignment is important, because self-identification with a discipline adds perceived value to the work that students do in class. In other words, if a student sees themselves as *a mathematician* (or a budding mathematician), they are more likely to continue to study mathematics further. Questions can function as scripts for our students to practice taking on this type of positive math identity; motivation to ask questions comes from wanting to continue feeling like a competent mathematician, which in turn fosters a classroom community of motivated budding mathematicians that promotes risk taking, asking questions, and collaboration.

The classroom community has the potential to both limit and empower student participation in math tasks. As it stands, our classroom might make our students reluctant to ask questions publicly. This is typically the case when activities during math lessons expect students to be passive learners who sit down and listen to the teacher, which might not even be the teacher's intent. By celebrating moments when students ask questions and by encouraging active participation in math lessons, we can create inquisitive classroom environments that support every learner (Reiser et al., 2017). Our own questions that we ask our students scaffold students' task engagement and increase opportunities for higher-order thinking and learning, which shape the nature of the learning environment into one that is supportive and comforting (Franke et al., 2009; Reiser et al., 2017).

But how can we become more aware of and purposeful in our own questioning? According to researchers Teodoro and colleagues (2011), we can enhance our positive questioning habits by recording, processing, sorting, and analyzing the questions that we ourselves pose to our students and that students themselves provide. It is helpful to record what questions are asked and, in turn, assess whether they are relevant and answerable collectively—we cannot just accept answers as right or wrong without explanation, nor can we simply accept answers that simply name or categorize the content. Additionally, teachers need to revisit their questions as well as those that students pose, which builds trust in how students can rely on you to guide their learning without forgetting the individual learner. Furthermore, by building on previous questions or connecting new questions to already explained phenomena, we help shape students' problem-solving perspectives into inquisitive excitement. Our 22 Questions activity (Appendix A.42) helps educators practice building on the questions posed by students and allows numerous opportunities for students to work together actively to come up with best solutions.

We want our students to ask questions and, in turn, perform their math identities through active participation, so we as educators need to teach our students through collaborative work how to go about asking good questions and responding to them genuinely with a growth-focused, strengths-based mindset. Over time, these habits create an environment that celebrates taking chances and holding students accountable for their learning. As students develop their skills, their math attitudes increase in tandem; their enjoyment flourishes, as does their confidence and perceived value of the discipline of mathematics, all of which support higher math scores, and all of which benefit from increased physical activity opportunities.

## Can You Prove Your Answer... Fearlessly?

As we've discussed in previous chapters, anxiety and fear have for too long become expected associates of student (dis)engagement in the math classroom. Fear, of course, is a complex emotion that impacts behavior in a multitude of ways. Quite often within the math classroom this fear manifests as disengagement in math tasks. According to Thomas and colleagues (2019), "the focus in recent trauma-informed discipline resources shifts educator perspectives from viewing students' undesirable behaviors (e.g., avoidance, aggression, disengagement) as inherently bad or oppositional toward viewing each student as having been affected in some way by their experiences" (p. 428). This conclusion melds nicely into our understanding of brain science; undesirable behaviors like disengagement are often indicators of unmanageable stress or previous adverse experiences. When we intentionally empower, support, question, coach, and guide our students when they engage in unwanted behaviors, our students no longer think of discipline as punishment but rather as one more opportunity to learn. Students no longer think of their teacher as a punitive agent but as a role model—a hero—who cares about their well-being and learning. In turn, the classrooms of these teachers become *fearless spaces* where students are empowered to take risks.

But how can this *fearlessness* take shape within our math curricula? For many math students, the topic of proofs and proofing can be intimidating and fear-inducing, especially if students have had no prior experience with it. What we mean by *proof* here comes from the works of Stylianides (2007; 2016), who defines proof as a "mathematical argument" or a connected sequence of assertions for or against a mathematical claim. Mathematical proofs provide (Stylianides, 2016; Zaslavsky et al., 2021)

- Justification, refutation, or validation.
- Explanations.
- Discovery opportunities.
- Communication practice.
- Systemization or structuring.
- Illustration of new methods of deduction.
- Defense of axiom systems.
- A means for promoting understanding by showing *why* an assertion is true or false.

Proof and the act of proofing one's answer help students internalize the *how* and *why* of mathematical processes while burgeoning their transferable argumentation skills (Sowder & Harel, 1998). For a proof to be meaningful, it needs to use statements that are accepted by your classroom community to be true and available. The proof also needs to employ forms of reasoning that are accessible to all of your students as well as be communicated in ways that are appropriate and known to the classroom community. Under this definition, proof can take *many* forms, but it is appropriate in school math (even in lower grades) because (Stylianides, 2007; 2016)

- It considers both math as a discipline and students as mathematical learners.
- It promotes consistent definitions of proof across grade levels.
- It prevents empirical arguments from being considered as proofs.
- It supports analysis of classroom instruction related to proof and study of the role of teachers in managing proofing.

Proofs are *tools* that teachers and students use to become knowledgeable of mathematical phenomena and shouldn't be used simply as an exercise in explaining the obvious (Zaslavsky et al., 2021). When we frame proofs as tools for gaining knowledge, our students will become more confident learners when tackling complex concepts—and they will have the capacity to utilize multiple schemes to make sense of the world around them (Sowder & Harel, 1998), which is an extremely transferable skill. Our Ready, Set, Sudoku! activity (Appendix A.43) provides students opportunities to build the foundational logical reasoning and communication skills required of proofing, the functions of which are multivarious and support the increased perceived value of mathematics among students.

Proofs are usually a tool that *higher*-level classrooms employ in their lessons, so most students who reach that level of mathematical experience are stopped in their tracks when encountering formal proofing activities. The benefits of proofs are massive, so why don't we get our students to begin writing proofs at an earlier age? The lack of consistent and coherent experiences with the reasoning processes that proofs provide has the potential to cause difficulties in higher-level classes, like geometry and trigonometry (Bieda et al., 2013). The lack of experience can be attributed—at least partly—to a relatively low number and unequal distribution of proof/reasoning problems in our math textbooks and curricula. How can we expect our students to embrace proofs as a legitimate tool and proofing as a valuable skill if there are few formal opportunities for them to practice generating and evaluating mathematical claims?

Proofs have been pushed to the back of our curriculum into a marginalized position. This is due in part to teachers' own lackluster knowledge about proofs and effective proofing strategies as well as low self-confidence in their own ability to formulate proofs (Zaslavsky et al., 2021). There are also presumed beliefs that many educators hold that limit student participation in proofing activities, namely that elementary students will not (or are not able to) understand proofs, when this has been proven over time to not be the case (Stylianides, 2016). Additionally, for those teachers who want their students to engage in proofing, there are a number of high pedagogical demands that are placed on those teachers as well as inadequate instructional support for such classroom endeavors. Because of these issues, the activity of proofing has become an exercise in confirming assertions that lack intellectual purpose (Zaslavsky et al., 2021). For there to be purpose in a proof, students need to both appreciate the mathematical problem at hand and be fully engaged in the solution attempt. We can promote this engagement by providing our students opportunities for hands-on math practice that is physically demanding and collaborative. One activity that provides such an opportunity for collaborative, movement-based proofing is Cutout Conundrum. (Appendix A.44).

So, *how* can we teach proofs in a way that sets up our students for success later in their mathematical careers? If we are to instill knowledge of important mathematical procedures in our students, it would be quite counterproductive to not also support the reasoning and sense making that our students engage in (Sowder & Harel, 1998). We need to first be perceptive of our students' own perspectives toward proofs, the need for proofs, and what sort of situations and tasks encourage students to look for proofs (Zaslavsky et al., 2021). Even younger students have a number of intellectual needs that proofs satisfy—namely, students' need for certainty, interest in causality, and desire for computation, communication, and structure. By making proofs part of our math curriculum, we can get our students to accept the activity of proofing as a worthwhile problem-solving and reflective strategy, thus increasing their perceived value of mathematics as a useful discipline.

Again, collaboration in small groups provides students with numerous opportunities to discuss and cooperate on proofing while simultaneously removing the teacher as the sole focus of authority (Sowder & Harel, 1998). Small-group work empowers students to take risks and learn from others, and because proofing is a test in argumentation and persuasion, the social expectations of small-group work provides the perfect environment for proofing and reflection. Of course, our facilitation of proofing activities is crucial if we're to help our students develop their proofing abilities (Stylianides, 2007). A teacher needs to be explicit in what qualifies as proofs and what arguments could count as proofs. Decisions related to these aspects should come collaboratively from ourselves and our students. Our sole responsibility, then, is to provide students with a repertoire of action plans and interventions that advance students' proof-related math resources. As such, teachers function as a *bridge* between two communities—a bridge between the classroom community and the greater math community, which finds proofs to be the definitive activity of "authentic" mathematics. Teachers play the active role in judging, instructing, and guiding students on what arguments are valid and count as proof (Zaslavsky et al., 2021).

Our actions as teachers matter, as do the actions of our students and the classroom environment in which learning math takes place! In order to foster productive, positive attitudes toward proofs and mathematics more generally, it is important to promote and enact a classroom culture that encourages openly sharing and debating ideas (Bieda et al., 2013). Such a classroom includes a variety of math tasks that are closely related to math reasoning and proofing. Additionally, students should consistently use effective forms of questioning, and all should embrace an inquiry-based approach to problem solving, which includes opportunities to explore, conjecture, explain, validate, disprove, and experiment (Zaslavsky et al., 2021). Our 101 and Out activity (Appendix A.45) allows students to physically engage in this inquiry-driven problem solving in the mathematical context of adding, subtracting, and multiplying on a giant 100-number grid.

The activity of proofing and the resourceful use of proofs to understand the machinations of various math concepts play an important role in students' ongoing reflection and, in turn, learning of mathematics. By providing students with numerous opportunities to formulate proofs either individually or collectively, we can get our students to develop critical thinking skills and resilience in the inevitable face of error.

## Wrapping Up

Let's round off our chapter on review and reflection with a continuation of Maggie's story:

> During our math review times, Chris would use the skip-counting floor mats to practice his multiplication and division facts. When he worked on paper-pencil assignments, Chris would often get up and use the math mats for a few minutes to reenergize his brain and get additional fact practice. He would often ask to have a physical movement break, which indicated his self-awareness that he needed to stimulate his brain to learn. In addition, I also worked with Chris in a small group with three to four students to help him with math concepts. The consistent movement opportunities helped Chris enjoy math and increased his focus to learn. Chris ended the year by passing the math end-of-grade test, despite being on an intensive intervention plan during the previous years.
>
> Each year I always make an effort to ask my students if they know why it's important to know their multiplication and division facts. I usually get a range of different responses, such as "It will

help me next year," "I'll be able to get a good job someday," and so on. I also ask them if they would rather practice and review their facts on their own, at their desk, on a computer program, with flash cards, or with their own worksheet and pencil. Their quick response is always an emphatic *"No!"*

Time and time again they have asserted that their favorite way to review math is to work together and move around. Usually without further questioning, my students begin to list why, often citing that moving makes them feel more awake and not bored. They comment on how they worry less about getting something incorrect and just focus on what they are doing. I often have a few students in my class who say they like math, but they feel that they're slower than others at calculating answers, which definitely causes them anxiety. They say the movement review is "easy-going" and makes them feel good about themselves. Once I had a female student, who rarely participated in math discussions, who said she was having so much fun that at one point she chuckled and said she forgot that she was actually working on math.

This positive feedback is important not just for me as their teacher but also for the whole class because students will more likely learn any content when they are comfortable in their environment and fully engaged in the learning process. I also explain to my students why I have them practice math facts using movement. I think it's important for students to understand the science of the brain and how it needs extra oxygen from physical activity to quickly learn, think, and remember ideas. I believe this is a critical conversation to have with students, because they start to monitor their own focus and reflect on their own engagement. They start to take ownership of their learning. As the school years move on, my students will at times get up and quietly do some knee taps, full body twists, or no-impact jumping jacks if they begin to feel unproductive during work times. Sometimes they ask me to provide a three- or five-minute full-class movement break to get reenergized. This refocuses the entire classroom and reorients attention toward what needs to be practiced.

This self-awareness is important for young people as they move forward through their educational journey. By being informed about how the brain works, students can independently regulate themselves and identify what they need to help them be more efficient learners. Such knowledge is the foundation of a growth mindset. We always begin the school year talking about working hard and persevering along the paths and processes to mastering new information. I feel it is my obligation as a teacher to inform my students about the positive impact physical movement has on their learning. This, in turn, enhances their growth mindset and positive attitude toward obtaining new knowledge. I feel that we need this in our math classrooms now more than ever.

We can support our students' review and reflection of their math content by reframing how we approach making mistakes, how we ask and answer math-related questions, and how we implement and engage with proving on a consistent basis. Maggie consistently questioning *why* in harmony with movement-based learning strategies assisted her classroom's reflection and review competencies by increasing student enjoyment, task engagement, and social cohesion. The classroom community that Maggie fostered is indicative of the power of collaborative, fearless questioning and engagement. This was made manifest through her consistent incorporation of physical activity both as the framework for facilitation and as a vehicle for students to engage fully and fearlessly with the math content. The beauty of this story, we feel, is that *all* of us can be Maggie.

# Conclusion

In this book we've covered a variety of instructional strategies, explored a wealth of research, and pondered many personal stories of growth and achievement as they relate to movement in the mathematics classroom. We first investigated how physical activity influences the relationship between stress and the developing brains of our students. We then proposed our research-based instructional framework of the three Moving and Learning Teacher Powers and introduced our active math framework with the Five Catalysts of Movement-Based Instruction. We discovered how movement stimulates student engagement through motivating and focusing minds. We discovered how movement scaffolds student learning when implemented collaboratively and creatively. We discovered how movement expands student learning and opens up connections to other content. We discovered how movement enriches student learning in how it helps to minimize math anxiety, boost trust, and support the development of lifelong learning attitudes. We also discovered how movement stimulates reflection through the normalization of mistake making, question asking, and exploration. All along the way, we provided inspirational stories from powerhouse kinesthetic teachers and dozens of movement-based math activities that readers can immediately implement in their classrooms.

We hope these discussions have provided a comprehensive foundation from which you can confidently enrich your mathematics instruction with multisensory activities and instructional strategies. Based on what you've read here, we also hope you try out these activities and play around with their implementation in different learning contexts. We've found success as they are, but we ask that you adapt them as you see fit so that every one of your students, regardless of skill or ability level, can participate.

We anticipate that your students will have few issues buying into these activities, and you can expect them to catch on to these movements and games rather quickly. When students reach that observable point of effort-lessness in their physical movements and their math fact recall, it's time to increase the rigor and complexity!

Knowing when students have reached that point is a matter of practice; your students will be quick to tell you how the activities make them feel, and you will see their enjoyment and engagement in the games and their relevant math content. Use that joy as a starting point to engage the classroom in deep discussions and collaborative reflection. When we focus on joy as an anchor for learning, we actively foster classroom environments of trust, risk taking, and inquiry, which set the stage for accelerated learning and positive attitude development. You, too, will experience joy as a facilitator of these activities. We sincerely hope that you run with this joy and that you use the practical frameworks described in this book to maximize the impact of your teacher powers.

In the fast-paced, tumultuous world of today, it has become a habit of sorts to keep our students seated for most of their time in school. Such a response is not unreasonable—when students are sitting still and silent, there is observable *order* in behaviors and *structure* to the learning environment. Such an environment is enticing, especially for educators who work with students who need additional support, who struggle with behavioral challenges, or who have ACEs. Much like mathematics as a discipline, which has historically been presented to young learners as an orderly, systematic, even rigid field of study, it's not that surprising that students in the average math classroom are expected to sit quietly in their seats and do so habitually. This is how it's always been—"This is how *I* was taught mathematics," we say to ourselves and to our students. Sitting in our seats has been the status quo for American math classrooms.

The problem is that this approach doesn't work. If our goal is for students to become competent and confident learners who are motivated to continue learning and growing (and actually stay in school), sitting idly does not do the job. Motivation requires engagement, and sitting still is not engaging. For those students who *can't* sit still, attempting to do so is excruciating! We see this daily in students' disruptive behaviors and their disengagement from math tasks and classroom participation; we see them fidgeting in their seats or poking at others, we see the glazed-over look in their eyes, and we hear silence—not the type of silence that comes from contemplation, but the fearful silence of feeling lost in what is being taught.

The teachers we supported in Florida saw this firsthand on a regular basis, which compelled them to reach out to us to learn more about alternatives and how to support their educators and, in turn, their students. That conversation led to a successful movement-based multiplication intervention that not only changed math scores but also changed attitudes and behaviors toward learning in general. In response to the success witnessed during this intervention, one such educator enthusiastically offered us his own "call to action" to educators who might be interested in incorporating movement into their classroom:

> I sincerely hope that you'll open up your eyes and your heart and try something different. Not for your sake, but for the sake of your children. It's that big of a difference. You can change lives that quickly. It's not even been two weeks, and there's a change in the dynamics of my class.... I can't stress enough how important it is for our students, how important it is for the parents, how important it is for the teacher, because it makes your job easier to do, more efficient to do, more fun to do. It minimizes stress and increases pride. These are the things that we talk about as educators that we hope to achieve. This is your opportunity to try something different because the old way is not working. (Mr. Mills, 3rd grade teacher)

It's high time we rid math classrooms of the desk-bound status quo. Structured movement and cross-disciplinary practices like learning science, neurobiology, and physical education provide an evidence-based alternative to stationary mathematics. Movement taps into the natural inclination of our students—the natural inclinations of *all of us*—that set us up for accelerated learning at the most foundational, physiological level. Let's harness this need and desire to move, and let's capitalize on the observable benefits of regular physical activity throughout the school day.

To remain sedentary is to remain limited or confined to a particular way of thinking and participating in math—a way of thinking that does not account for the well-evidenced physical and physiological needs of all of us learners. Being sedentary is being *bounded*, like a mathematical function, and where's the fun in that?

# Appendix: Movement-Based Activities

## A.1: Zero Heroes

### Overview

This activity helps students model zero pairs using their own bodies as manipulatives. It's a blast to do collaboratively with students at different levels of support requirements.

### Required Materials

Masking tape; construction paper; pens/pencils; index cards (preferably different colors for positive and negative numbers)

### Preparation

Create a number line on the floor for numbers negative 10 to positive 10 (see Figure A.1). Lay masking tape on the floor or tape down construction paper to measure equivalent distances, and label them accordingly.

On 10 index cards (the same color), write the individual numbers –10 to –1. On 10 other (differently colored) index cards, write the individual numbers 1 to 10. On the last index card, write 0.

FIGURE A.1

**Zero Heroes**

## Activity Steps

1. Introduce your students to the two rules of adding positive and negative numbers kinesthetically:
   - When *adding*, you will face the positive end of the number line; when *subtracting*, you will face the negative end.
   - When you encounter a *negative sign* before a number, you make a 180-degree turn.
2. Have a student stand on the number line on the first number in the equation. Ask the student, "Are you adding or subtracting?" If subtracting, the student will face the negative end of the line.
3. Ask, "Is the second number positive or negative?" Make a 180-degree turn when the second number is negative. Then they will hop the number of spaces equal to the second number of the equation.

# A.2: Double Dutch Duos

## Overview

This partner activity supports student collaboration and coordination using jump ropes to practice skip-counting by 3s, 4s, 6s, and 7s.

## Required Materials

Jump ropes

## Preparation

Make sure that your students have enough space to hop using jump ropes. This activity is perfect for PE or during recess, but it can be done in any open space indoors or outdoors.

## Activity Steps

1. **Alternating 3s:** Stand side by side with your partner, each holding one handle of the rope. Begin with the rope down behind your feet. Partner A holds the rope in the right hand; partner B holds the rope in the left hand. As the rope comes down in front, partner A brings the right arm down across the body to the left side, and only partner B jumps over the rope. Both whisper, "One." As the rope comes down again, partner A brings the right arm back to the right side, and partner B brings the left arm down and across to the right side. This time only partner A jumps over the rope. Both whisper, "Two." As the rope comes down again, both partners return to the starting position and complete a single bounce jump. Both say, "Three!" Continue until 30.

2. **Face-to-Face by 4s:** With one jumper holding the rope and both partners facing each other, turn the rope overhead and jump together. Count by 4s each time a jump is completed. Continue until 40.

3. **Side by Side by 6s:** Stand side by side with your partner. Each jumper holds one handle of the rope. Begin with the rope down behind both jumpers' feet. Turn the rope overhead and jump together. Count by 6s each time a jump is completed. Continue until 60.

4. **Back-to-Face by 7s:** With one jumper holding the rope, the other jumper turns their back to the turner's face. Turn the rope overhead and jump together. Count by 7s each time a jump is completed. Continue until 70.

## Possible Variations

The more participants the better! Consider involving more students in the activity as either holders of the rope or counters of the jumps; those who are not actively involved in jumping rope can still participate by jumping in place, clapping, and counting out loud.

Additionally, to practice fractions, the rope holders can swing the jump rope around four times, for example, and the jumper would have to time their jump through the rope once per every four counts (i.e., one-*fourth* of the total swings); in other words, after every four revolutions of the rope, a student would hop through the rope to indicate ¼, a hop through the rope every three revolutions would equal ⅓, and so on.

# A.3: Mathematicians from Outer Space

## Overview

This activity will teach students about building trust through problem-solving strategies and effective communication. You can play an active role in this activity as a speechless facilitator of the math tasks.

## Required Materials

Index cards; writing materials; tape, chalk, or construction paper for creating the 10-by-10-foot 100 number grid

## Preparation

Create a 10-by-10-foot 100 number grid (with chalk if outside or with tape or construction paper if inside). Draw a box at the top left edge of the grid (or place another piece of construction paper) and write 0 in the box (see Figure A.3).

Ask your students to sit around in a circle on the floor or have them arrange their desks in a circle. Introduce the scene by telling them that they have been transported to a different planet far beyond our solar system where they are now role-playing as alien mathematicians. As such, they can no longer speak out loud and can only communicate through *actions* (see A.9 for some example gestures). In groups of four, students can be tasked with various mathematical problems that they need to solve together on the 100 number grid. You can play with the design of the number grid to have your alien mathematicians navigate an asteroid field or explore a new planet.

## Activity Steps

1. Assign pairs of students to secretly come up with a specific number pattern (or an equation for students who would like an additional challenge); they can use the 100 number grid as a reference and whisper to one another during the planning phase. For example, the two students could come up with a pattern of three hops along the rows of the grid ("multiples of 3s") or both hop on numbers that are only even or odd ("odd and even numbers") or move across numbers below 50 ("< 50").

2. Once the pair has decided on a pattern, pairs of students will take turns to demonstrate their pattern to the whole class (or other pairs) without speaking.

3. Considering that the demonstrations could yield multiple correct answers, students in the class (or the other pair) can silently take note on index cards what patterns, qualities, language, or equations they think are correct.

4. After students have had a chance to observe the behaviors and made their guesses, they can break up into small groups to quietly discuss their findings and guesses.

5. After some idea sharing, the class will come together to present their "translations," which could be done orally or on the board; the pairs/ groups that answer correctly will then have the opportunity to lead the next round.

FIGURE A.3
**Mathematicians from Outer Space**

| 0 | 1 | 2 | 3 | 4 | 5 | 6 | 7 | 8 | 9 | 10 |
|---|---|---|---|---|---|---|---|---|---|---|
|  | 11 | 12 | 13 | 14 | 15 | 16 | 17 | 18 | 19 | 20 |
|  | 21 | 22 | 23 | 24 | 25 | 26 | 27 | 28 | 29 | 30 |
|  | 31 | 32 | 33 | 34 | 35 | 36 | 37 | 38 | 39 | 40 |
|  | 41 | 42 | 43 | 44 | 45 | 46 | 47 | 48 | 49 | 50 |
|  | 51 | 52 | 53 | 54 | 55 | 56 | 57 | 58 | 59 | 60 |
|  | 61 | 62 | 63 | 64 | 65 | 66 | 67 | 68 | 69 | 70 |
|  | 71 | 72 | 73 | 74 | 75 | 76 | 77 | 78 | 79 | 80 |
|  | 81 | 82 | 83 | 84 | 85 | 86 | 87 | 88 | 89 | 90 |
|  | 91 | 92 | 93 | 94 | 95 | 96 | 97 | 98 | 99 | 100 |

## Possible Variations

Time permitting, have one group that did particularly well completing their tasks take the *whole class* through their solution to their problem without speaking; you can format this whole-group activity as a speechless "panel" of experts.

For students who need additional support, the teacher could begin the activity by pointing to items in the room all with the same characteristics/qualities. When someone thinks they have to point to something that would fit that category (e.g., something blue, something that starts with the letter *L*) the teacher can nod if correct or shake their head for the student to try again; this activity could be framed around mathematical language/terms that you're covering in your curriculum (e.g., "how many," "count," "multiple").

# A.4: Fantastic High-Fivers

## Overview

In this activity, students practice evens and odds while simultaneously boosting positive mathematics beliefs and class cohesion through high-energy high fiving. This game is part mystery; sometimes it will be possible for everyone to get a high five, sometimes not. The difference is that it is *only* possible if there are an even number of people giving high fives.

## Required Materials

Whiteboard/blackboard (if you want to write down patterns for the class)

## Preparation

Make sure that students have enough space to move around to high-five other students in the class.

## Activity Steps

1. Have students stand out of their seats and introduce to them the activity; each student is tasked to give a high five to five different classmates. When students have given/received five high fives, they do a jumping jack and then sit down.

2. Start with a prediction; have students count out how many students (including the teacher) are in the classroom. Will everyone be able to give five high fives to *different* classmates? Or will there be students left over?

3. Begin the activity after a brief countdown. Give students as much time as they need to complete the task. Students who give/receive five high fives immediately sit down.

4. The student who remains standing (because the multiple is *odd*) gets to choose the next number of high fives that the class will seek out.

5. Try this game for different multiples (2s, 4s, 6s, 7s, etc.) and let students guess whether they think everyone will get the requisite number of high fives or not before they actually do the activity. Why does it only work sometimes and not always? If you make it four or six high fives instead of five (that is, an even number), then everyone will be able to get their high fives every time.

## Possible Variations

Have students arrange themselves into groups with an even number of people and then an odd number. Have them try the activity again, but it can't be the same number they made last time!

# A.5: Who Wants to Be a 100 Millionaire?

## Overview

This activity fosters positive mathematics attitudes by supporting students' engagement, enjoyment, and self-confidence completing math tasks collaboratively (and competitively).

## Required Materials

None, other than any particular manipulatives that you would like your students to use to answer the questions you pose during the game

## Preparation

Prepare a set of 15 multiple-choice math questions for a particular math concept you're working on (e.g., place values). The questions and their multiple-choice answers can be written on the board as they're delivered, or they can be printed or written on pieces of paper or index cards and then displayed for all to see as the questions are posed.

Some students might find individual participation in this activity a bit nerve-wracking, which is why we suggest partnering students together or in small groups (no more than four) to participate in the game show as teams. Organize the chairs in your classroom in a circle around a few chairs in the middle (which will be for you as the host and for the team competing). Playing music in the background is a great way to increase student engagement!

## Activity Steps

1. You will act as a game show host and ask for a math contestant (or small team of contestants) to join you in the middle of the circle of seats.

2. You will ask your students math questions (or math terminology questions) around a particular concept (e.g., place values, fractions, probability, etc.) in the form of a multiple-choice question.

3. The students have the option to ask other students in the "audience" for assistance (called *lifelines*) if they do not know the answer, encouraging collaboration. Lifelines can only be used once in a game. These lifelines can include

   - **Phone a friend:** the contestant can speak to one student in the audience for 30 seconds to try to agree on an answer.
   - **50–50:** remove two incorrect answers, leaving the correct answer and one remaining one answer.
   - **Ask the audience:** ask a poll of answers from the audience.
   - **Double dip:** the contestant can give another answer if their first answer is incorrect, but they cannot walk away on that question if they use it, nor is the lifeline reusable if the first answer is correct.
   - **Move instead:** the contestant can do an active math movement or a physical activity in lieu of answering the question.

4. Students who answer a question correctly (or incorrectly) can be tasked with a particular physical activity, such as doing 10 squats or jumping jacks.

5. Like the game show, an incorrect answer will result in losing the game, so the team who answers incorrectly will sit in the audience and the next team will come up to play (time permitting).

## Possible Variations

Reverse the roles! Students have to come up with the questions and quiz their teacher in this version. Students will collaborate on making the questions and have to know the correct answers to quiz their instructor; this could be a homework or group activity that could tie together a whole unit around a particular concept.

# A.6: Ifs and Thens

## Overview

This activity helps students practice the logical foundations of proofing ("if, then" statements) in a way that is physically active and relatable to students' own knowledge/life experiences.

## Required Materials

Index cards; writing materials; whiteboard/blackboard

## Preparation

On index cards, prepare a number of "if" statements for students; these statements could start with more relevant connections (e.g., "If it is 1:00 on a Saturday…" or "If I have \$5 in my pocket…"). Prepare enough index cards for each student to hold. Split students into pairs or small groups, and give each individual an index card with an "if" statement on it.

## Activity Steps

1. Ask each pair/grouping to come up with a "then" statement and write it on the back of the card.
2. After a student writes their "then" statement on the back of the card, they can hand it to their partner, who will create their own (different) "then" statement under their partner's response.

3. Once the team has completed the task, collect the index cards and regroup the class. On the whiteboard/blackboard, write the "if" statement of each card like you would a mathematical proof.

4. Read the two answers provided by the students on the "then" side of the cards; students can vote on their favorite/most logical response. After the "then" statement is decided, record that answer on the other side of the proof on the board

5. Repeat this process for each "if, then" statement

6. After students become familiar with the logic of such statements, provide them with new index cards with "if" statements that are mathematical in nature (e.g., "If I multiply three groups by five,…"). Repeat the steps as needed.

## Possible Variations

Break students up into small groups (at least four per group) and split the groups into teams; one team will construct the "if" statement while the other team is tasked to construct the "then" statement. To highlight the possible "ifs" that could result in a particular "then," you can have students first draft a "then" statement and work collaboratively to come up with a variety of "if" statements that could result in that "then" response. Be sure to highlight the mathematical language/terms throughout the facilitation of this activity.

# A.7: Where's the Overlap?

## Overview

This activity builds students' multiplication skills and confidence through collaborative problem solving using manipulatives, their own bodies, and a large Venn diagram for visualization.

## Required Materials

A red hula hoop and a blue hula hoop (or two different colors if possible; this activity also works with two different colors of string if the circles need to be larger); index cards; markers; skip-counting charts (see downloadable resources)

## Preparation

Divide students into two teams. One team works together to write on index cards the multiples of 6 (i.e., 0, 6, 12, 18, 24, 30, 36, 42, 48, 54, 60) and five other numbers between 1 and 500. The second team works together to write on index cards the multiples of 7 (i.e., 0, 7, 14, 21, 28, 35, 42, 49, 56, 63, 70) and five other numbers between 1 and 500. Collect the index cards. From the pile of index cards, remove two index cards, a 0 and a 42. Lay out the hula hoops (or string) on the floor in the shape of a Venn diagram (see Figure A.7); mix up the cards.

FIGURE A.7
**Where's the Overlap?**

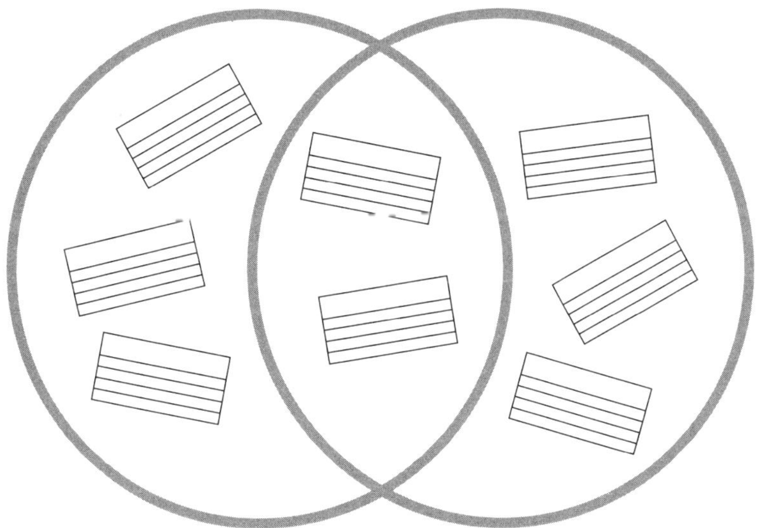

## Activity Steps

1. Display the skip-counting chart by 6s on the whiteboard or smart-board (or print and laminate as cards). Instruct students to look at the chart and chant the multiples of 6s as they engage in cross-body movements with their arms (see activities A.10 and A.28 for some examples).

2. Display the skip-counting chart by 7s on the smartboard. Instruct students to look at the chart and chant the multiples of 7s as they jump up and down.

3. Explain to students that the red circle represents multiples of 6, the blue circle represents multiples of 7, and the intersection of the Venn diagram represents numbers that are both multiples of 6 and 7.

4. Hand one index card to each student.

5. Students decide where to place the card on the Venn diagram on the floor; alternatively, students can tape the card to their chest and stand on the Venn diagram where they feel it should be placed. Note that, if students themselves are going to stand on the diagram, make sure that the circle is large enough with string instead of hula hoops. Students can collaborate and check each other's work.

## Possible Variations

Repeat the steps for different pairs of multiples. You can also spread out the index cards randomly throughout the Venn diagram and have students rearrange them to their correct positions. Alternatively, you split the class into two teams; one team will have the index cards and stand on the Venn diagram wherever they want, while the other team has to rearrange their classmates on the Venn diagram. For a competitive edge, you can time each round to see which team is the quickest to correctly organize the numbers/students on the diagram.

# A.8: Groovy Groupings

## Overview

This activity is a bit similar to the Fantastic High-Fivers (A.4) but with added difficulty in that students will be tasked with responding to multi-step commands. This activity promotes collaboration and communication and allows the teacher to participate with students as either the facilitator or a group member.

## Required Materials

None

## Preparation

Make sure students have enough room to move around and form groups. For some more physical rigor, you can arrange the desks/tables in such a way to make traversing the room more difficult for students to get to point A or B.

## Activity Steps

1. To begin, you will call out a number (e.g., 3), and the students have 10 seconds to get themselves into groups of that size. You can play music in the background like Musical Chairs. It might be impossible for everyone to get in a group every time, but each new number gives everyone another chance.

2. Once students get the gist, you can call out addition or subtraction problems (e.g., "Get into groups of 7 – 4"). Don't forget to call out a group of 1 and a group of however many students are in the entire class at some point in the game. The "remainder" students get to go to the board and write out the equation of all the groups, and the whole class works together to solve for the total (which won't change).

## Possible Variations

In the basic game, just call out single numbers, but you can increase the difficulty of the activity by building from previous answers and incorporating different concepts (e.g., "Get into groups of 10 – 4; now get into groups *half* that number").

# A.9: Strategize, Gesture-ize!

## Overview

This activity uses gestures to strengthen students' mathematics communication skills and embodied cognition. Students will collaboratively build questions and communicate individual problem-solving strategies about adding and subtracting, but this activity can also be adapted for students who need a challenge with more complex mathematical concepts like multiplication and division or adding and subtracting fractions.

### Required Materials

Index cards; markers; masking tape (or construction paper)

### Preparation

Create a number line on the floor for numbers 1–20 (see Figure A.9; you can place masking tape on the floor or use construction paper to measure equivalent distances for each space). Write addition and subtraction problems on cards or on a smartboard.

FIGURE A.9
**Strategize, Gesture-ize!**

| 1 | 2 | 3 | 4 | 5 | 6 | 7 | 8 | 9 | 10 | 11 | 12 | 13 | 14 | 15 | 16 | 17 | 18 | 19 | 20 |
|---|---|---|---|---|---|---|---|---|----|----|----|----|----|----|----|----|----|----|----|

### Activity Steps

1. Teach students the following gestures for communicating addition/subtraction strategies:
   - **Counting on/counting back:** Students raise one hand with their thumb up and lower their other hand with their thumb down.
   - **Make 10:** Students raise both hands above their heads with all 10 fingers outstretched and wiggling.
   - **Partial sums/partial differences:** Students place both hands on their head and pull their hands apart (embodying breaking apart the numbers into 100s, 10s, and 1s).
   - **Compensation:** Students cross their arms across their chests (because they are very clever to do compensation).
   - **Inverse math strategy for subtraction:** Students put two thumbs up and then immediately two thumbs down.
   - **Doubling:** Students put one fist on top of the other.

2. Display an addition or subtraction problem on a smartboard or whiteboard and take the class through the solution of the problem via each of the strategies listed above; ask your students how *they* would initially approach solving the problem. What strategy would they use? Are there strategies that they find particularly interesting? Are there strategies that seem easier or more efficient than others?

3. After students have familiarized themselves with the strategies, write another problem on the board and ask them to use gestures to communicate what strategy they would employ to solve the problem.

4. Call on a variety of students to explain their thinking/preferences.

5. Repeat until multiple students have had a chance to share.

6. Break students up into pairs and provide them with an index card that has an addition/subtraction problem on it. Students will work together to identify a strategy (through gesturing) that they feel helps solve the problem; they will then navigate to the number line on the floor to solve the problem together.

7. Once they've identified the answer, they will write that answer as well as the strategy they used to solve for it on the index card and sit back in their seats.

8. After students have completed the activity, collect the index cards and present the problems and answers to the whole class, giving each pair a chance to explain their reasoning/strategy for their solution.

## Possible Variations

For an extra challenge, have students carry out the activity steps while on a positive and negative number line on the floor (see A.1 Zero Heroes).

# A.10: Cat Scratch Fever!

## Overview

For this activity, students will make a circle around the classroom and pretend to be cats! This activity supports skip-counting concept development and math fact recall by approaching skip-counting in a *multisensory* way.

## Required Materials

None

## Preparation

Because this activity requires students to move cross-laterally, make sure that students have enough room around them to move their bodies.

## Activity Steps

1. Invite students to pull out their cat claws (make cat claws with their fingers).
2. Have students cross their right cat claw over to the left side of their body and whisper *1*.
3. Have them cross their left cat claw over to the right side of their body and whisper *2*.
4. Have students bring their claws together and count *3*, making sure to shout out the multiple.
5. Have students repeat this cross-body movement up to 30, whispering all nonmultiples and shouting out all multiples of 3.

## Possible Variations

You can modify the movements to be more *physically intensive*, such as incorporating squats on every nonmultiple of three and jumping up on every multiple.

You can have students start counting at numbers other than one or count backward.

You can modify these movements for different multiples. For example, a movement that practices skip-counting by 6s could include the following movements: students cross their left cat claw over their midline (whispering *1*), cross their right cat claw (whispering *2*), cross their left leg (whispering *3*), cross their right leg (whispering *4*), scratch with both hands forward in front of their body (whispering *5*), and then jump up and clap (shouting *6*).

# A.11: Race to 100

## Overview

This (typically) competitive activity engages students in math fact practice related to addition and subtraction of single- and double-digit numbers. This game can be played individually, with partners, or in teams.

## Required Materials

Painter's tape and construction paper (if inside); chalk (if outside); dice (6–20-sided)

## Preparation

Create a 100 number grid on the floor or ground. With chalk (if outside), create a 10-by-10-feet 100 number grid (you can use tape or construction paper with numbers on the individual sheets if inside). Have students write the numbers 1–100 in the boxes moving from left to right across the rows (see Figure A.11).

FIGURE A.11
**Race to 100**

| 1 | 2 | 3 | 4 | 5 | 6 | 7 | 8 | 9 | 10 |
|---|---|---|---|---|---|---|---|---|---|
| 11 | 12 | 13 | 14 | 15 | 16 | 17 | 18 | 19 | 20 |
| 21 | 22 | 23 | 24 | 25 | 26 | 27 | 28 | 29 | 30 |
| 31 | 32 | 33 | 34 | 35 | 36 | 37 | 38 | 39 | 40 |
| 41 | 42 | 43 | 44 | 45 | 46 | 47 | 48 | 49 | 50 |
| 51 | 52 | 53 | 54 | 55 | 56 | 57 | 58 | 59 | 60 |
| 61 | 62 | 63 | 64 | 65 | 66 | 67 | 68 | 69 | 70 |
| 71 | 72 | 73 | 74 | 75 | 76 | 77 | 78 | 79 | 80 |
| 81 | 82 | 83 | 84 | 85 | 86 | 87 | 88 | 89 | 90 |
| 91 | 92 | 93 | 94 | 95 | 96 | 97 | 98 | 99 | 100 |

## Activity Steps

1. Have players line up on the grid standing on the 1.
2. Each player or team rolls the dice. Whoever gets the highest number goes first.
3. The first player (or team) rolls the dice and takes that number of steps across the grid, adding the number they rolled to the number they are standing on.

4. The second player rolls the dice and takes that many steps across the grid, adding that number to where they were.

5. Have your students continue rolling the dice and stepping forward until the first player (or team) reaches 100.

## Possible Variations

Race to 1: Replay the activity beginning at 100 and subtracting numbers until the first player (or team) reaches 1. To add complexity to the addition/subtraction (or multiplication), students can play the game with more dice or multiply the numbers before taking their steps forward on the grid.

# A.12: Kinesthetic Number Path

## Overview

This activity supports the development of cooperative problem-solving (and associated social) skills, as well as one-to-one correspondence and adding and subtracting within 20 (or beyond).

## Required Materials

Printer paper; laminator; index cards; any classroom items that can be counted up to 20 and can be gathered and placed on the floor

## Preparation

Print or write the numbers 0–20 on sheets of paper. Make the numbers very large. You can laminate the numbers if you will have your students jumping on them. Tape the laminated cards in order on the floor to make a number path. Using 21 index cards, write the numbers 0–20, putting one number on each card (see Figure A.12). Make sure that there are quantities of items in your classroom that can match each number (e.g., there are at least 20 of something, 19 of something else, etc.).

## Activity Steps

1. Each student should have an index card that matches a number on the number path. Students can choose their number by picking from the pile of index cards, or you can assign numbers to each student.

2. Have each student locate items in the classroom to place on the number path. For example, they could place three books on the number 3.

3. As students place their items on the path, have them each physically jump on numbers on the number path while saying each number.

4. After the number path has been completed, provide students with addition and subtraction problems related to their accumulated items. When adding kinesthetically, students should be facing and hopping toward the 20; and when subtracting, they should hop toward the 0.

FIGURE A.12

**Kinesthetic Number Path**

| 1 | 2 | 3 | 4 | 5 | 6 | 7 | 8 | 9 | 10 | 11 | 12 | 13 | 14 | 15 | 16 | 17 | 18 | 19 | 20 |
|---|---|---|---|---|---|---|---|---|----|----|----|----|----|----|----|----|----|----|----|

## Possible Variations

Consider including an ELA or art component to this activity by having students practice spelling the item names and associated numbers, telling a story or writing a short poem about the item, or drawing a picture of the item.

# A.13: Skip-Counting Parade

## Overview

This activity helps build class cohesion and trust through the cooperative design of a skip-counting parade pathway. Individual students have the opportunity to showcase their interests and identities as parade participants.

## Required Materials

Chalk (outdoors); painter's tape (indoors)

## Preparation

Unlike other kinesthetic activities, students' *themselves* prepare the stage for this activity.

FIGURE A.13
**Skip-Counting Parade**

| 24 | 36 | 48 | 60 | 72 | 84 |
| 22 | 33 | 44 | 55 | 66 | 77 |
| 20 | 30 | 40 | 50 | 60 | 70 |
| 18 | 27 | 36 | 45 | 54 | 63 |
| 16 | 24 | 32 | 40 | 48 | 56 |
| 14 | 21 | 28 | 35 | 42 | 49 |
| 12 | 18 | 24 | 30 | 36 | 42 |
| 10 | 15 | 20 | 25 | 30 | 35 |
| 8 | 12 | 16 | 20 | 24 | 28 |
| 6 | 9 | 12 | 15 | 18 | 21 |
| 4 | 6 | 8 | 10 | 12 | 14 |
| 2 | 3 | 4 | 5 | 6 | 7 |
| 0 | 0 | 0 | 0 | 0 | 0 |

## Activity Steps

1. Have students create a path of 13 boxes that are around 22 × 15 inches using either chalk or painter's tape.
2. Within each box, have your students write the multiples of 2, beginning with 0 and ending with 24 (see Figure A.13).
3. Have students create a path for multiples of 3 next to the previous pathway. They will construct the boxes and write the multiples of 3 within them.

4. Have them continue to create additional paths for the remaining multiples that they have learned thus far in your multiplication unit (e.g., 2–12). These pathways *do not* have to be in a straight line or immediately next to one another.

5. Once students have created their paths, they will pretend to be in a parade. Have them jump along the paths on each of the boxes, chanting out loud the corresponding multiple. You can even invite students to dress up in costumes for their parade or perform an active math movement associated with the multiples (see A.10 for an example).

## Possible Variations

Have a number parade for other kinds of numbers. Create paths for odd numbers, even numbers, tally marks, ordinal numbers, Fibonacci numbers, prime numbers, composite numbers, square numbers, triangular numbers, cubed numbers, pentagonal numbers, Roman numerals, halves (i.e., ½, 1, 3/2, 2, etc.), trigonometric numbers, factorials, positive numbers, or negative numbers. If it is possible to keep the parade path up or available to your students, you can add to it as you progress through the relevant units; this can culminate in an end-of-unit celebration!

# A.14: Double It, Half It

## Overview

This activity is a collaborative game that requires cooperation and co-strategizing solutions to problems associated with halving and doubling.

## Required Materials

Timer; chalk (outdoors); painter's tape (indoors); index cards

## Preparation

Write the numbers 1–50 individually on index cards. With chalk (if outside), have students create a large number grid with numbers from 1 to 100 (see Figure A.14). Divide your students into two teams.

FIGURE A.14
**Double It, Half It**

| 1 | 2 | 3 | 4 | 5 | 6 | 7 | 8 | 9 | 10 |
|---|---|---|---|---|---|---|---|---|---|
| 11 | 12 | 13 | 14 | 15 | 16 | 17 | 18 | 19 | 20 |
| 21 | 22 | 23 | 24 | 25 | 26 | 27 | 28 | 29 | 30 |
| 31 | 32 | 33 | 34 | 35 | 36 | 37 | 38 | 39 | 40 |
| 41 | 42 | 43 | 44 | 45 | 46 | 47 | 48 | 49 | 50 |
| 51 | 52 | 53 | 54 | 55 | 56 | 57 | 58 | 59 | 60 |
| 61 | 62 | 63 | 64 | 65 | 66 | 67 | 68 | 69 | 70 |
| 71 | 72 | 73 | 74 | 75 | 76 | 77 | 78 | 79 | 80 |
| 81 | 82 | 83 | 84 | 85 | 86 | 87 | 88 | 89 | 90 |
| 91 | 92 | 93 | 94 | 95 | 96 | 97 | 98 | 99 | 100 |

## Activity Steps

1. Have Team 1 draw an index card. They will be given five seconds to work together to double the number. You can adjust the time given to each group for age and ability.

2. One of the team members should stand on their answer on the 100 number grid; have them say the full equation out loud once they stand on the number. If the first team has correctly answered the question *and* is standing on the correct box on the 100 number grid, they receive one point. If they are incorrect or the team member is standing on an incorrect box, they receive zero points.

3. If Team 1 is incorrect, give Team 2 the option to stand on the correct number. If that team stands on the correct answer, they receive two points.

4. Repeat the above steps with Team 2.

Alternatively, students can play the game Half It. They will repeat the steps above with index cards that have the numbers from 51 to 100. If the answer is 50.5, for example, then the student stands on the line between 50 and 51.

## Possible Variations

Use two different colors of index cards. Write the numbers 1–50 on one color of index cards. Write the numbers 51–100 on the other color. Mix up the cards. If the index card is one color, the student will play Half It. If it is the other color, the game is Double It. This activity will help students learn to pivot operations quickly and efficiently.

Shuffle the deck of cards. One student from each team will draw a card from the top of the deck. Repeat the steps of this activity. Remember, students must stand on the answer. The first team member to stand on the correct answer receives one point for their team. If a student stands on an incorrect answer, the other team is given the opportunity to answer. If correct, they earn two points.

# A.15: Exploring Eights

## Overview

This activity provides students with collaborative multiplication practice spotlighting multiples of eight.

## Required Materials

Chalk (outside) or painter's tape (inside); index cards

## Preparation

Write numbers 1–12 on index cards. Create three sets of cards. With chalk (if outside), create a 10-by-10-foot 100 number grid. Draw a box at the top left edge of the grid and write 0 in the box (see Figure A.15).

## Activity Steps

1. Have one student stand on the 0 box.
2. Beginning at 0, have that student count out eight boxes.

3. That student (or another) will then write the number *8* in the box and then stand on that number.

4. Have the same (or a different student) count out another eight boxes. Have another student write *16* in the box and stand on that number.

5. Continue to have your students count out 8 boxes. Choose a student to write the multiple and then stand on the box, moving up to 96.

6. As a whole group, encourage your students to skip-count by 8s. The student standing on 0 shouts, "Zero!" The student standing on 8 shouts, "Eight!" The student standing on 16 shouts, "Sixteen!" and so on up to 96.

7. Repeat this exercise while having your students skip-count forward and backward.

8. Next, invite students to jump on each multiple, moving across the 100 number grid and chanting the multiple out loud.

FIGURE A.15
**Exploring Eights**

| 0 | 1 | 2 | 3 | 4 | 5 | 6 | 7 | 8 | 9 | 10 |
|---|---|---|---|---|---|---|---|---|---|---|
|  | 11 | 12 | 13 | 14 | 15 | 16 | 17 | 18 | 19 | 20 |
|  | 21 | 22 | 23 | 24 | 25 | 26 | 27 | 28 | 29 | 30 |
|  | 31 | 32 | 33 | 34 | 35 | 36 | 37 | 38 | 39 | 40 |
|  | 41 | 42 | 43 | 44 | 45 | 46 | 47 | 48 | 49 | 50 |
|  | 51 | 52 | 53 | 54 | 55 | 56 | 57 | 58 | 59 | 60 |
|  | 61 | 62 | 63 | 64 | 65 | 66 | 67 | 68 | 69 | 70 |
|  | 71 | 72 | 73 | 74 | 75 | 76 | 77 | 78 | 79 | 80 |
|  | 81 | 82 | 83 | 84 | 85 | 86 | 87 | 88 | 89 | 90 |
|  | 91 | 92 | 93 | 94 | 95 | 96 | 97 | 98 | 99 | 100 |

## Possible Variations

Teach students how to solve multiplication problems by 8s. For example, what is three groups of eight (or 3 × 8)? Have a student stand on the 0 box then move to 8 and say, "One group of eight." Then have them move to 16 and say, "Two groups of eight." The student will then move to 24 and say, "Three groups of eight," followed by the full equation: "3 times 8 equals 24!"

To further gamify this activity, divide your students into teams. Mix up the number cards. Each team takes a card from the deck. Task them to multiply the number they drew by eight. One team member will then stand on the answer. If a student is standing on the correct answer, then their team receives one point. If the answer is incorrect, the other team has a chance to stand on the correct number and receive two points.

# A.16: Let's Go Shopping

## Overview

In this activity, students will create their own shopping cards after investigating shopping catalogs. They will then use these cards to practice adding and subtracting money.

## Required Materials

Shopping catalogs; scissors; glue; white copy paper; green construction paper; black markers; place value manipulatives; chalk (outside) or painter's tape (inside)

## Preparation

1. Have students cut out the items, glue the items to a sheet of white copy paper, and mark the price of the item ($1–100.) You can laminate the students' shopping cards too.

2. Have your students cut the green construction paper into rectangles about three-by-seven inches large.

3. Using these pieces, have students create their own play money by writing the denomination of each bill on the green paper and drawing a face in the center (see Figure A.16a). Alternatively, you can use play money.

**Let's Go Shopping: Play Money Cards**

4. With chalk (if outside), have students create a 10-by-10-foot 100 number grid, with the numbers 1–100 written individually in the boxes; the first row of the grid will contain the numbers 1–10 (see Figure A.16b).

## Activity Steps

1. Invite your students to look through catalogs in search of items that the class may want to purchase.
2. Give students the shopping cards of items to purchase. The prices of these items will be $1–100.
3. Have each student match their card and the price of their item with the corresponding number on the 100 number grid.
4. Then have students use the place value blocks and play money to build the numbers/prices of their items.
5. Ask students to brainstorm other denominations of money that they can use to purchase the item.

## Possible Variations

Repeat the game using decimals. Play a game where all items are on sale for 10 percent off, 25 percent off, or 60 percent off. What is the sale price of each item?

FIGURE A.16b
**Let's Go Shopping: 100 Grid**

| 1 | 2 | 3 | 4 | 5 | 6 | 7 | 8 | 9 | 10 |
|---|---|---|---|---|---|---|---|---|---|
| 11 | 12 | 13 | 14 | 15 | 16 | 17 | 18 | 19 | 20 |
| 21 | 22 | 23 | 24 | 25 | 26 | 27 | 28 | 29 | 30 |
| 31 | 32 | 33 | 34 | 35 | 36 | 37 | 38 | 39 | 40 |
| 41 | 42 | 43 | 44 | 45 | 46 | 47 | 48 | 49 | 50 |
| 51 | 52 | 53 | 54 | 55 | 56 | 57 | 58 | 59 | 60 |
| 61 | 62 | 63 | 64 | 65 | 66 | 67 | 68 | 69 | 70 |
| 71 | 72 | 73 | 74 | 75 | 76 | 77 | 78 | 79 | 80 |
| 81 | 82 | 83 | 84 | 85 | 86 | 87 | 88 | 89 | 90 |
| 91 | 92 | 93 | 94 | 95 | 96 | 97 | 98 | 99 | 100 |

# A.17: The Skip-Counting Zookeeper

## Overview

This activity provides students with a scenario-based (practical) experience using multiplication and skip-counting strategies to solve problems.

## Required Materials

Painter's tape (inside) or chalk (outside); paper

## Preparation

Have your students create a skip-counting outline for multiples of two; with chalk (if outside), students will create a path of 12 boxes, each of which will contain a multiple of two from 2 to 24 (see Figure A.17).

FIGURE A.17

**The Skip-Counting Zookeeper**

<table>
<tr><td>24</td></tr>
<tr><td>22</td></tr>
<tr><td>20</td></tr>
<tr><td>18</td></tr>
<tr><td>16</td></tr>
<tr><td>14</td></tr>
<tr><td>12</td></tr>
<tr><td>10</td></tr>
<tr><td>8</td></tr>
<tr><td>6</td></tr>
<tr><td>4</td></tr>
<tr><td>2</td></tr>
</table>

## Activity Steps

1. Take some time to explore your students' personal experiences with zoos, asking questions like "Who has been to a zoo before?" and focusing students on the details of a zookeeping job: "What is going on there?" "What kinds of things are involved?" "Which roles/ responsibilities are involved in zookeeping?"

2. Develop a story (or script) with your students based on shared previous experiences. It can be played out by referring to a common zoo story or by opening the scene with a particular act at the zoo (e.g., the teacher enters the scene as the owner of the zoo who needs to prepare

the zoo for opening day). You can also prepare a script with information about the zoo prior to the activity.

- These tasks can involve taking an inventory of the animals at the zoo or getting the animals cleaned and fed.
- Continue asking your students questions as they plan: What are we going to do? How many animals are there in the zoo? How many animals are in each enclosure?

3. Give your students time to play together and imagine acting out the role of zookeepers. Encourage them to think about the realities of zookeeping responsibilities, such as size of enclosures for specific animals and how to decorate them with foliage, informative posters, and warnings (e.g., do not feed the lions!). A zookeeper might want to count all the animals that enter each cage (you or other students can pretend to usher animals into the cages).

4. Provide students with paper to make enclosure signage to practice writing and drawing specific practice-related texts.

5. After the scene is set and these logistics have been set, transition into discussions around math in this setting:
   - There are six enclosures in the mammal area of the zoo. There are two lions in one enclosure, two tigers in another, two elephants in another, two pandas in another, two sloths in another, and two prairie dogs in the last. How many animals in total need to return to their enclosures?
   - If there are five enclosures in the reptile area of the zoo, and there are two reptiles in each enclosure, how many reptiles are at the zoo?
   - Toucans require seven cups of seed per day. There are two toucans in the bird exhibit. How many cups of seed do you need to feed both toucans?

     To solve these questions, students can hop across the multiples of two pathway that they created using chalk or painter's tape. Students will stand at the beginning of the path in front of the box with a 2 in it. To solve the math problems, students will hop the multiplicand to arrive at the answer; for example, to solve the toucan problem (7 × 2), students will hop seven boxes forward, landing on 14.

6. Involve your students in little moments of discourse about the activity, and help them reflect on how they can apply multiplication in the context of their activities. You can ask questions like "How is it going?" "Is this what you want?" "Can you do it otherwise?" "What else can the skip-counting by 2s outline be used for at the zoo?" "What does this mean?" "Are you sure?"

## Possible Variations

Create outlines for other multiples, such as 6s or 8s. Have your students continue role-playing as zookeepers but ask different math problems related to the multiples. An example question could be "If there are eight monkeys in one enclosure and each monkey drinks four cups of water each day, how much water does the zookeeper have to provide daily for the monkeys?"

# A.18: Talent Show

## Overview

In this activity, students will create their own Active Math Movements in the form of a dance, a cheerleading movement, or any action that they feel like they are talented in. This activity provides students an opportunity to express their interests and present collaboratively with friends.

## Required Materials

Your imagination!

## Preparation

Make sure your students are familiar with the design and practice of Active Math Movements (see Appendix A.10) before doing this activity. Their task here is to design a dance move that has the same number of steps as the multiple of focus.

## Activity Steps

1. Have your students determine what kind of movement they want to showcase.

2. Depending on the multiple of focus in your unit/lesson, you will then assign a specific multiple that the student will practice with their

Active Math Movement. For example, if you're practicing multiples of four, the student's dance steps could include them first crossing their right leg to the left, then crossing their left leg to the right, twirling around, and finally jumping and clapping. Make sure that students say the number of the steps out loud as they move, whispering the nonmultiples and shouting out loud the multiples.

3. Let students practice their movements for a few minutes.

4. You can have them perform the movements they created for everyone else during a classroom talent show.

## Possible Variations

If your students are shy about performing individually, you can partner up students to develop their own movements together. After designing their movement around a particular multiple, they can then present (or lead the class through) their movement.

# A.19: Math Positive Affirmations

## Overview

This activity integrates the science of positive affirmations into our classic Active Math Movement framework, in which students will strengthen their physical balance and neural networks through multisensory, cross-body movements.

## Required Materials

None

## Preparation

Before starting this activity, take some time explaining to your students about the benefit of "crossing the midline." All humans have a left and a right hemisphere in our brain. We also have a *corpus callosum* connecting these hemispheres. The corpus callosum is a web of white matter that acts as a bridge for neurons traveling across the hemispheres of the brain. We can imagine this line between our brain's hemispheres as extending all the way down our body, which we call the *midline*. When we cross that imaginary line using our body, information in our brain moves from one hemisphere to the other. It is healthy for our brain when we cross the midline. We cross the midline when we do cross-body movements with our arms or our legs. By repeating these movements, we build up balance and strengthen the neural pathways connecting our brain's hemispheres.

## Activity Steps

1. Have students practice crossing their midlines. For example, you can have students take their right hand and touch the left side of their body. Students can then take their left hand and cross it over to the right side of their body. Moving one's foot from one side of their body to the other also crosses the midline.

2. Next, have students add positive affirmations to the exercise detailed in step 1. For example, you might choose the affirmation "I am persistent." Have your students cross their right arm to the left side of their body, touching their waist, while saying, "I." Then, have them cross their left arm to the right side of your body while saying, "Am." Then, have them raise both arms over their head while shouting out loud, "Persistent!"

3. Repeat this exercise at least three times.

Additional affirmations related to math could include the following:
- I am a problem solver.
- I am hardworking.
- I like to solve challenging math problems.
- My perseverance pays off!
- Math is fun!
- I am curious.
- Solving problems grows my brain!

## Possible Variations

Most students enjoy asking *why* questions. Cross-body movements provide a wonderful stepping stone into the study of neuroscience and learning. For students looking for an added challenge, consider having them do a mini research project related to brain science (e.g., the corpus callosum, BDNF, dopamine) to bring context to these activities. Have them draw pictures of the brain or make a presentation to the class. Consider incorporating brain breaks during lessons, and be sure to include a variety of positive affirmations and movements that challenge the balance and coordination of your students. Just remember that, the more time students practice crossing their midline, the more balanced and in control of their bodies they become!

# A.20: Multiplication Moles

## Overview

Inspired by the game Battleship, this teams-based competitive activity strengthens students' multiplication skills.

## Required Materials

Paper or bean bags; chalk (outside), painter's tape (inside); index cards or construction paper; sticky notes

## Preparation

Have students use chalk or painter's tape to create a 10-by-10-foot multiplication grid (see Figure A.20). Have students write multiplication products in chalk in each of the boxes. If the grid is created with painter's tape, then have students write the products on index cards and place them in the boxes. Above the top row (or the *x*-axis) write/place a letter for each unit (from A to J). Along the leftmost column (the *y*-axis), write/place a number for each unit from 1 to 10; these axis labels will assist students with communicating their identification of specific units within the grid (e.g., C8 identifies a specific box on the grid). Use a piece of tape or string to divide the grid into halves horizontally (i.e., there will be a top half and a bottom half)

On a separate set of index cards, write *Find* and *Miss*, which students will use to mark decisions on the grid

## Activity Steps

1. Have students partner up with a classmate; then position a pair of students on opposite sides of the grid.

2. Have the teams secretly write down four coordinates from the quadrant on a piece of paper or notecard; these coordinates will function as locations of the hidden "moles."

3. Once the hidden moles have been secretly placed, the teams will alternate asking one another multiplication problems, the *products* of which will be where they think the hidden moles of the opposing team are located. For example, one team thinks that a mole is located in square D8. In order to select that space, they will need to say out loud to the other team the *equation* that yields the product illustrated on that space. "The mole is hiding in four times eight!"

4. Once the equation has been stated, the opposing team must mark that space as either a "Find" or a "Miss" with an index card. If either team incorrectly connects an equation to a product (e.g., "The mole is hiding in three times three!" and the other team marks "Miss" on the square with *12* in it), the team that made the mistake loses a turn!

5. Have students repeat these steps, alternating turns guessing and marking, until all four moles have been identified (or a certain amount of time has passed or a specific number of guesses have been made). The team that identifies all four moles of the opposing team is the winner.

## Possible Variations

Consider restructuring the game around playing cards. Put objects at several points all around the multiplication grid (small cubes or even animal figurines work well). Set two decks of cards next to the grid (make sure that the face cards are taken out, but keep the aces in—to serve as 1). Have students take turns turning over a card from each deck. The numbers they turn over will be their coordinates; the first number they draw will be their $x$-axis point and the second card their $y$-axis point. For students who require an additional challenge, black cards can function as positive numbers and red as negative for this game. If they hit one of the blocks on the mat, they get to collect it. The person with the most objects collected at the end of the game wins.

FIGURE A.20
**Multiplication Moles**

| x | A | B | C | D | E | F | G | H | I | J |
|----|----|----|----|----|----|----|----|----|----|----|
| 1 | 1 | 2 | 3 | 4 | 5 | 6 | 7 | 8 | 9 | 10 |
| 2 | 2 | 4 | 6 | 8 | 10 | 12 | 14 | 16 | 18 | 20 |
| 3 | 3 | 6 | 9 | 12 | 15 | 18 | 21 | 24 | 27 | 30 |
| 4 | 4 | 8 | 12 | 16 | 20 | 24 | 28 | 32 | 36 | 40 |
| 5 | 5 | 10 | 15 | 20 | 25 | 30 | 35 | 40 | 45 | 50 |
| 6 | 6 | 12 | 18 | 24 | 30 | 36 | 42 | 48 | 54 | 60 |
| 7 | 7 | 14 | 21 | 28 | 35 | 42 | 49 | 56 | 63 | 70 |
| 8 | 8 | 16 | 24 | 32 | 40 | 48 | 56 | 64 | 72 | 80 |
| 9 | 9 | 18 | 27 | 36 | 45 | 54 | 63 | 72 | 81 | 90 |
| 10 | 10 | 20 | 30 | 40 | 50 | 60 | 70 | 80 | 90 | 100 |

# A.21: Change for $100

## Overview

This activity helps students practice a variety of strategies individually or collectively to solve money-related problems. There are a ton of combinations of patterns that students could use to determine change (or the answer to the equation), so encourage students to think of more strategies for solving these problems by exploring the grid. Notice that, although we use many strategies, we always receive the same answer!

## Required Materials

Number/index cards ranging 1–100; place value blocks or other manipulatives (popsicle sticks, rubber bands); chalk (outside) or painter's tape (inside)

## Preparation

Have students create a 10-by-10 100 number grid (see Figure A.21) using painter's tape (inside) or chalk (outside). Have students write the numbers 1–100 on pieces of paper to fill in the grid.

FIGURE A.21
## Change for $100

| 1 | 2 | 3 | 4 | 5 | 6 | 7 | 8 | 9 | 10 |
|---|---|---|---|---|---|---|---|---|---|
| 11 | 12 | 13 | 14 | 15 | 16 | 17 | 18 | 19 | 20 |
| 21 | 22 | 23 | 24 | 25 | 26 | 27 | 28 | 29 | 30 |
| 31 | 32 | 33 | 34 | 35 | 36 | 37 | 38 | 39 | 40 |
| 41 | 42 | 43 | 44 | 45 | 46 | 47 | 48 | 49 | 50 |
| 51 | 52 | 53 | 54 | 55 | 56 | 57 | 58 | 59 | 60 |
| 61 | 62 | 63 | 64 | 65 | 66 | 67 | 68 | 69 | 70 |
| 71 | 72 | 73 | 74 | 75 | 76 | 77 | 78 | 79 | 80 |
| 81 | 82 | 83 | 84 | 85 | 86 | 87 | 88 | 89 | 90 |
| 91 | 92 | 93 | 94 | 95 | 96 | 97 | 98 | 99 | 100 |

## Activity Steps

1. We can first determine what would be the change if we were to buy one item with a 100-dollar bill. For example, let's say the cost of one item is $68. Ask your students what change we would receive if we paid for the item with a 100-dollar bill?

2. One student can stand on the number 68 on the number grid. The answer to the question would be the number of steps or boxes it would take the student to reach 100.

3. Have the student take one step down to 78 (counting 10), another step to 88 (counting 20), and another step to 98 (counting 30). While standing on 98, the student would then take 1 step to 99 and count 31,and then take another step to 100 and count 32. The answer to the question would be $32 in change.

4. Ask your students to consider if there are other strategies involving addition on the grid that they can use to determine the change for $100. You can demonstrate another one of these strategies by having a student stand on 68. The student may walk out the following pathway: First count the 1s, then count the 10s. They would then stand on 68 and move to 69, 70, 80, 90, 100 (counting out 1, 2, 12, 22, 32 as they move along).

5. Alternatively, a student could count by 11s, stand first on 68, and then move to 79, 90, and 100 (counting out 11, 22, 33). Students might find counting *backward* from 100 to be another strategy. A student could first count by 10s and then 1s, standing first on 100 and then moving to 90, 80, 70, and then by 1s to 69, 68 (counting out 10, 20, 30, 31, 32).

## Possible Variations

Repeat activity with decimal cards (such as 0.27 or 0.55) and by making change for a dollar. Or use larger denominations of money. What would be the change for a 500-dollar bill?

# A.22: Math Investigators

## Overview

This activity gets students to work together to uncover missing numbers on a large 100 number grid. For students who need additional support, identifying the missing number provides wonderful one-to-one correspondence practice, and this activity practices pattern identification and communication via mathematical language.

## Required Materials

Chalk (outside) or painter's tape (inside); construction paper (preferably black); writing paper or journal

## Preparation

Using chalk or painter's tape, have students create a 10-by-10 100 number grid with the numbers 1–100 written inside the boxes (see Figure A.22). Alternatively, you can have students write numbers on pieces of paper to fill in the grid.

FIGURE A.22
**Math Investigators**

| 1 | 2 | 3 | 4 | 5 | 6 | 7 | 8 | 9 | 10 |
|---|---|---|---|---|---|---|---|---|---|
| 11 | 12 | 13 | 14 | 15 | 16 | 17 | 18 | 19 | 20 |
| 21 | 22 | 23 | 24 | 25 | 26 | 27 | 28 | 29 | 30 |
| 31 | 32 | 33 | 34 | 35 | 36 | 37 | 38 | 39 | 40 |
| 41 | 42 | 43 | 44 | 45 | 46 | 47 | 48 | 49 | 50 |
| 51 | 52 | 53 | 54 | 55 | 56 | 57 | 58 | 59 | 60 |
| 61 | 62 | 63 | 64 | 65 | 66 | 67 | 68 | 69 | 70 |
| 71 | 72 | 73 | 74 | 75 | 76 | 77 | 78 | 79 | 80 |
| 81 | 82 | 83 | 84 | 85 | 86 | 87 | 88 | 89 | 90 |
| 91 | 92 | 93 | 94 | 95 | 96 | 97 | 98 | 99 | 100 |

## Activity Steps

1. Divide students into groups, with enough students to make two teams within each group.
2. Team 1 will be tasked to cover up specific numbers on the 100 number grid. Team 2 will be tasked to investigate the missing numbers and determine what numbers are missing.
3. Begin by covering up one number (your choice).

4. Have your students in Team 1 gradually cover more numbers at one time. Covering up a large segment of numbers helps students to visualize specific math patterns.

5. After each pattern is identified, have the investigators record the specific pattern in their journal and label it. Their next task is to identify where one could find that pattern *outside* the math classroom. For example, Fibonacci numbers are a pattern that can be identified on the number grid. The Fibonacci sequence is a series of numbers where each number is the sum of the previous two. It begins with 0 and 1. The next number is 0 + 1 = 1. The next number is 1 + 1 = 2. The next number is 1 + 2 = 3, and it continues on in this manner. The first 12 Fibonacci numbers in the series are 0, 1, 1, 2, 3, 5, 8, 13, 21, 34, 55, 89. Fibonacci sequences can be found in nature (e.g., spiral arrangements in sunflower seeds, pinecones, and pineapples).

6. After identifying a real-world instance of the pattern, each investigator will provide a brief verbal report of their findings with a description of the pattern. Students can work in pairs to research these patterns.

## Possible Variations

For students looking for an added challenge, you can have Team 2 come up with an equation with an answer that is a covered number instead of saying the missing number. Team 1 can solve the equation to double-check whether Team 2 is correct.

# A.23: Timekeepers

## Overview

This collaborative activity showcases the breadth of mathematics as a way to tell time and solve for elapsed time along a circle.

## Required Materials

Toy hoop; chalk; yard stick; ruler

## Preparation

Have your students use a large hoop to make the outline of a clock with chalk (if outside). With the yardstick, have them mark off four equal quadrants within the circle. Then, have your students draw lines from the origin of the circle outward, dividing each of the four quadrants into three equal parts. Mark each line around the circle by 5s (see Figure A.23). Students will use the ruler and yardstick as the hands of the clock for the following activity. Choose one student to be the timekeeper.

FIGURE A.23
**Timekeepers**

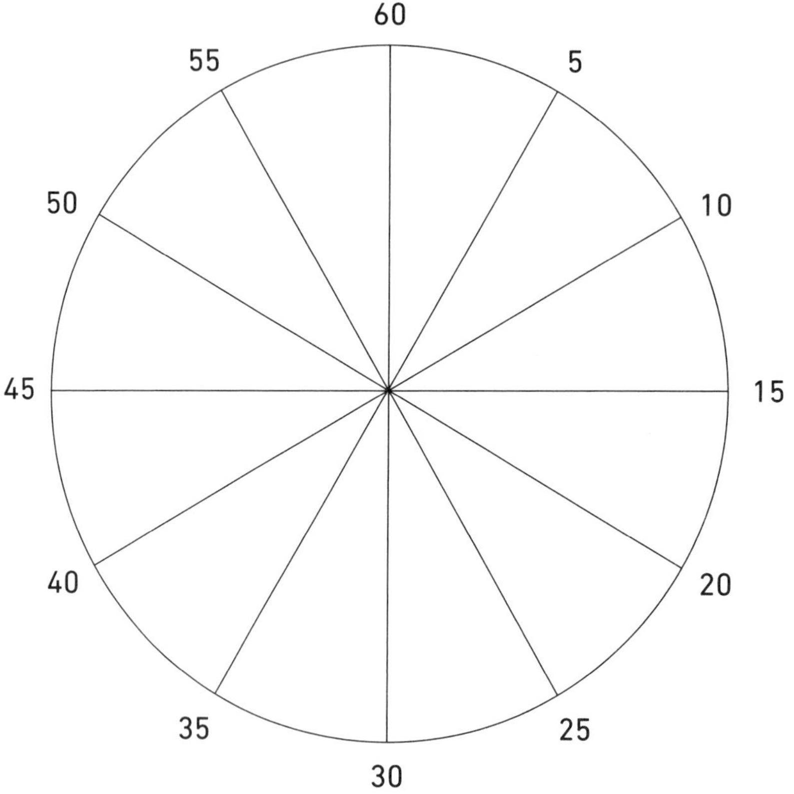


## Activity Steps

1. Have the timekeeper place the yardstick and ruler on the chalked-out clock to resemble hands pointing to the time 3:10. If the student

struggles with creating the time, have them hop from the 60-minute position (the top of the circle) to the hours and minutes individually.

2. Ask the class a few questions related to elapsed time. For example, "What time will it be in 10 minutes, 12 minutes, 27 minutes, or 52 minutes?" To solve these questions, the student on the clock would hop clockwise by 5s across the chalked lines by minutes (and hours, if necessary).

3. Encourage students to think of their own questions to ask, and switch up the timekeeper after each question is answered correctly. Consider asking students what routines they have during the day, such as expected bedtimes, time allotted for movies or video games, or time spent doing homework, to make time (and the math associated with elapsed time) relatable.

4. To help students understand elapsed time word problems, have students act out the word problems on the chalk clock. For example, if it is 6:35 a.m. and the bus comes at 7:25 a.m., how much time do you have to get ready for school?

5. What other mathematical concepts can be visualized and kinesthetically practiced on this circle? Consider using the clock to practice
   - Angles.
   - Fractions and percents.
   - Multiplication and division.

## Possible Variations

If students are struggling with translating digital time to analog time, you can modify your questions to assist with this translation and with their development of time-telling terminology. A common misconception among students first introduced to telling time is to think that "a quarter after 3:00" is actually 3:25. This is typically due to the word *quarter* having been associated with money prior to telling time. Hopping across the clock and saying out loud the numbers (or portions of the clock) helps students recognize that a clock is divided into four parts, so a quarter of an hour is actually 15 minutes.

# A.24: Clipboard Math

## Overview

This activity illustrates how easy it is to implement supplementary kinesthetics in a math classroom. Students can engage in movement-based learning without having to discard tried-and-true instructional methods or traditionally successful tools.

## Required Materials

Chalk (outside) or painter's tape (inside); clipboard; multiplication worksheets or paper with math problems on them

## Preparation

Have students use chalk (or painter's tape) to create a path of 13 boxes that are around 22 by 15 inches large. Within each box, students will write the multiples of two, beginning with 0 and ending with 24 (see Figure A.24). Using this method, you can have your students continue to create additional paths for different multiples that they have learned thus far in your multiplication unit (e.g., $3 \times 12$). Students will use these number lines to solve a variety of addition, subtraction, multiplication, and division problems. Depending on what concept you want to focus on for this activity, write one or a few math problems on a piece of paper or index card for each student; make sure to have plenty extra so they can continue practicing after solving their first few problems!

## Activity Steps

1. Hand out a worksheet or index card with an addition, a subtraction, a multiplication, or a division problem (or a set of problems) to each student.

2. If the question asks, for example, "What is $8 \times 3$?" have the student choose a chalked-out number line and stand on 8. To multiply, they will move three spaces forward on the path, counting out loud, "1, 2, 3," as they step across the 8, 16, and 24 boxes.

3. Upon landing on the 24 box, students will hop in place, clapping and shouting out loud, "8 times 3 equals 24!" The physicality of

the activity helps students with the misconception that one begins counting on the first number.

FIGURE A.24
**Clipboard Math**

| | | | | | |
|---|---|---|---|---|---|
| 24 | 36 | 48 | 60 | 72 | 84 |
| 22 | 33 | 44 | 55 | 66 | 77 |
| 20 | 30 | 40 | 50 | 60 | 70 |
| 18 | 27 | 36 | 45 | 54 | 63 |
| 16 | 24 | 32 | 40 | 48 | 56 |
| 14 | 21 | 28 | 35 | 42 | 49 |
| 12 | 18 | 24 | 30 | 36 | 42 |
| 10 | 15 | 20 | 25 | 30 | 35 |
| 8 | 12 | 16 | 20 | 24 | 28 |
| 6 | 9 | 12 | 15 | 18 | 21 |
| 4 | 6 | 8 | 10 | 12 | 14 |
| 2 | 3 | 4 | 5 | 6 | 7 |
| 0 | 0 | 0 | 0 | 0 | 0 |

## Possible Variations

This activity can be used for a variety of math concepts and skill levels. Once students become familiar with how to solve problems using the number lines with their bodies, you can add a competitive edge to the activity by timing them as they complete their worksheets. Timed tests can be stressful for students, but moving their bodies in a fun way helps minimize this anxiety! See how many problems students can solve by hopping within one minute!

# A.25: Math Is Everywhere!

## Overview

This activity sets the stage for a project-based learning unit involving math concepts that you're actively covering in your curriculum. Consider the following steps a basic guideline to develop your own project that helps students see the real-world application of mathematics.

## Required Materials

Journals; pen/pencil; whiteboard

## Preparation

Have students partner up with one another.

## Activity Steps

1. Have students brainstorm jobs/careers that interest them. Encourage them to ask questions about what the day-to-day work would include and what aspects of the job they would find appealing.

2. Ask your students how they would use math or problem-solving skills at that job.

3. Have your students conduct some research to determine how each profession uses mathematical concepts. For example, firefighters use math to calculate tank volumes and flow rates. They would then need to determine pump pressure and do hydraulic calculations, understand coordinates, and be able to estimate slopes.

4. Students should summarize their research on a large whiteboard, in their journals, or make a slideshow presentation for the class.

5. After reviewing your students' projects, consider crafting real-world math problems associated with their professions or breaking your students up into groups and having them develop different math problems that they could expect to solve as experts in their profession.

## Possible Variations

For students who need additional support, the first step in seeing how math can be used in different contexts is seeing *where* math and all of its variables happen. Consider challenging your students to look for instances of math (e.g., numbers, operations, measurements, adding, subtracting) around the room or as they spend time outside school. Consider having students record in a journal instances when they encounter math; for example, a student could record that they went to the doctor's office over the weekend and were measured by a nurse. Alternatively, a student could identify numbers on the clock hanging on the wall. After students have recorded their examples, create a classroom list of these examples.

# A.26: Travel Agents

## Overview

Students will decide on a location around the globe where they (or you, as their client) would like to go for a one-week vacation. This activity takes students through the responsibilities and processes associated with this task as a travel agent.

## Required Materials

Chalk (outdoors), or painter's tape (indoors); construction paper (green); markers; journals; blank checks for a greater challenge

## Preparation

Have students create a 10-by-10 100 number grid using painter's tape (inside) or chalk (outside). Have students write the numbers 1–100 on pieces of paper to fill in the grid (see Figure A.26).

## Activity Steps

1. In their journal, have your students write down the advantages and disadvantages of visiting their chosen location.
2. In their journal, task them to figure out the estimated cost of *every possible* aspect of their holiday. Have them consider the following questions:

- What is the cost of travel? How will they travel there?
- What is the cost of where they will stay?
- Where will they stay? At a hotel, an Airbnb, or somewhere else?
- Will they go to restaurants to eat, or will they purchase food and make it for themselves?
- Do they have to purchase additional clothing for their trip, such as bathing suits for the beach or winter gear for Antarctica?
- What will they do for entertainment on their holiday? What will be the cost for entertainment?

3. Using the blank check templates, have students fill out checks for each category.

4. Have students go to the "classroom bank" to cash each of the checks in return for play money.

5. Have students count the play money to determine the total cost of the vacation. Students can use the number grid to add up their money by laying out their money on the 100 number grid. When their money reaches $100, they will go back to the classroom bank and exchange it for a 100-dollar bill.

6. After they've collected their money from the bank, have students count their 100-dollar bills. When they have ten 100s, then they go back to the bank and exchange the ten 100s for a 1,000-dollar bill. Students will complete their project when they have added up all their money.

7. Consider having your students reflect on the process of calculating the total cost of their holiday. Are there any areas where they could cut costs?

## Possible Variations

To make the game more challenging, have students write checks with dollars *and* cents.

**Travel Agents**

| 1 | 2 | 3 | 4 | 5 | 6 | 7 | 8 | 9 | 10 |
|---|---|---|---|---|---|---|---|---|---|
| 11 | 12 | 13 | 14 | 15 | 16 | 17 | 18 | 19 | 20 |
| 21 | 22 | 23 | 24 | 25 | 26 | 27 | 28 | 29 | 30 |
| 31 | 32 | 33 | 34 | 35 | 36 | 37 | 38 | 39 | 40 |
| 41 | 42 | 43 | 44 | 45 | 46 | 47 | 48 | 49 | 50 |
| 51 | 52 | 53 | 54 | 55 | 56 | 57 | 58 | 59 | 60 |
| 61 | 62 | 63 | 64 | 65 | 66 | 67 | 68 | 69 | 70 |
| 71 | 72 | 73 | 74 | 75 | 76 | 77 | 78 | 79 | 80 |
| 81 | 82 | 83 | 84 | 85 | 86 | 87 | 88 | 89 | 90 |
| 91 | 92 | 93 | 94 | 95 | 96 | 97 | 98 | 99 | 100 |

# A.27: Math Buddies

## Overview

Our Math Buddy program partners students from different groups (by grade, age, skill level, etc.). With Math Buddies, students can create and participate in a kinesthetic learning game *together*. All of the activities included in the book could be refocused as buddy games.

## Required Materials

Varies depending on the kind of activity presented

## Activity Steps

1. For example, 8th graders could partner with 3rd graders to carry out the Skip-Counting Parade activity (see Appendix A.13). Have *both*

students use chalk to create a path of 13 boxes that are around 22 by 15 inches.

2. Within each box, have students write the multiples of 2, beginning with 0 and ending with 24.

3. Have your students create a path for multiples of 3 next to the previous pathway. They will construct the boxes and write the multiples of 3 within them.

4. Have them continue to create additional paths for the remaining multiples that they have learned thus far in your multiplication unit (e.g., 2–12). These pathways *do not* have to be in a straight line or immediately next to one another.

5. Once students have created their paths, they will pretend to be in a parade. The 8th grader can assist the 3rd grader in jumping along the paths on each of the boxes, chanting out loud the corresponding multiple.

## Possible Variations

Any opportunity for students to work together toward a common goal benefits all parties. Consider extending the buddy framework beyond the math classroom; there are many other disciplines that students currently engage in that do not prioritize collaborative work (e.g., the language arts classroom provides many opportunities to read and practice literacy skills). Consider having your students create similar kinesthetic pathways that practice sight words rather than skip-counting multiples.

# A.28: Nines Twist

## Overview

For this activity, students will make a circle around the classroom. This activity supports skip-counting concept development and math fact recall by approaching skip-counting in a multisensory way.

## Required Materials

None

## Preparation

Because this activity requires students to move cross-laterally, make sure that students have enough room around them to move their bodies.

## Activity Steps

1. Have students cross their right hand to the bottom of their left foot and whisper, "One."
2. Have students cross their left hand to the bottom of their right foot and whisper, "Two."
3. Have students touch their right elbow to their left knee, whispering, "Three."
4. Have students touch their left elbow to their right knee, whispering, "Four."
5. Have students twist to the left, whispering, "Five."
6. Have students twist to the right, whispering, "Six."
7. Have students reach their hands upward and sway to their left, whispering, "Seven."
8. Have students then sway to their right, whispering, "Eight."
9. Then, have them clap their hands together above their heads, shouting, "Nine!"
10. Continue these steps up to 90.

## Possible Variations

Students can repeat the these steps counting forward starting at *different* numbers, counting backward from 90, or counting backward from 0 (that is, counting negative numbers).

# A.29: Affirming Journalists

## Overview

This activity is an extension of A.19 that helps students develop a positive sense of self in the context of the mathematics classroom.

## Required Materials

Journals and writing utensils

## Preparation

Choose five positive affirmations. Display the positive affirmations on the whiteboard, smartboard, or large poster paper.

## Activity Steps

1. Follow the instructions from activity A.19. Have students engage in cross-body movement while chanting each of the positive affirmations displayed. Repeat the chanting and cross-body movements three times for each positive affirmation.

2. After students have practiced these affirmations and movements, have them transition to their desks or a writing space. Students will choose one positive affirmation that they found particularly meaningful and spend time reflecting on their own life experiences related to the positive affirmation that they chose.

3. As students journal, you can assist their reflections with a number of questions:
   - "Why did you choose to reflect on this affirmation?"
   - "Describe a time when you were embodying this affirmation."
   - "Describe the situation you were in when you were embodying this affirmation."
   - "How old were you when you felt that way?"
   - "How did it make you feel?"

## Possible Variations

Consider kicking off the activity with a scavenger hunt, where you print off individual affirmations and hide them around the room. Give students time to locate an affirmation to then reflect on. Also consider pairing up students and having them find or decide on an affirmation that they both identify with or aspire to be. Each student can take some time to reflect and write down their thoughts before returning to their partner. After sharing, the pair can create their own active math movement that embodies their chosen positive affirmation. After designing and practicing the movement, you can have the partners share their movement with the class, leading everyone through the steps and celebrating their creations.

# A.30: The Algebra Dance

## Overview

This activity is a physically engaging opportunity for students to practice algebraic problem solving and PEMDAS processes through the collaborative creation of dance choreography. Using movements as variables, students will design their own algebraic equations that the class as a whole can solve together.

## Required Materials

Index cards

## Preparation

Make sure that students have enough space to move around in partners or in small groups.

## Activity Steps

1. Break students up into partners or small groups and supply them with a few index cards.
2. Share the following rules:
   - $f(x) = twirl$
   - $f(y) = leap$
   - $f(z) = slide$
3. With their partners, have students choreograph a dance using the movements and variables provided. They can be as creative as they want as long as they write down their dance as an algebraic formula on the index cards.
4. Give students time to practice their routines; once students are comfortable and once you have a chance to review their choreography/equation, have students write their algebraic equation on the board.
5. After every pairing or group has written their equation on the board, have the whole class dance through each equation. You can have the group who created the equation lead the class if they're comfortable doing so.

6. Once all equations have been danced through, provide some example numbers to associate with the given variables as a way to transition into solving these equations mathematically. For example, what is $3x + 3y$ if $f(x) = 2$ and $f(y) = 6$? What is $3(x + y)$ if $f(x) = 2$ and $f(y) = 6$?

## Possible Variations

Have your students create their own rules for the variables before they begin creating their dance/equation. Students will then create their dance/equation but will not share it with the class. Have each pair group up with another pair of students; once variable rules have been shared, the one team will dance the equation without speaking, and the other will try to write out the dance as an algebraic equation. There is a possibility that these equations could be written out (or notated) differently, so push students to think of alternative ways to depict the equation via PEMDAS rules.

# A.31: The Beanpole Method

## Overview

This quick regulatory exercise functions as a powerful introduction to any kinesthetic activity you plan on implementing in your classroom. Once students learn the easy steps listed below, you can call out, "Beanpole!" whenever you need to grab their attention and focus them on the task at hand.

## Required Materials

None

## Preparation

Students should be standing out of their seats for this exercise; like bean poles, they should also be *silent*.

## Activity Steps

1. Explain and model the following instructions:
   - Have students put both hands at their sides and stand up straight with their chins up.
   - The whole class will take a deep breath together.

- The whole class will take a deep exhale together; you can count out loud quietly to 10 to assist students as they breath out.

2. Students will then look at their teacher for the next instruction.

## Possible Variations

The Beanpole Method activity is a regulatory exercise that derives most of its efficacy from students' mindful breathing. Consider including a conscious breathing component to the other activities we've shared thus far. It also benefits students to talk about these mindfulness components, so do not hesitate to share the *why* behind these activities.

# A.32: The Five Rites

## Overview

This activity is an adapted version of the Five Tibetan Rites that centers the intentional, conscious breathing practices of yantra yoga and skip-counting by 5s; this particular activity follows the same regulatory principles of The Beanpole Method (A.31), but it is a bit more physically rigorous and much more numbers-focused. This activity works wonderfully as a cool-down activity at the end of class.

## Required Materials

None

## Preparation

Make sure students have space to spread out and ideally a soft space on the floor to stretch. Students will mirror you as you demonstrate the individual movements.

## Activity Steps

1. Remind students of the importance of counting and moving *collectively* at a slower, structured pace; students will whisper-count by 5s during each phase of the individual movements:

2. **Twirling:** Have students extend their arms out to the sides with their palms down. They should relax their shoulders and bring their arms in line with their shoulders (like a T-pose). Have students turn slowly

in place in a clockwise direction, whisper-counting up to five for one full rotation. Have students make three full rotations (counting up to 15 total). After rotating, with hands together, have students raise their arms over their heads while inhaling for five counts. Then they will exhale for five counts, lowering their arms to shoulder height and then down to their sides.

3. **Leg Raises:** Students will lie flat on their backs with their arms extended alongside their body with their palms down. While breathing inward and whisper-counting by 5s, they will raise their head off the floor. At the same time, have them lift their legs off the ground, keeping their legs straight as best they can. After they reach five, they will exhale, counting by 5s (up to 10) and lower their heads and legs back down, keeping their legs straight as they go down as best they can. They can relax their muscles for a moment and then repeat the movements two more times (three stretches total), continuing to count by 5s while raising and lowering their heads and legs.

4. **Dynamic Camel:** Have students kneel on the ground with their knees under their hips and their toes tucked under their feet as best they can. Their hands can support their lower back as they stretch. While exhaling and counting to five, students will lower their chin toward their chest. Then, while counting 5–10 and inhaling, students will arch their back and drop their head slowly backward, using their hands on their back for support. Repeat these two phases two more times, counting by 5s for each phase.

5. **Tabletop:** Have students sit on the floor with their legs extended in front of them and their feet about hip-width apart. Their palms should be placed flat alongside their body with their fingers pointing forward. While exhaling for five counts, students will tuck their chin toward their chest. Then, while slowly inhaling for five counts, students will raise their torso (sliding their hips forward and lifting them off the ground) while dropping their head back. Have students hold this position for five counts. Then while exhaling for five counts, have them slowly lower their body back down to the starting position. Have them repeat these two phases two more times.

6. **Upward/Downward Dog:** Have students start in a table position with their hands shoulder-width apart and knees directly under their hips. Then, while inhaling and counting by 5s, have them lift their tailbone up and press their heels down into an inverted V position. Their chin will tuck in toward their chest. Then, while exhaling and counting by 5s, have them lower their body forward and down, arching their back and tiling their head back to look upward as much as they can. Their shoulders should remain broad, and their toes should remain tucked under their feet. Repeat these two phases two more times.

7. After completing the movements, have the class collectively stand up, take a deep breath in together, and take a deep exhale together before returning to their seats.

## Possible Variations

Consider having students record their thoughts and feelings in a journal before and after participating in these stretches. Providing students a space to reflect on these activities will help them see their own growth over time as they continue to practice these movements, which can be quite empowering and motivating for students to continue practicing and pushing themselves to new heights.

# A.33: The Five Animals

## Overview

This activity is a natural extension of activity A.32 that engages students in more physically rigorous movements while still centering conscious breathing. However, instead of pulling from the wisdom of yantra yoga, these short activities (or *stances*) are inspired by Shaolin Kung Fu routines. The combination of balance strengthening (which increases the heart rate and stretches the muscles), breath control, and whisper-counting strengthens students' emotional regulation and conscious discipline skills while building flexibility, making this particular activity a wonderful warm-up or cooldown activity in a classroom setting.

## Required Materials

None

## Preparation

Make sure students have space to spread out to where they can fully extend their arms/legs without touching others. Students will mirror you as you demonstrate the individual movements. Note: These movements should be done *slowly* and *fluidly*.

## Activity Steps

1. Remind students of the importance of counting out loud during the following movements and moving *collectively* at a slower, structured pace. These movements are about synchrony of thought, breath, movement, and stillness. Students will whisper-count by 10s during each of the individual stances.

2. **Snake Stance:** From standing position, begin by having your students step back with their left leg and settle into a low crouch. Have students raise their right hand up to the right side of the face (fingers together and pointing forward, the wrist bent, and palm down, in Snake Hand form; see Figure A.33a).

FIGURE A.33a
**Snake Hand Form**

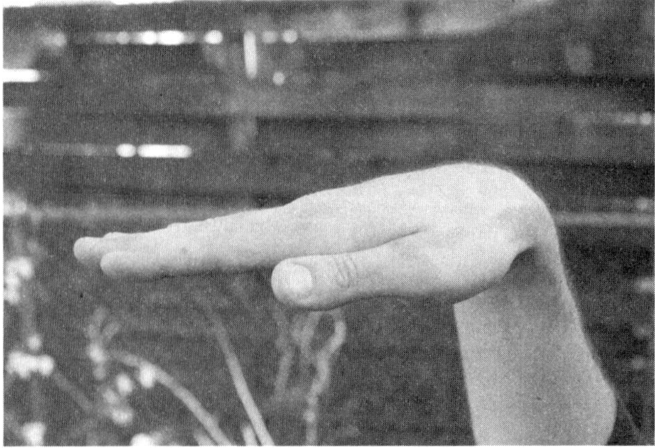

Their right elbow should be against their body. Then, have them move their left hand (with fingers together) to under their right elbow. While in this position, have students slowly raise their right foot at the heel so that their leg (when raised) is as parallel to the floor as they can (see Figure A.33b). Hold this pose for 10 counts.


**Snake Stance**

3. **Horse Stance:** From a standing position, have your students step outward with their left foot so that their legs are slightly wider than shoulder width. Then, have them slowly lower into a deep crouch with their hands as fists tucked against the sides of their body (by the floating ribs). Both thighs should be nearly parallel to the ground and their toes pointing forward as best they can. In this stance, the chest is slightly protruding, butt tucked in, and their back should be straight (see Figure A.33c).

Hold this position for 10 counts, and then have students fully extend their arms outward while slowly turning their fists downward. Hold this position for 10 counts before bringing the fists slowly back to the sides of the body (see Figure A.33d).

## Horse Stance 1

## Horse Stance 2

4. **Eagle Stance:** From a standing position, have your students slide their hands up to their waist with their fingers pointing downward. Then, have them bend over to touch their toes with their hands flat. As they unbend upward, have them extend their arms fully outward and up over their heads. Then, have them rub their hands together as they wiggle their bodies into a crouch (like a bird shaking water droplets off its down!). From a crouching position, have students slowly stand up straight and lift their hands up to the sides of their body in Eagle Hand form (see Figure A.33e).

FIGURE A.33e
**Eagle Hand Form**

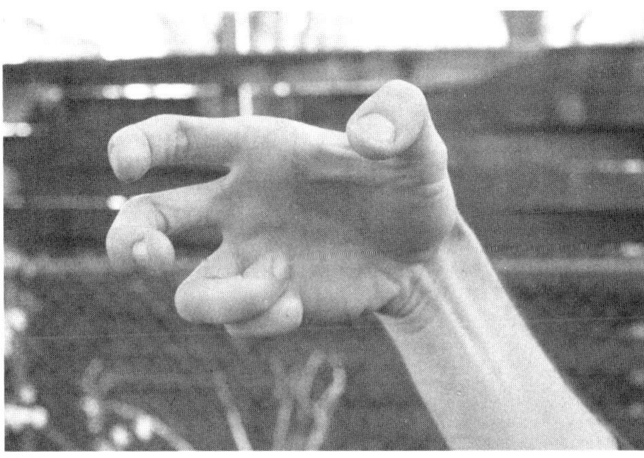

Then, once standing, they will slowly lift their left leg with the knee bent and toes facing downward. The upper part of their leg should be parallel to the ground. At the same time, they will extend their "claws" outward to the left and right sides of their bodies (see Figure A.33f). Hold this position for 10 counts.

5. **Tiger Stance:** From a standing position, have students move their left leg forward across the floor, keeping their hands as fists against the sides of their body (at the floating ribs). Then, have them slowly lower into a crouch with only the toes of the left foot touching the ground (i.e., have them raise the sole of their left foot as they crouch).

As they lower into the crouch, students' right hand will turn into Tiger Hand (see Figure A.33g).


**Eagle Stance**

**Tiger Hand Form**

Have them extend their right hand outward and then arch above their head, fingers and palm facing forward. At the same time, have students extend their left arm forward then place their left hand (in a fist) over their left knee. Their left elbow should be directly above their left hand and knee (see Figure A.33h). Have them hold this position for 10 counts.

FIGURE A.33h
**Tiger Stance**

6. **Dragon Stance:** From a standing position, have students move their right leg forward into a lunge position, with 90 percent of their weight forward on their right leg; their left leg should be fully extended backward (see Figure A.33i). As they lunge, their hands will circle one another in Dragon Hand form as if spinning a ball on the right side of their waist (see Figure A.33j).

Have them hold this position for 10 counts. Then, from the lunging position, have them redistribute their weight by standing upward slowly, inhaling deeply. As they slowly stand up, they will move both hands across their body to the left, with the left arm extending outward and the palm in the position of shaking someone's hand (see Figure A.33k). The right hand will move to cup the left elbow. Have them hold this position for 10 counts.

FIGURE A.33i
**Dragon Hand Form**

FIGURE A.33j
**Dragon Stance 1**

FIGURE A.33k
**Dragon Stance 2**

7. After completing the movements, have the class collectively stand up, take a deep breath in together, and take a deep exhale together before returning to their seats.

## Possible Variations

Much like the yoga poses and active math movements detailed in this book, these stances do not have to be carried out in sequence or all at once; consider using these stances individually as quick regulatory focusing exercises like the Bean Pole Method (A.31), or as a brain break in between units, tests, or lessons. When doing these stances, make sure that students are counting out loud as they hold the poses, and provide enough time in between them so that they can relax their muscles. In a typical kung fu routine, students of the forms would transition between each stance while inhaling slowly. These martial-arts-style activities are particularly helpful for students functioning at a brain stem or midbrain level, although all students benefit from the structured movements and synchronous breathing.

# A.34: To Chance or Not to Chance

## Overview

This activity helps students to understand the likelihood (or unlikelihood) of winning the lottery while giving them context to apply mathematical thinking to the real world, engage in logical reasoning, and use mathematical tools to solve tasks. This activity also helps build students' mathematical vocabulary around the concept of probability.

## Required Materials

Play money; pens/pencils; paper; whiteboard/blackboard

## Preparation

Make sure students have enough space to stand in a circle. Create a chart with headings on the whiteboard or blackboard with the following two headings: How many students are in a circle? What is the likelihood of one student being selected out of the total? It is also helpful to have a 100 number chart available for students to reference (see A.3).

## Activity Steps

1. Start with some introductory questions to gauge students' understanding of the lottery and chance. For example, you could ask students, "Do you know anyone who has purchased a lottery ticket?"
   - What is the likelihood of *winning* the lottery?
   - What is the likelihood of *losing* the lottery?
   - What do we mean when we say something happens *randomly*?
   - What do we mean when we say something happens *by chance*?
   - What do we mean when we say that the *probability* of something happening is low?
2. After some co-deliberation and co-defining terms, choose a record keeper to document on the chart the likelihood with each iteration of the problem. This student's additional responsibility is to explain their findings to the class.
3. Invite students to stand in a circle.

4. Ask one student to go into the center of the group. You can then ask, "What is the likelihood or *probability* that this student will be selected?" Is it 1/1? Or 100 percent? Or 1.00? The record keeper should write down any responses and conversations.

5. Invite another student to join the first student in the circle. You can then ask, "What is the likelihood or probability that *this* student will be selected?" Is it ½? Or 50 percent? Or 0.50? To help students understand that ½ is the same as 50 percent, you can have students cover 50 boxes on the 100 number grid with construction paper.

6. Invite a third student to join the circle. "What is the likelihood or probability of this student being selected?" Is it ⅓ or 33.333 percent or 0.333333?

7. Invite seven more students to stand in the circle (so that there are 10 total). "What is the likelihood or probability of one of the students being selected?" Is it 1/10 or 10 percent or 0.10?

8. Invite 10 more students into the center. Now there are 20 students in the circle. "What is the likelihood or probability of one of the students being selected?" Is it 1/20 or 5 percent or 0.05?

9. Ask your record keeper to share observations and reflections about the likelihood of being selected as the number of participants increases. Follow up this reflection time with an additional question: "Do you have a better chance of being selected if there are more or fewer people in the center?"

10. Ask students to imagine or form a hypothesis around 100 students within the circle. What is the likelihood or probability of one of the students being selected? Would it be 1/100 or 1 percent or 0.01? Any good hypothesis requires testing to prove its accuracy. How would students test this hypothesis? What strategies or explanations could they use in solving the problem?

11. Build on the previous inquiries with further questioning. Imagine if there were 1,000 students in the circle. What is the likelihood or probability of one of the students being selected? Is it 1/1000 or 0.1 percent or 0.001? Imagine if there were one million students in the circle. What is the likelihood or probability of one of the students being selected? Is it 1/1,000,000 or 0.0001 percent or 0.000001?

Imagine if there were 100 million students in the circle. What is the likelihood or probability of one of the students being selected? Is it 1/100,000,000 or 0.000001 percent or 0.00000001?

12. In actuality, the odds of winning the lottery are approximately one in 300 million. Have students take time to reflect with one another about this hefty number. Is it *really* worth spending your money to purchase a lottery ticket?

## Possible Variations

There are many other real-world connections to probability besides the lottery, some of which students might already have already been exposed to or thought about, such as the probability of a storm brewing next week or the probability that a favorite baseball team will win the World Series or the probability that they will be stuck in traffic on the way home. Other thought-provoking, more humorous examples include the probability of being struck by lightning, being attacked by a shark, or having the same birthday as another person in class. These examples can be applied to the activity steps, but there is also significant value in letting your students research real-world instances of probability and present their discoveries to the class using the 100 number grid or the line of logic and explanation detailed above. Alternatively, a brief introduction to Murphy's law (the adage that anything that can go wrong will go wrong) could provide a lighthearted introduction to the concept of probability and spur discussions around real-world applications of the concept.

# A.35: Leaping Arrays

## Overview

This activity helps students visualize and manipulate arrays collaboratively.

## Required Materials

Beanbags; paper; sticky notes; tape (indoors); chalk (outdoors)

## Preparation

You or your students should construct a 10-by-10 multiplication grid on the ground (see Figure A.35) where students can hop to complete the following steps.

FIGURE A.35
**Leaping Arrays**

| 1 | 2 | 3 | 4 | 5 | 6 | 7 | 8 | 9 | 10 |
|---|---|---|---|---|---|---|---|---|---|
| 2 | 4 | 6 | 8 | 10 | 12 | 14 | 16 | 18 | 20 |
| 3 | 6 | 9 | 12 | 15 | 18 | 21 | 24 | 27 | 30 |
| 4 | 8 | 12 | 16 | 20 | 24 | 28 | 32 | 36 | 40 |
| 5 | 10 | 15 | 20 | 25 | 30 | 35 | 40 | 45 | 50 |
| 6 | 12 | 18 | 24 | 30 | 36 | 42 | 48 | 54 | 60 |
| 7 | 14 | 21 | 28 | 35 | 42 | 49 | 56 | 63 | 70 |
| 8 | 16 | 24 | 32 | 40 | 48 | 56 | 64 | 72 | 80 |
| 9 | 18 | 27 | 36 | 45 | 54 | 63 | 72 | 81 | 90 |
| 10 | 20 | 30 | 40 | 50 | 60 | 70 | 80 | 90 | 100 |

## Activity Steps

1. Have students use beanbags or paper to make a rectangle on the grid, covering up all the numbers on the multiplication grid within that rectangle. This helps students visualize the arrays; if each box is a single unit, then the total number of boxes equals the *area* of the rectangle.

2. If the top left corner of the constructed rectangle falls on the top left corner of the multiplication grid (i.e., on the product *1*), have your

students reveal the bottom right corner of their rectangle to find that product is equal to the rectangle's area.

3. Give students time to construct different-sized rectangles and have them determine each rectangle's area either by counting the number of boxes within it or by multiplying arrays. Students can hop across the multiplication grid as they multiply the sides together.

4. Next, have students create a rectangle on the grid as before. Then, have them place yellow sticky notes (or pieces of paper, blocks, or other manipulatives on the floor mat) to make a rectangle with an equivalent area to the first one.

5. Have students play around with the shape and size of the rectangles, but make sure that their areas are consistent. Students can check for mistakes by counting the boxes or multiplying the arrays of their rectangles.

## Possible Variations

Have students find the area of various rectangles using the grid. Place a beanbag on some number near the middle of the grid. For example, if you choose 48, this is the area of the rectangle students will make. Use painter's tape or sticky notes to make an enclosed area with corners at 48, 6, ×, and 8. Students will then be able to connect the idea of the area model to multiplication. Challenge them to find rectangles with the same area but with different lengths of sides.

# A.36: Fast Fact Workout

## Overview

This activity helps to increase BDNF production via aerobically rigorous math practice for any fact-recall concept.

## Required Materials

None

## Preparation

Make sure students have enough space to move their bodies and carry out the various physical movements.

## Activity Steps

1. Inform your students that the number 10 is the magic number; when 10 is the answer to the following problems, students will do a squat.

2. Give your students a series of math problems that they should solve mentally. For each answer that equals 10, students should do a squat, but for any other answer, they should stay still (e.g., "7 + 3" or "14 – 5"). This is a great game to try to "trick" the students into squatting when they should be standing still.

3. Once students get a handle of the rules, increase the complexity of the problem by adding additional steps (e.g., 7 + 5 – 2). If students need a visual aid, you can write these questions on the board.

## Possible Variations

There are endless variations for this activity:

- Have students do a pushup when the number is larger than 5 or sit if it is 5 or below.
- Have students do a jumping jack when the number is even and stand still when it is odd.
- Have students do a lunge if the digit *1* appears in the number or sit down if it doesn't.

# A.37: Shapeshifters

## Overview

This collaborative activity builds on student knowledge of shapes, angles, and symmetry via formative, corrective feedback.

## Required Materials

Whiteboard or blackboard

## Preparation

Make sure that students have enough room on the floor to spread out and angle their bodies to create the shapes.

## Activity Steps

1. Split the class into two teams. One will be the "shapeshifters," and the other will be the guessers or drawers.

2. Team 1 will use their collective bodies to create a shape on the floor, while Team 2 has to collectively guess the name of the shape and its specific qualities (e.g., a pentagon, which has five sides and five vertices).

3. One member of Team 2 will draw the shape and write its name down (with any associated qualities) on the board. If their answer is incorrect, the team will keep trying until they get it correct.

## Possible Variations

You can also give the name of a shape to Team 1 to create on the floor or to Team 2 to draw on the board. Alternatively, you can split the class into three or four groups and have them race to create and identify the most shapes within a given time limit.

# A.38: Heads Up, Sevenths Up

## Overview

This activity takes an active, math-focused spin on the classic game Heads Up, Seven Up. This activity helps students practice adding and subtracting (or multiplying and dividing) fractions, beginning with 7s and 7ths, while simultaneously building noticing skills.

## Required Materials

Index cards

## Preparation

On each index card, write out an equation that adds, subtracts, multiplies, or divides fractions with 7 in the numerator or denominator (depending on the difficulty level). Then, on other cards, write out the answer to each equation (see Figure A.38); make sure that the equations and answers are coupled together.

FIGURE A.38
**Heads Up, Sevenths Up**

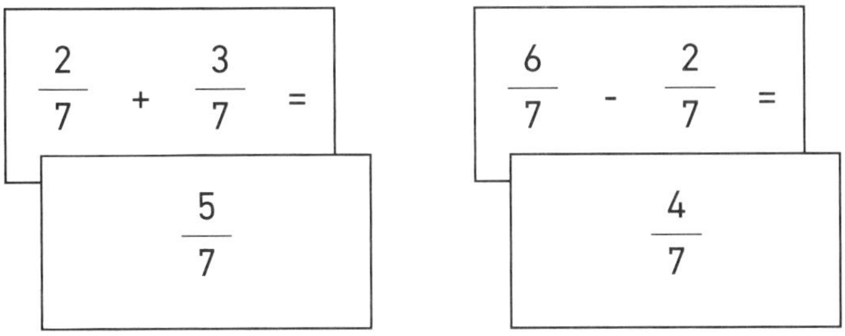

$$\frac{2}{7} + \frac{3}{7} = \qquad \frac{6}{7} - \frac{2}{7} =$$

$$\frac{5}{7} \qquad\qquad \frac{4}{7}$$

## Activity Steps

1. Choose seven students to be the "seven up." Alternatively, you can choose the first picker and then each picker chooses an additional picker until there are seven of them total. Give each of the seven pickers an equation card and an answer card.

2. Instruct the picking phase by announcing the rhyme "Heads down, hands cupped, time to play sevenths up." All of the players (besides the pickers) put their heads down on their arms on the table and close their eyes. The facilitator can also turn off or dim the light to make it harder for players to cheat and see the pickers.

3. Once everyone at the desks has their heads down and hands open, the pickers will each select one person by handing them their answer index card. The pickers' goal is to make their selection in a stealthy way that does not give away their identity and then return to the front of the room. Guessers can pay attention to clues that will help them identify their picker, such as footsteps, giggles, or other sounds.

4. Once all seven pickers have selected a guesser by giving out their answer card and returning to the front of the room, the facilitator will announce "Heads up, sevenths up," and everyone who had their eyes closed takes their heads off the table and opens their eyes.

5. All of the people who were given a card stand up. Each guesser gets one attempt to identify the person who gave them the card by matching their answer card to one of the equations displayed by the seven pickers. If they guess their associated equation correctly, they're a

picker for the next round, and the current pickers sit down. If they guess incorrectly, they sit back down, and the picker remains a picker in the next round. You can have students do specific physical activities if they answer correctly or incorrectly!

## Possible Variations

To make it easier, students can be asked to connect *equivalent* fractions rather than identify answers to equations. To increase the difficulty of the game, consider adding place values into the fraction cards; just change the seven player cards to place values in numerical form and have the seven students hand out cards with the place values written out alphabetically.

# A.39: Wait! That Doesn't Add Up

## Overview

This activity helps foster appreciation for making mistakes by getting students to work collaboratively to identify (and create!) mistakes as they solve multiple math problems. This activity will help students learn to ask good questions when they see a mistake instead of just pointing it out. This is an excellent review after a test where students love to share their "best mistakes"—and see that other students made similar mistakes!

## Required Materials

Index cards; pen/pencils and paper for drafting ideas and answering questions; a whiteboard or blackboard

## Preparation

Mark each corner of the classroom as A, B, C, and D. On index cards provide a math problem related to the concepts you're covering in class. Divide the index cards into groups of four and label each A, B, C, and D.

## Activity Steps

1. Have students work in small groups to complete a set of four math problems (each group gets a full set labeled A, B, C, and D) around a specific math concept your class is currently covering.

2. In each small group, students will share their individual solutions with their group and write their solution on the back of each of the four index cards.

3. The team will then choose *one* solution and make one *intentional mistake* in that solution. They can choose a mistake that one of their members made (this leads to a discussion of who had the "best" mistake), or they can think of a mistake other students might make. They can make as many *unintentional* mistakes as they like.

4. Bring everyone into a whole-class discussion, but keep the teams together.

5. As each group shares their solutions for each group of problems to the class as a whole, the rest of the class listens and attempts to find their mistake. When they find their mistake, they (as a team) must move to the corner of the room that corresponds to the letter on that index card. You can write the options on the board for students to see.

6. After time is allotted for students to move across the classroom and decide on a corner, they must agree on a question to ask in order to get the group to admit their mistake. For example, "Why did you…?" "Can you explain how you…?"

7. If a team correctly identifies which equation *and* the mistake made, they get a point. If the class correctly identifies the equation but does not correctly identify the specific mistake, another team gets a chance to steal the point.

## Possible Variations

Alternatively, you can facilitate a kinesthetic version of the classic game Two Truths and a Lie. Each team comes up with two correct number sentences and one incorrect one. The rest of the class stands up when they think they have found the mistake. Once everyone is standing, the teacher directs the standing students to jump once if they think it is the first problem, jump twice if they think it is the second, and three times if it is the third. Be sure to let each presenting group choose the physical action; this could be jumping, clapping, snapping, or any other movement.

# A.40: Geometry Taboo

## Overview

In this conversation-centered activity, students try to get their teammates to guess a specific geometric term by giving clues. But students have to be careful not to use any of the "taboo" words in their description. This activity can be done as a whole class or in groups.

## Required Materials

Index cards; paper and pens/pencils (if you want students to show their work)

## Preparation

Create sets of cards, each with a geometry term at the top and a list of two or three related taboo words below.

## Activity Steps

1. Split students into pairs or small groups with their own set of taboo cards.
2. One student will choose a card and will then try to get their teammate to guess the term at the top of the card without using any of the words listed below. Students can't use any part of the word or give "sounds like" or "rhymes with" clues.
3. Each team gets two minutes to get as many words as possible, earning one point per correctly guessed word. If they accidentally say a taboo word, they have to switch seats or do a specific physical action (e.g., a jumping jack, a pushup, a squat). If the clue giver succeeds without saying any taboo words, the group gets a 20-second silent dance party!

## Possible Variations

In addition to having students vocalize their clues, you can have students *draw* clues to get their group to correctly guess the word.

# A.41: Guess Who, Place Value!

## Overview

This activity is a more active, whole-body adaptation of the classic game Guess Who that builds students' question-asking skills and helps strengthen mathematics language and terminology comprehension.

## Required Materials

Tape, chalk, or construction paper for creating the 10-by-10 100 number grid indoors or outdoors; index cards (23 in total) with numbers written on them big enough to see from a distance; whiteboard or blackboard

## Preparation

With chalk (if outside), create a 10-by-10-foot 100 number grid (you can use tape or construction paper with numbers on the individual sheets if inside). Draw a box at the top left edge of the grid and write 0 in the box (see Figure A.41).

Up to 23 students will be given an index card with a number on it ranging 1–100; they will stand on the 100 number grid that matches their specific number. Identify one of the students *secretly* to be the mystery number. Another student (or a small group of no more than three students) will be chosen as the guesser.

## Activity Steps

1. Have the students standing on the grid hold their index card in their hands; they will be responsible for knowing their number.
2. The guesser(s) will ask a series of questions to try to identify the mystery number. Some example questions could include the following:
   - Is it less than…?
   - Is it an even number?
   - Does it have a 7 in the 10s place?
   - Does it come after the number 32?
   - Is it divisible by 5?
3. Students whose numbers do not correspond to the questions will sit down on their number, and those whose numbers do correspond to the questions will remain standing. For added stakes, you can give

the guesser(s) a limited number of guesses before ultimately deciding on a number.

4. For every question that yields *no* action on the part of the students on the mat, the guesser(s) have to do 10 jumping jacks.

5. The guesser(s) win the game if they can identify the mystery number (or the last student that remains standing) and get to choose the next guesser(s).

FIGURE A.41
**Guess Who, Place Value!**

| 0 | 1 | 2 | 3 | 4 | 5 | 6 | 7 | 8 | 9 | 10 |
|---|---|---|---|---|---|---|---|---|---|---|
|  | 11 | 12 | 13 | 14 | 15 | 16 | 17 | 18 | 19 | 20 |
|  | 21 | 22 | 23 | 24 | 25 | 26 | 27 | 28 | 29 | 30 |
|  | 31 | 32 | 33 | 34 | 35 | 36 | 37 | 38 | 39 | 40 |
|  | 41 | 42 | 43 | 44 | 45 | 46 | 47 | 48 | 49 | 50 |
|  | 51 | 52 | 53 | 54 | 55 | 56 | 57 | 58 | 59 | 60 |
|  | 61 | 62 | 63 | 64 | 65 | 66 | 67 | 68 | 69 | 70 |
|  | 71 | 72 | 73 | 74 | 75 | 76 | 77 | 78 | 79 | 80 |
|  | 81 | 82 | 83 | 84 | 85 | 86 | 87 | 88 | 89 | 90 |
|  | 91 | 92 | 93 | 94 | 95 | 96 | 97 | 98 | 99 | 100 |

## Possible Variations

Split the class into small groups and use the 100 number grid for a game of kinesthetic Simon Says. One group will be "Simon" and secretly come up with a number that they want the rest of the class to identify by marking the 100 number grid with a piece of colored construction paper.

The Simon group will need to give directives to the rest of the class, and they can quickly deliberate among themselves about which orders to give. Some examples could be "Simon says stand on a number greater than 50." "Simon says to stand on an even number." "Simon says that the digits of the number add up to 7."

Make sure that the Simon group gives the class enough time to move around, deliberate, and mark the numbers. You can also appoint a student (or yourself) to write the list of commands for everyone to keep track of what's been asked so that they can identify the specific number.

# A.42: 22 Questions

## Overview

A collaborative spin on the classic game 20 Questions, this activity helps build class cohesion and strengthen students' question-asking skills as they relate to mathematics terminology.

## Required Materials

Numbered record sheets and pencils for recording questions and responses; math vocabulary lists with definitions for the relevant terms (optional but recommended); sticky notes or paper and tape

## Preparation

Write math vocabulary words or expressions connected to the current unit of study on sticky notes or slips of paper. Place easier terms near the top of the stack and more difficult terms near the bottom of the stack so you can give each student an appropriate challenge when play begins. Make sure students have enough space to move around.

## Activity Steps

1. Play one demonstration round as a class to model useful questions that start out broad and gradually narrow the field. Most questions will target math concepts, but a few might address linguistic matters, such as "Am I just one word?" or "Am I a noun?"
2. Pass out vocabulary lists and numbered sheets for recording questions and answers.

3. Place a mystery word or expression on each student's back, drawing from the top, middle, or bottom of the stack as needed to accommodate different proficiency levels.

4. The students circulate while asking questions, recording responses, and answering questions.

5. As students figure out their mystery words, they may receive a new word or expression from the teacher and begin a new round.

6. Students who cannot guess correctly within 22 questions may opt to keep guessing or to "give up" and see their words then start over with new mystery words or expressions.

7. For each correct and incorrect guess, students have to do a specific physical activity (e.g., jumping jacks, a squat, a pushup).

8. After you've led this game with the whole class, you can break students up into groups or partners to play this game together.

## Possible Variations

Instead of writing vocabulary words on slips of paper, consider providing the words on a bingo card. In order to mark off the word on the card, students have to ask the teacher a question about a word. For instance, "Can I mark off the shape that has three sides?" That student can mark it off, and any other student who knows what the word is can mark theirs too. Students who know the most vocabulary will be able to ask the right questions to get bingo first. The other students will learn it as the game progresses. After each question, you have students discuss their reflections in pairs or in groups. You can also break the class up into small groups to complete a single bingo card to support collaborative problem solving and inquiry.

# A.43: Ready, Set, Sudoku!

## Overview

An important skill that plays a significant role in the proof-making process is the ability to concisely write one's reasoning for why a specific step was taken to solve a problem. This activity helps students build their writing and communication skills through a collaborative, kinesthetic game of sudoku.

## Required Materials

Tape, chalk, or construction paper for creating the nine-by-nine-unit Cartesian coordinate grid; writing utensils

## Preparation

With chalk (if outside), create a nine-by-nine-unit Cartesian coordinate grid (you can use tape or blank pieces of construction paper if inside) to mimic a sudoku puzzle (including "nonets"). Fill the grid with specific numbers to kickstart the sudoku-solving process (see Figure A.43; there are a number of free sudoku generators online to get started).

Above the top row (or the x-axis), write or place a letter A–I for each unit. Along the leftmost column (the y-axis), write or place a number 1–9 for each unit. These axes labels will help students communicate specific units within the grid (e.g., "We wrote a 7 in square C8").

FIGURE A.43
**Ready, Set, Sudoku!**

|   | A | B | C | D | E | F | G | H | I |
|---|---|---|---|---|---|---|---|---|---|
| 1 |   |   |   | 6 | 5 | 1 | 4 | 9 |   |
| 2 | 3 |   | 1 | 7 |   | 9 | 6 |   |   |
| 3 | 9 |   |   |   |   | 3 | 7 |   |   |
| 4 |   | 3 |   |   | 6 |   |   |   |   |
| 5 | 1 |   |   | 9 | 2 |   |   | 7 |   |
| 6 |   |   |   |   | 3 | 4 | 2 | 8 | 1 |
| 7 | 8 |   |   | 4 |   | 5 |   | 3 | 7 |
| 8 | 4 |   |   | 8 | 7 |   |   |   |   |
| 9 |   |   | 7 |   |   | 2 |   |   | 4 |

You can do this activity as a whole class, or you can split the class into no more than four groups to complete the puzzle. If you decide to break the class up into groups, you might want to consider constructing a smaller sudoku grid for each individual group.

## Activity Steps

1.  Introduce your students to the four rules of sudoku:
    - Each row must contain the numbers 1–9 without repetitions.
    - Each column must contain the numbers 1–9 without repetitions.
    - The digits can only occur once per nonet.
    - The sum of every single row, column, and nonet must equal 45.
2.  The students' task is to complete the puzzle by filling in the squares of the grid with the correct numbers (1–9) based on what numbers are initially provided.
3.  Have each team elect a note taker.
4.  Students will work collaboratively to complete the puzzle while the note taker records the group's choices. The note taker must record the steps/reasoning as a list (like a two-column proof). The other group members can help the note taker provide the rationale through discussion. The rationale must be presented concisely and clearly so that others can follow the logic to solve the problem themselves. Don't worry if there are mistakes!
5.  With each number added to the grid, students will do that many jumping jacks together (or any physical activity that would be appropriate).
6.  After the group has finished completing the puzzle, check their work. If they made a mistake, give students a chance to find it themselves based on the rules. Have a student show their mistake by standing on the specific unit. Where in their written logic (recorded by the note taker) was this decision made? How did the team come to this conclusion? The notes in this case provide students a chance to go back and check their reasoning!
7.  After some reflection, let the students work together to correct their mistake by doing jumping jacks or some other movement for the number they put down.

## Possible Variations

After every group has completed their puzzle, have teams share their notes with another team. The new task is for them to complete the puzzle using the "directions" (or rationale) provided by the other team as a list. If clarity is required to make sense of the notes, the teams can ask each other questions as they progress through the steps. This approach can also be helpful for students to practice constructive feedback if they come across any mistakes or are confused by the rationale.

# A.44: Cutout Conundrum

## Overview

This activity helps model proofing to support students' comprehension of the practice. The application of "cutouts" for the proof parts provides students with manipulatives to aid in collaborative problem solving and communicating their rationale for each step of the proof.

## Required Materials

Whiteboard or blackboard; proof cutouts and "prove/given" statement cutouts; writing paper and utensils for students to show their work; tape, chalk, or string for creating a space for students to place their cutouts on the floor.

## Preparation

Using tape, chalk, or string (depending on whether it's indoors or outdoors), create a two-column table on the floor, with the first column labeled *Statements* and the second labeled *Reasons* (see Figure A.44). This should model a typical two-column proof. Group students into pairs.

## Activity Steps

1. Give each pair of students one cutout piece of the proof (connected to a specific prove/given statement, which you can write on the whiteboard).
2. Each pair will look at their cutout and move to the side of the two-column table depending on whether their cutout is a statement or a

reason (there will ultimately be two larger groups, one on each side of the table).

3. The statement group will work together to arrange the statements on the floor to prove the provided answer. The pairs in charge of each cutout will move the cutout to the correct place through collaborative discussion.

4. Once the statement group is confident of their order, the reason group can start matching up the reasons for each statement. While the reason group waits for the statement group to arrange their cutouts, they can discuss the order among themselves and come up with questions or corrections for the other team.

5. For each correct placement of a cutout, everyone will do three jumping jacks. Alternatively, once both sides have attempted to order their cards, you can check their work; if they make a mistake or multiple mistakes, you can provide the *number* of incorrect placements and have students work together to check their collaborative work.

6. Once the teams are confident in their answers, they can ask you to check their work again; repeat these steps until the students have correctly arranged the cutouts.

FIGURE A.44

## Cutout Conundrum

| Statements | Reasons |
| --- | --- |
|  |  |
|  |  |
|  |  |
|  |  |
|  |  |
|  |  |
|  |  |

## Possible Variations

To maximize students' collaboration (and minimize your "omniscient" status as instructor), consider providing the statement group the answer key for the reason cutout order and vice versa. This gives the class *partial* knowledge of the whole solution, which will then force them to work together to complete the proof. To keep students from giving away the answers to the other team, have students suggest corrections by *asking questions* that are relevant to the information given in the cutouts and the order in which they're placed. This helps students practice giving affirmative, constructive feedback to their peers and opens up more possibilities to explain and reflect on answers given.

# A.45: 101 and Out

## Overview

This exciting, strategic thinking activity gets students to work cooperatively in a competitive setting while allowing the space to explore, conjecture, and explain their reasoning with others and practice their addition, subtraction, and multiplication skills.

## Required Materials

Painter's tape (if inside) or chalk (if outside); dice (6–20-sided); paper/pencils to write out explanations

## Preparation

Create a 100 number grid on the floor/ground (see Figure A.45). Have students write the numbers 1–100 in the boxes moving from left to right across the rows. Add a box with 0 to the left of the 1 space and a box with 101 to the right of the 100 space. Divide your class into two groups.

## Activity Steps

1. Group 1 will roll one of the dice. They will strategize together to count the number at face value *or* multiply it by 10. For example, a student who rolls a 4 can either keep it a 4 or turn it into 40.
2. Once the roll is decided, another student from that group hops on the 100 number grid and stands on the decided number.

3. Group 2 will roll and strategize, with one student moving to the number on the grid.

4. The first team to reach 101 *without going over* wins the game. If a team goes over, they have to start back at 0.


**101 and Out**

| 0 | 1 | 2 | 3 | 4 | 5 | 6 | 7 | 8 | 9 | 10 | |
|---|---|---|---|---|---|---|---|---|---|---|---|
| | 11 | 12 | 13 | 14 | 15 | 16 | 17 | 18 | 19 | 20 | |
| | 21 | 22 | 23 | 24 | 25 | 26 | 27 | 28 | 29 | 30 | |
| | 31 | 32 | 33 | 34 | 35 | 36 | 37 | 38 | 39 | 40 | |
| | 41 | 42 | 43 | 44 | 45 | 46 | 47 | 48 | 49 | 50 | |
| | 51 | 52 | 53 | 54 | 55 | 56 | 57 | 58 | 59 | 60 | |
| | 61 | 62 | 63 | 64 | 65 | 66 | 67 | 68 | 69 | 70 | |
| | 71 | 72 | 73 | 74 | 75 | 76 | 77 | 78 | 79 | 80 | |
| | 81 | 82 | 83 | 84 | 85 | 86 | 87 | 88 | 89 | 90 | |
| | 91 | 92 | 93 | 94 | 95 | 96 | 97 | 98 | 99 | 100 | 101 |

## Possible Variations

Students can play the same game but *subtract* their rolls or multiples starting from 100. The goal is to score as close to 0 as possible without going under. If students go *under,* they have to start over at 100. Alternatively, you (or your students) can create multistep rules to add complexity to the game. For example, groups will roll three dice; the first is a stable number, the second is a multiplier to the first, and the third can be a multiplier or added to the total of the other two dice.

# Acknowledgments

For more than two decades, our work has been enriched by the dedication and expertise of so many professionals. We deeply appreciate and want to acknowledge *all* who have tirelessly supported our mission, whether that support has come through in-person or virtual workshops and conference meetups; through collaborations around family engagement events, research projects, and fundraising campaigns; or through impassioned Zoom chats about the state of education and the growing need for change, we are forever grateful.

Special thanks is in order for our close friends and colleagues who have helped bring this work to life. Thank you, Stephanie, for your unyielding support of our cause and years of steadfast advocacy for the creation of this very book. Thank you, Ken, Rudy, Dave, Eli, and Millie, for your years of leadership, friendship, and wisdom. Thank you, Fayth, Jeff, Luvelle, Sean, Jennie, Kimberly, Maggie, and Sally, for your service not only as stellar educators and school leaders but also as community bridge builders. And, finally, we want to share our appreciation for the love and support of our families, our friends, and the many, many communities that have made us who we are today; we hope that this book lives up to your high—yet necessary—expectations.

# References


Ajzen, I. (1985). From intentions to actions: A theory of planned behavior. In J. Kuhl & J. Beckmann (Eds.), *Action control* (pp. 11–39). Springer.

Akin, A., & Kurbanoglu, I. (2011). The relationships between math anxiety, math attitudes, and self-efficacy: A structural equation model. *Studia Psychologica, 53*(3), 263–273.

Akos, P. (2000). Building empathic skills in elementary school children through group work. *Journal for Specialists in Group Work, 25*(2), 214–223.

Allen-Lyall, B. (2018). Helping students to automatize multiplication facts: A pilot study. *International Electronic Journal of Elementary Education, 10*(4), 6.

Alvidrez, M., Louie, N., & Tchoshanov, M. (2022). From mistakes, we learn? Mathematics teachers' epistemological and positional framing of mistakes. *Journal of Mathematics Teacher Education, 27*, 111–136. https://doi.org/10.1007/s10857-022-09553-4

Arnsten, A. F. T. (2015). Stress weakens prefrontal networks: Molecular insults to higher cognition. *Nature Neuroscience, 18*(10), 1376–1385. http://www.nature.com/doifinder/10.1038/nn.4087

Ashcraft, M., & Moore, A. (2009). Mathematics anxiety and the affective drop in performance. *Journal of Psychoeducational Assessment, 27*(3), 197–205.

Bachman, J., O'Malley, P., Freedman-Doan, P., Trzesniewski, K., & Donnellan, M. B. (2011). Adolescent self-esteem: Differences by race/ethnicity, gender, and age. *Self Identity, 10*(4), 445–473. https://doi.org/10.1080/15298861003794538

Bandura, A. (1982). Self-efficacy mechanism in human agency. *American Psychologist, 37*(2), 122–147. https://doi.org/10.1037/0003-066X.37.2.122

Bandura, A. (Ed.). (1995). *Self-efficacy in changing societies*. Cambridge University Press.

Barry-Jester, A. M. (2019). California looks to lead nation in unraveling childhood trauma. *California Healthline.* https://californiahealthline.org/news/california-looks-to-lead-nation-aces-screening-childhood-trauma/

Baumann, C. E., & Boutellier, R. (2011). Physical activity—The basis of learning and creativity. *The Future of Education*. Pixel International Conferences. https://conference.pixel-online. net/conferences/edu_future/common/download/Paper_pdf/ITL59-Baumann.pdf

Baumeister, R., Campbell, J., Krueger, J., & Vohs, K. (2003). Does high self-esteem cause better performance, interpersonal success, happiness, or healthier lifestyles? *Psychological Science in the Public Interest, 4*(1), 1–44.

Bay-Williams, J., & Kling, G. (2019). *Math fact fluency: 60+ games and assessment tools to support learning and retention.* ASCD.

Beernaert, Y. (1994). *Lifelong learning as a contribution to quality education in Europe* [European Lifelong Learning Monograph].

Beilock, S., & Willingham, D. T. (2014). Math anxiety: Can teachers help students reduce it? Ask the cognitive scientist. *American Educator, 38*(2), 28–32.

Beilock, S., Gunderson, E., Ramirez, G., & Levine, S. (2010). Female teachers' math anxiety affects girls' math achievement. *PNAS, 107*(5), 1860–1863.

Bekdemir, M. (2010). The pre-service teachers' mathematics anxiety related to depth of negative experiences in mathematics classroom while they were students. *Educational Studies in Mathematics, 75*, 311–328. https://doi.org/10.1007/s10649-010-9260-7

Benson-O'Connor, C., McDaniel, C., & Carr, J. (2019). Bringing math to life: Provide students opportunities to connect their lives to math. *Networks: An Online Journal for Teacher Research, 21*(2). https://doi.org/10.4148/2470-6353.1299

Bergen, D. (2009). Play as the learning medium for future scientists, mathematicians, and engineers. *American Journal of Play, 1*(4), 413–428.

Bethell, C., Newacheck, P., Hawes, E., & Halfon, N. (2014). Adverse childhood experiences: Assessing the impact on health and school engagement and the mitigating role of resilience. *Health Affairs, 33*(12), 2106–2115. https://doi.org/10.1377/hlthaff.2014.0914

Bieda, K., Ji, X., Drwencke, J., & Picard, A. (2013). Reasoning-and-proving opportunities in elementary mathematics textbooks. *International Journal of Educational Research, 64*, 71–80.

Bingölbali, E., & Bingölbali, F. (2020). Divergent thinking and convergent thinking: Are they promoted in mathematics textbooks? *International Journal of Contemporary Educational Research, 7*(1), 240–252.

Birch, S., & Ladd, G. (1997). The teacher-child relationship and children's early school adjustment. *Journal of School Psychology, 35*(1), 61–79.

Blair, C., & Razza, P. (2007). Relating effortful control, executive function, and false belief understanding to emerging math and literacy ability in kindergarten. *Child Development, 78*(2), 647–663. https://doi.org/10.1111/j.1467-8624.2007.01019.x

Blazer, C. (2011). Strategies for reducing math anxiety. *Miami-Dade County Public Schools, Information Capsule, 1102.* https://eric.ed.gov/?id=ED536509

Blodgett, C., & Lanigan, J. (2018). The association between adverse childhood experience (ACE) and school success in elementary school children. *School Psychology Quarterly, 33*(1), 137–146. https://doi.org/10.1037/spq0000256

Bollimbala, A., James, P. S., & Ganguli, S. (2021). Impact of physical activity on an individual's creativity: A day-level analysis. *American Journal of Psychology, 134*(1), 93–105.

Bonny, J., Lindberg, J., & Pacampara, M. (2017). Hip hop dance experience linked to sociocognitive ability. *PLoS ONE, 12*(2), 1–26. https://doi.org/10.1371/journal.pone.0169947

Bragg, L. (2007). Students' conflicting attitudes towards games as a vehicle for learning mathematics: A methodological dilemma. *Mathematics Education Research Journal, 19*(1), 29–44.

Brattico, E., Bonetti, L., Ferretti, G., Vuust, P., & Matrone, C. (2021). Putting cells in motion: Advantages of endogenous boosting of BDNF production. *Cells, 10*(183), 16.

Broman-Fulks, J., Berman, M., Rabian, B., & Webster, M. (2004). Effects of aerobic exercise on anxiety sensitivity. *Behaviour Research and Therapy, 42*(2), 125–136. https://doi.org/10.1016/S0005-7967(03)00103-7

Brooks, S. J., Parks, S. M., & Stamoulis, C. (2021). Widespread positive direct and indirect effects of regular physical activity on the developing functional connectome in early adolescence. *Cerebral Cortex, 31*, 4840–4852. https://doi.org/10.1093/cercor/bhab126

Brown, S., & Vaughan, C. (2009). *Play: How it shapes the brain, opens the imagination, and invigorates the soul.* Penguin.

Bubikova-Moan, J., Hjetland, H. N., & Wollscheid, S. (2019). ECE teachers' views on play-based learning: A systematic review. *European Early Childhood Education Research Journal, 27*(6), 776–800. https://doi.org/10.1080/1350293X.2019.1678717

Burns, R. D., Brusseau, T. A., Fu, Y., Myrer, R. S., & Hannon, J. C. (2016). Comprehensive school physical activity programming and classroom behavior. *American Journal of Health Behavior, 40*(1), 100–107. https://doi.org/10.5993/AJHB.40.1.11

Camera, L. (2019, October 30). Across the board, scores drop in math and reading for U.S. students. *U.S. News World Report.* https://www.usnews.com/news/education-news/articles/2019-10-30/across-the-board-scores-drop-in-math-and-reading-for-us-students

Carr, J. M., Schoephoerster, K., & Riegel, C. (2024). The impact of kinesthetic instructional strategies and manipulatives on fourth graders' self-efficacy and self-confidence toward multiplication. *Mathematical Thinking and Learning, 27*(3), 361–377. https://doi.org/10.1080/10986065.2024.2343036

Causton, J., & Macleod, K. (2020). *Building a positive and supportive classroom* (quick reference guide). ASCD.

Center for Youth Wellness. (2014). A hidden crisis: Findings on adverse childhood experiences in California. Author. https://cwlibrary.childwelfare.gov/permalink/01CWIG_INST/3508qr/alma991000101349707651

Centers for Disease Control and Prevention (CDC). (2024). Making physical activity part of a child's life. *Centers for Disease Control and Prevention.* https://www.cdc.gov/physical-activity-basics/adding-children-adolescents/index.html

Centers for Disease Control and Prevention (CDC). (2025, September 24). Adverse childhood experiences. Author. https://www.cdc.gov/aces/about/index.html

Chapman, K. (2022). "Wait—it's a math problem, right?": Negotiating school frames in out-of-school places. *Educational Studies in Mathematics, 109*, 661–676.

Ciarrochi, J., Heaven, P., & Davies, F. (2007). The impact of hope, self-esteem, and attributional style on adolescents' school grades and emotional well-being: A longitudinal study. *Journal of Research in Personality, 41*, 1161–1178. https://doi.org/10.1016/j.jrp.2007.02.001

Ciotto, C. M., & Fede, M. H. (2017). Integrating CSPAP into the PETE Programs at Southern Connecticut State University and Central Connecticut State University. *Journal of Physical Education, Recreation & Dance, 88*(1), 20–28. https://doi.org/10.1080/07303084.2017.1250520

Cohn, M., & Fredrickson, B. (2006). Beyond the moment, beyond the self: Shared ground between selective investment theory and the broaden-and-build theory of positive emotions. *Psychological Inquiry, 17*(1), 39–44.

Cohn, M., Fredrickson, B., Brown, S., Mikels, J., & Conway, A. (2009). Happiness unpacked: Positive emotions increase life satisfaction by building resilience. *Emotion, 9*(3), 361–368. https://doi.org/10.1037/a0015952

Colella, D., Monacis, D., & Massari, F. (2019). Assessment of motor performances in Italian primary school children: Results of SBAM project. *Advances in Physical Education, 9*, 117–128. https://doi.org/10.4236/ape.2019.92009

Colvin, R. L. (1999). Math wars: Tradition vs. real-world applications. *School Administrator, 56*(1), 26.

Cortez, C., Shao, I. Y., Seamans, M. J., Dooley, E. E., Gabriel, K. P., & Nagata, J. M. (2023). Moderate-to-vigorous intensity physical activity among U.S. adolescents before and during the COVID-19 pandemic: Findings from the Adolescent Brain Cognitive Development Study. *Preventive Medicine Reports, 35*(102344), 5. https://doi.org/10.1016/j.pmedr.2023.102344

Curby, T., Rimm-Kaufman, S., & Ponitz, C. (2009). Teacher–child interactions and children's achievement trajectories across kindergarten and first grade. *Journal of Educational Psychology, 101*(4), 912–925. https://doi.org/10.1037/a0016647

Cutter-Mackenzie, A., & Edwards, S. (2013). Toward a model for early childhood environmental education: Foregrounding, developing, and connecting knowledge through play-based learning. *The Journal of Environmental Education, 44*(3), 195–213. https://doi.org/10.1080/00958964.2012.751892

Darragh, L. (2014). Asking questions and performing mathematics identity. *Proceedings of the 37th Annual Conference of the Mathematics Education Research Group of Australasia*, 175–182.

Day, C. (1999). *Developing teachers: The challenges of lifelong learning*. Falmer Press.

De Corte, E., Verschaffel, L., & Greer, B. (2000). Connecting mathematics problem solving to the real world. *Mathematics for Living*, 66–73.

Demarin, V., Morovic, S., & Raphael, B. (2014). Neuroplasticity. *Periodicum Biologorum, 116*(2), 209–211.

Demir-Lira, O. E., Suarez-Pellicioni, M., Binzak, J., & Booth, J. (2020). Attitudes toward math are differentially related to the neural basis of multiplication depending on math skill. *Learning Disability Quarterly, 43*(3), 179–191.

Dempsey, A. (2017). *Movement and attention: An examination of the relationship between movements and ADHD manifestations in middle school students with ADHD* [Unpublished doctoral dissertation]. Carson-Newman University.

Dewey, J. (1902). *The child and the curriculum*. University of Chicago Press.

Dewey, J. (1897). My pedagogical creed. *The School Journal, 54*(3), 77–80.

Doménech-Betoret, F., Abellán-Roselló, L., & Gómez-Artiga, A. (2017). Self-efficacy, satisfaction, and academic achievement: the mediator role of students' expectancy-value beliefs. *Frontiers in Psychology, 8*(1193), 1–12. https://doi.org/10.3389/fpsyg.2017.01193

Donnelly, J., & Lambourne, K. (2011). Classroom-based physical activity, cognition, and academic achievement. *Preventive Medicine, 52*, S36–S42.

Donohoo, J., & Katz, S. (2017). When teachers believe, students achieve: Collaborative inquiry builds teacher efficacy for better student outcomes. *The Learning Professional, 38*(6), 20–27.

Dunn, R., & Dunn, K. (1993). *Teaching secondary students through their individual learning styles: Practical approaches for grades 7–12*. Pearson.

Dutrisac, S., Bearden, A., Borgel, J., Weddell, R., Jones, M., & Oddie, S. (2023). A tailored physical education program enhances elementary students' self-efficacy, attitudes, and motivation to engage in physical activity. *Psychology in the Schools, 60*(9), 3419–3434. https://doi.org/10.1002/pits.22927

Edwards, S. (2017). Play-based learning and intentional teaching: Forever different? *Australasian Journal of Early Childhood, 42*(2). https://doi.org/10.23965/AJEC.42.2.01

Eggleston, K., Green, E. J., Abel, S., Poe, S., & Shakeshaft, C. (2021). *Developing trauma-responsive approaches to student discipline: A guide to trauma-informed practice in Pre-K–12 schools* (Vol. 1). Routledge.

Ekowati, D. W. (2017). The mathematical connection ability in multiplication material at the elementary school. *The Social Sciences, 12*(12), 2212–2217.

Enloe, E. (2021). Social and emotional learning through creative movement in the physical education classroom. *A Journal for Physical and Sport Educators, 34*(1), 37–39. https://doi.org/10.1080/08924562.2021.1843340

Ewing, A., & Taylor, A. (2009). The role of child gender and ethnicity in teacher–child relationship quality and children's behavioral adjustment in preschool. *Early Childhood Research Quarterly, 24*(1), 92–105.

Fesseha, E., & Pyle, A. (2016). Conceptualising play-based learning from kindergarten teachers' perspectives. *International Journal of Early Years Education, 24*(3), 361–377. https://doi.org/10.1080/09669760.2016.1174105

Forbes, H. (2012). *Help for Billy: A beyond consequences approach to helping challenging children in the classroom.* Beyond Consequences Institute, LLC.

Franke, M., Webb, N., Chan, A., Ing, M., Freund, D., & Battey, D. (2009). Teacher questioning to elicit students' mathematical thinking in elementary school classrooms. *Journal of Teacher Education, 60*(4), 380–392.

Froiland, J., & Oros, E. (2014). Intrinsic motivation, perceived competence and classroom engagement as longitudinal predictors of adolescent reading achievement. *Educational Psychology, 34*(2), 119–132. https://doi.org/10.1080/01443410.2013.822964

Ganley, C., & Vasilyeva, M. (2014). The role of anxiety and working memory in gender differences in mathematics. *Journal of Educational Psychology, 106*(1), 105–120. https://doi.org/10.1037/a0034099

García, E., & Weiss, E. (2019). The teacher shortage is real, large and growing, and worse than we thought. *Economic Policy Institute.* https://files.epi.org/pdf/163651.pdf

Gardner, H. H. (2012). *Multiple intelligences: New horizons* (2nd ed.). Basic Books.

Ginsburg, H. (2006). Mathematical play and playful mathematics: A guide for early education. In D. Singer, R. Michnik Golinkoff, & K. Hirsh-Pasek (Eds.), *Play = Learning: How play motivates and enhances children's cognitive and social-emotional growth* (pp. 145–165). Oxford University Press.

Ginsburg, K. (2007). The importance of play in promoting healthy child development and maintaining strong parent-child bonds. *American Academy of Pediatrics, 119*(1), 182–191. https://doi.org/10.1542/peds.2006-2697

Goetz, T., Bieg, M., Lüdtke, O., Pekrun, R., & Hall, N. (2013). Do girls really experience more anxiety in mathematics? *Psychological Science, 24*(10), 2079–2087. https://doi.org/10.1177/0956797613486989

Goh, T. L., Leong, C. H., Fede, M. H., & Ciotto, C. M. (2022). Before-school physical activity program's impact on social and emotional learning. *Journal of School Health, 92*(7), 674–680. https://doi.org/10.1111/josh.13167

Goh, T. L., Moosbrugger, M., & Mello, D. (2020). Experiences of preservice and in-service teachers in a comprehensive school physical activity infusion curriculum. *Education Sciences, 10*, 290. https://doi.org/10.3390/educsci10100290

Good, T., & Slavings, R. (1988). Male and female student question-asking behavior in elementary and secondary mathematics and language arts classes. *Journal of Research in Childhood Education, 3*(1), 5–23. https://doi.org/10.1080/02568548809594783

Goodykoontz, E. N. (2008). *Factors that affect college students' attitude toward mathematics* [Unpublished doctoral dissertation]. West Virginia University. https://researchrepository.wvu.edu/etd/2837

Hammett, C. T. (2009). *The effects of physical movement during story time on vocabulary acquisition of primary students in grades K-1: An exploratory investigation in one school location* [Unpublished doctoral dissertation]. Lewis and Clark College.

Harper, N., & Daane, C. J. (1998). Causes and reduction of math anxiety in preservice elementary teachers. *Action in Teacher Education, 19*(4), 29–38. https://doi.org/10.1080/01626620.1998.10462889

Harris, N. B. (2019). *The deepest well: Healing the long-term effects of childhood adversity.* Mariner Books.

Heinze, A. (2005). Mistake-handling activities in the mathematics classroom. *Proceedings of the 29th conference of the International Group for the Psychology of Mathematics Education, 3,* 105–112.

Herzog, J., & Schmahl, C. (2018). Adverse childhood experiences and the consequences on neurobiological, psychosocial, and somatic conditions across the lifespan. *Frontiers in Psychiatry, 9*(420). https://doi.org/10.3389/fpsyt.2018.00420

Hillman, C. H., Erickson, K. I., & Kramer, A. F. (2008). Be smart, exercise your heart: Exercise effects on brain and cognition. *Nature, 9,* 58–65. https://doi.org/10.1038/nrn2298

Hochanadel, A., & Finamore, D. (2015). Fixed and growth mindset in education and how grit helps students persist in the face of adversity. *Journal of International Education Research, 11*(1), 47–50.

Hoza, B. (2007). Peer functioning in children with ADHD. *Journal of Pediatric Psychology, 32*(6), 655–663. https://doi.org/10.1093/jpepsy/jsm024

Hwang, S., & Son, T. (2021). Students' attitude toward mathematics and its relationship with mathematics achievement. *Journal of Education and E-Learning Research, 8*(3), 272–280.

Idaho Youth Ranch. (n.d.). ACEs and education. Author. https://www.youthranch.org/educational-impacts-of-aces

Ihme, H., Olie, E., Courtet, P., El-Hage, W., Zendjidjian, X., Mazzola-Pomietto, P., Consoloni, J.-L., Deruelle, C., & Belzeaux, R. (2022). Childhood trauma increases vulnerability to attempt suicide in adulthood through avoidant attachment. *Comprehensive Psychiatry, 117,* 152333.

Isoard-Gautheur, S., Ginoux, C., Gerber, M., & Sarrazin, P. (2019). The stress–burnout relationship examining the moderating effect of physical activity and intrinsic motivation for off-job physical activity. *Workplace Health & Safety, 67*(7), 350–360. https://doi.org/10.1177/2165079919829497

Jackson, C. D., & Leffingwell, R. J. (1999). The role of instructors in creating math anxiety in students from kindergarten through college. *The Mathematics Teacher, 92*(7), 583–586.

Jacobs, J., Greef, J., & Heyman, R. (2018). Interactive game for children with difficulty crossing the midline. Institute of Electrical and Electronics Engineers (IEEE). https://doi.org/10.1109/SeGAH.2018.8401348

Jensen, E. (2005). *Teaching with the brain in mind* (Revised 2nd ed.). ASCD.

Jensen, F., & Sjaastad, J. (2013). A Norwegian out-of-school mathematics project's influence on secondary students' STEM motivation. *International Journal of Science and Mathematics Education, 11*(6), 1437–1461.

Jimenez, K. (2023, April 17). Most Americans are unhappy with the math taught in classrooms, new survey shows. *USA Today.* https://www.usatoday.com/story/news/2023/04/17/families-unsatisfied-way-us-teaches-math/11666787002/

Jin, Q., & Kim, M. (2018). Metacognitive regulation during elementary students' collaborative group work. *Interchange, 49,* 263–281.

Kaiser Permanente. (n.d.). Adverse childhood experiences (ACEs). *Thriving Schools.* https://thrivingschools.kaiserpermanente.org/mental-health/aces/

Keefe, J. (1987). Learning style theory and practice. NASSP.

Kimura, Y. (2010). Expressing emotions in teaching: Inducement, suppression, and disclosure as caring profession. *Educational Studies in Japan: International Yearbook, 5,* 63–78.

Kinzer, C. J., & Stanford, T. (2013). The distributive property: The core of multiplication. *Teaching Children Mathematics, 20*(5), 302–309. https://doi.org/10.5951/teacchilmath.20.5.0302

Kitayama, N., Brummer, M., Hertz, L., Quinn, S., Kim, Y., & Bremner, J. D. (2007). Morphologic alterations in the corpus callosum in abuse-related posttraumatic stress disorder: A preliminary study. *Journal of Nervous and Mental Disease, 195*(12), 1027–1029. https://doi.org/10.1097/NMD.0b013e31815c044f

Klamm, M., Duck, A., Welsch, M., Yan, Y., Torres, E., Wade, B., Stewart, M., Clayton, J., & Zhang, L. (2022). Dispersion of daily physical activity behaviors in school-age children: A novel approach to measure patterns of physical activity. *Journal for Specialists in Pediatric Nursing, 27*(2), e12364. https://doi.org/10.1111/jspn.12364

Koch, S., Mars, R., Toni, I., & Roelofs, K. (2018). Emotional control, reappraised. *Neuroscience and Biobehavioral Reviews, 95,* 528–534.

Körük, S. (2017). The effect of self-esteem on student achievement. In E. Karadağ (Ed.), *The factors effecting student achievement* (pp. 247–257). Springer International Publishing.

Kumaş, Ö., & Ergül, C. (2021). Effectiveness of the big math for little kids program on the early mathematics skills of children with risk group. *Athens Journal of Education, 8*(4), 385–400. https://doi.org/10.30958/aje.8-4-3

Kwon, O. N., Park, J. S., & Park, J. H. (2006). Cultivating divergent thinking in mathematics through an open-ended approach. *Asia Pacific Education Review, 7*(1), 51–61.

Laal, M., & Salamati, P. (2012). Lifelong learning; Why do we need it? *Procedia—Social and Behavioral Sciences, 31,* 399–403.

Lakeside. (2025). The science behind. *Lakeside Training.* https://lakesidetraining.org/neurologic/the-science-behind/

Larina, G. (2016). Analysis of real-world math problems: Theoretical model and classroom applications. *Voprosy Obrazovaniya/ Educational Studies Moscow, 3,* 151–168. https://doi.org/10.17323/1814-9545-2016-3-151-168

Li, J.-B., Bi, S.-S., Willems, Y. E., & Finkenauer, C. (2021). The association between school discipline and self-control from preschoolers to high school students: A three-level meta-analysis. *Review of Educational Research, 91*(1), 73–111. https://doi.org/10.3102/0034654320979160

Licari, M., & Larkin, D. (2008). Increased associated movements: Influence of attention deficits and movement difficulties. *Human Movement Science, 27*(2), 310–324. https://doi.org/10.1016/j.humov.2008.02.013

Liew, J., Lench, H. C., Kao, G., Yeh, Y.-C., & Kwok, O. (2014). Avoidance temperament and social-evaluative threat in college students' math performance: A mediation model of math and test anxiety. *Anxiety, Stress, & Coping, 27*(6), 650–661. https://doi.org/10.1080/10615806.2014.910303

Linder, S. M., Cribbs, J., & Smart, J. B. (2015). A multi-method investigation of mathematics motivation for elementary age students. *School Science and Mathematics, 115*(8), 392–403.

Lombardo, T. W., & Drabman, R. S. (1985). Teaching LD children multiplication tables. *Academic Therapy, 20*(4), 437–442. https://doi.org/10.1177/105345128502000406

Lunkenheimer, L., & Kuntz, S. (2022). Building resilience through movement: Classroom-based instructional practices [Webinar]. Classroom-Based Instructional Practices, Virtual.

Luttenberger, S., Wimmer, S., & Paechter, M. (2018). Spotlight on math anxiety. *Psychology Research and Behavior Management, 11*, 311–322. https://doi.org/10.2147/PRBM.S141421

Lyons, I., & Beilock, S. (2012). When math hurts: Math anxiety predicts pain network activation in anticipation of doing math. *PLoS ONE, 7*(10), e48076. https://doi.org/10.1371/journal.pone.0048076

MacNeill, J. (2019). Practical strategies for regulating students' brains. Paper presented at the 2019 Spring Trauma Informed School Conference, St. Louis.

Maddock, R., Casazza, G., Fernandez, D., & Maddock, M. (2016). Acute modulation of cortical glutamate and GABA content by physical activity. *The Journal of Neuroscience, 36*(8), 2449–2457. https://doi.org/10.1523/JNEUROSCI.3455-15.2016

Marsh, H. W., & Hau, K.-T. (2004). Explaining paradoxical relations between academic self-concepts and achievements: Cross-cultural generalizability of the internal/external frame of reference predictions across 26 countries. *Journal of Educational Psychology, 96*(1), 56–67. https://doi.org/10.1037/0022-0663.96.1.56

Math & Movement. (2024). Kinesthetic learning boosts multiplication skills in Sarasota. Author.https://mathandmovement.com/kinesthetic-learning-boosts-multiplication-mastery-and-confidence-in-sarasota/

May, D. (2009). *Mathematics self-efficacy and anxiety questionnaire* [Unpublished doctoral dissertation]. University of Georgia.

Mazana, M. Y., Montero, C. S., & Casmir, R. O. (2019). Investigating students' attitude towards learning mathematics. *International Electronic Journal of Mathematics Education, 14*(1), 207–231.

McCormick, M. P., O'Connor, E. E., Cappella, E., & McClowry, S. G. (2013). Teacher–child relationships and academic achievement: A multilevel propensity score model approach. *Journal of School Psychology, 51*, 611–624. https://doi.org/10.1016/j.jsp.2013.05.001

McTighe, J. (2017). *Designing and using essential questions* (quick reference guide). ASCD. https://ascd.org/books/designing-and-using-essential-questions?variant=QRG118025

Mendez Colmenares, A., Voss, M. W., Fanning, J., Salerno, E. A., Gothe, N. P., Thomas, M. L., McAuley, E., Kramer, A. F., & Burzynska, A. Z. (2021). White matter plasticity in healthy older adults: The effects of aerobic exercise. *NeuroImage, 239*, 118305. https://doi.org/10.1016/j.neuroimage.2021.118305

Metcalfe, D., McKenzie, K., McCarty, K., & Pollet, T. (2019). Emotion recognition from body movement and gesture in children with Autism Spectrum Disorder is improved by situational cues. *Research in Developmental Disabilities, 86*, 1–10. https://doi.org/10.1016/j.ridd.2018.12.008

Meyer, S., Grob, A., & Gerber, M. (2021). No fun, no gain: The stress-buffering effect of physical activity on life satisfaction depends on adolescents' intrinsic motivation. *Psychology of Sport & Exercise, 56*, 102004. https://doi.org/10.1016/j.psychsport.2021.102004

Moon, J., Webster, C. A., Herring, J., & Egan, C. (2022). Relationships between systematically observed movement integration and classroom management in elementary schools. *Journal of Positive Behavior, 24*(2), 122–132. https://doi.org/10.1177/1098300720947034

Moore, B., Dudley, D., & Woodcock, S. (2023). The effects of a martial arts-based intervention on secondary school students' self-efficacy: A randomised controlled trial. *Philosophies, 8*(43). https://doi.org/10.3390/philosophies8030043

Moore, M., & Russ, S. (2008). Follow-up of a pretend play intervention: Effects on play, creativity, and emotional processes in children. *Creativity Research Journal, 20*(4), 427–436.

Morony, S., Kleitman, S., Lee, Y. P., & Stankov, L. (2013). Predicting achievement: Confidence vs self-efficacy, anxiety, and self-concept in Confucian and European countries. *International Journal of Educational Research, 58,* 79–96. https://doi.org/10.1016/j.ijer.2012.11.002

Mottet, T., & Beebe, S. (2000). Emotional contagion in the classroom: An examination of how teacher and student emotions are related. *Annual Meeting of the National Communication Association, 36.* https://files.eric.ed.gov/fulltext/ED447522.pdf

National Center for Education Statistics (NCES). (2022). Reading and mathematics scores decline during COVID-19 pandemic. Nation's Report Card. https://www.nationsreport-card.gov/highlights/ltt/2022/

National Child Traumatic Stress Network (NCTSN). (n.d.). Creating trauma-informed systems. Author. https://www.nctsn.org/trauma-informed-care/creating-trauma-informed-systems

National Math Foundation (NMF). (2023). Mighty multiplication project. Author. https://drive.google.com/file/d/1Lws8fszvjDtvZrdix3s46qiFH4EXpRmq/view

Newcombe, N. S. (2010). Picture this: Increasing math and science learning by improving spatial thinking. *American Educator, 34*(2), 29.

Notaras, M., & van den Buuse, M. (2020). Neurobiology of BDNF in fear memory, sensitivity to stress, and stress-related disorders. *Molecular Psychiatry, 25,* 2251–2274. https://doi.org/10.1038/s41380-019-0639-2

Novak, M. (2017). *Case studies listening to students using kinesthetic movement while learning to graph linear functions* [Unpublished doctoral dissertation]. Kent State University.

O'Connor, E., Dearing, E., & Collins, B. (2011). Teacher-child relationship and behavior problem trajectories in elementary school. *American Educational Research Journal, 48*(1), 120–162. https://doi.org/10.3102/0002831210365008

Pásztor, A., Molnár, G., & Csapó, B. (2015). Technology-based assessment of creativity in educational context: The case of divergent thinking and its relation to mathematical achievement. *Thinking Skills and Creativity, 18,* 32–42. https://doi.org/10.1016/j.tsc.2015.05.004

Peterman, C., & Ewing, J. (2019). Effects of movement, growth mindset and math talks on math anxiety. *Journal of Multicultural Affairs, 4*(1), 1–24.

Peters, A., Ren, X., Bessette, K., Goldstein, B., West, A., Langenecker, S., & Pandey, G. (2019). Interplay between pro-inflammatory cytokines, childhood trauma, and executive function in depressed adolescents. *Journal of Psychiatric Research, 114,* 1–10. https://doi.org/10.1016/j.jpsychires.2019.03.030

Picha, G. (2018). Recognizing and alleviating math anxiety: Math anxiety affects almost half of elementary school students. Spot the symptoms and use these strategies to counteract it. *Edutopia.* https://www.edutopia.org/article/recognizing-and-alleviating-math-anxiety

Pickersgill, J., Turco, C., Ramdeo, K., Rehsi, R., Foglia, S., & Nelson, A. (2022). The combined influences of exercise, diet and sleep on neuroplasticity. *Frontiers in Psychology, 13,* 1–17. https://doi.org/10.3389/fpsyg.2022.831819

Pinxten, M., Marsh, H. W., De Fraine, B., Van Den Noortgate, W., & Van Damme, J. (2013). Enjoying mathematics or feeling competent in mathematics? Reciprocal effects on mathematics achievement and perceived math effort expenditure. *British Journal of Educational Psychology, 84,* 152–174. https://doi.org/10.1111/bjep.12028

Piya-amornphan, N., Santiworakul, A., Cetthakrikul, S., & Srirug, P. (2020). Physical activity and creativity of children and youths. *BMC Pediatrics, 20*(118), 7.

Place, J. (2021). *Supporting emotional regulation in the classroom* (quick reference guide). ASCD.

Quane, K. (2022). Evaluating factors that influence young children's attitudes towards mathematics: The use of mathematical manipulatives. Proceedings of the 44th Annual Conference of the Mathematics Education Research Group of Australasia. https://www.researchgate.net/publication/363334300_Evaluating_Factors_that_Influence_Young_Children%27s_Attitudes_Towards_Mathematics_The_Use_of_Mathematical_Manipulatives#fullTextFileContent

Rafa, A. (2019). The status of school discipline in state policy [Policy Report]. *Education Commission of the States*. https://www.ecs.org/the-status-of-school-discipline-in-state-policy/

Ramirez, G., Gunderson, E., Levine, S., & Beilock, S. (2013). Math anxiety, working memory and math achievement in early elementary school. *Journal of Cognition and Development, 14*(2), 187–202. https://doi.org/10.1080/15248372.2012.664593

Raney, J. H., Testa, A., Jackson, D. B., Ganson, K. T., & Nagata, J. M. (2022). Associations between adverse childhood experiences, adolescent screen time and physical activity during the COVID-19 pandemic. *Academic Pediatrics, 22*(8), 1294–1299.

Ratey, J. J., & Hagerman, E. (2013). *Spark: The revolutionary new science of exercise and the brain* (Reprint edition). Little, Brown.

Reiser, B., Brody, L., Novak, M., Tipton, K., & Adams, L. (2017). Asking questions. In B. Reiser & C. Passmore (Eds.), *Helping students make sense of the world using next generation science and engineering practices* (pp. 87–108). NSTA.

Rimm-Kaufman, S., Baroody, A., Curby, T., Ko, M., Thomas, J., Merritt, E., Abry, T., & DeCoster, J. (2014). Efficacy of the responsive classroom approach: Results from a 3-year, longitudinal randomized controlled trial. *American Educational Research Journal, 51*(3), 567–603. https://doi.org/10.3102/0002831214523821

Rodrigo-Ruiz, D. (2016). Effect of teachers' emotions on their students: Some evidence. *Journal of Education & Social Policy, 3*(4), 73–79.

Rolston, A., & Lloyd-Richardson, E. (n.d.). What is emotion regulation and how do we do it? *Cornell Research Program on Self-Injury and Recovery*. https://www.selfinjury.bctr.cornell.edu/perch/resources/what-is-emotion-regulationsinfo-brief.pdf

Rutherford, K. (2015). Why play math games? *Teaching Children Mathematics*. https://www.nctm.org/Publications/TCM-blog/Blog/Why-Play-Math-Games_/

Sahin, M., Akbasli, S., & Yanpar Yelken, T. (2010). Key competences for lifelong learning: The case of prospective teachers. *Educational Research and Review, 5*(10), 545–556.

Saidmamatov, O., Rodrigues, P., & Vasconcelos, O. (2022). Motor skills training program reinforces crossing the body's midline in children with developmental coordination disorder. *Symmetry, 14*, 1259. https://doi.org/10.3390/sym14061259

Salciccioli, M., Mahoney, Walters, K., & Salazar, L. (2020). NBA math hoops: Findings from the Philadelphia area. *WestEd*.

Sanaeifar, F., Pourranjbar, S., Pourranjbar, M., Ramezani, S., Mehr, S. R., Wadan, A.-H. S., & Khazeifard, F. (2024). Beneficial effects of physical exercise on cognitive-behavioral impairments and brain-derived neurotrophic factor alteration in the limbic system induced by neurodegeneration. *Experimental Gerontology, 195*, 112539. https://doi.org/10.1016/j.exger.2024.112539

Scheiner, T. (2023). Shifting the ways prospective teachers frame and notice student mathematical thinking: From deficits to strengths. *Educational Studies in Mathematics, 114*, 35–61.

Schwartz, S. (2024, November 15). Which nation's students are defying the math anxiety trend? *Education Week*. https://www.edweek.org/teaching-learning/which-nations-students-are-defying-the-math-anxiety-trend/2024/11

Sege, R., & Browne, C. H. (2017). Responding to ACEs with HOPE: Health outcomes from positive experiences. *Academic Pediatrics, 17*(7S), S79–S85.

Sheldrake, R., Mujtaba, T., & Reiss, M. J. (2015). Students' intentions to study non-compulsory mathematics: The importance of how good you think you are. *British Educational Research Journal, 41*(3), 462–488. https://doi.org/10.1002/berj.3150

Sinha, K. (2014). Kinesthetic learning: Moving toward a new model for education. *Edutopia*. https://www.edutopia.org/blog/kinesthetic-learning-new-model-education-kirin-sinha-?crlt.pid=camp.f0xBSIluBjXW

Skarr, A., Zielinski, K., Ruwe, K., Sharp, H., Williams, R., & McLaughlin, T. F. (2014). The effects of direct instruction flashcard and math racetrack procedures on mastery of basic multiplication facts by three elementary school students. *Education and Treatment of Children, 37*(1), 77–93.

Slavin, R. (2014). Cooperative learning and academic achievement: Why does groupwork work? *Anales de Psicología, 30*(3), 785–791.

Slepian, M., & Ambady, N. (2012). Fluid movement and creativity. *Journal of Experimental Psychology: General, 141*(4), 625–629.

Smith, S. Z., & Smith, M. E. (2006). Assessing elementary understanding of multiplication concepts. *School Science and Mathematics, 106*(3), 140–149. https://doi.org/10.1111/j.1949-8594.2006.tb18171.x

Sneck, S., Viholainen, H., Syväoja, H., Kankaapää, A., Hakonen, H., Poikkeus, A.-M., & Tammelin, T. (2019). Effects of school-based physical activity on mathematics performance in children: A systematic review. *International Journal of Behavioral Nutrition and Physical Activity, 16*(109).

Sowder, L., & Harel, G. (1998). Types of students' justifications. *The Mathematics Teacher, 91*(8), 670–675.

Spilt, J., Koomen, H., & Thijs, J. (2011). Teacher wellbeing: The importance of teacher–student relationships. *Educational Psychology Review, 23*, 457–477. https://doi.org/10.1007/s10648-011-9170-y

Steffen, P. R., Hedges, D., & Matheson, R. (2022). The brain is adaptive not triune: How the brain responds to threat, challenge, and change. *Frontiers in Psychiatry, 13*, 802606. https://doi.org/10.3389/fpsyt.2022.802606

Stempel, H., Cox-Martin, M., Bronsert, M., Dickinson, L. M., & Allison, M. (2017). Chronic school absenteeism and the role of adverse childhood experiences. *Academic Pediatrics, 17*(8), 837–843. https://doi.org/10.1016/j.acap.2017.09.013

Stormont, M. (2001). Social outcomes of children with AD/HD: Contributing factors and implications for practice. *Psychology in the Schools, 38*(6), 521–531. https://doi.org/10.1002/pits.1040

Ströhle, A., Feller, C., Onken, M., Godemann, F., Heinz, A., & Dimeo, F. (2005). The acute anti-panic activity of aerobic exercise. *American Journal of Psychiatry, 162*(12), 2376–2378.

Stylianides, A. (2007). Proof and proving in school mathematics. *Journal for Research in Mathematics Education, 38*(3), 289–321.

Stylianides, A. (2016). The importance and meaning of proving, and the role of mathematics tasks. In *Proving in the elementary mathematics classroom* (pp. 7–25). Oxford University Press.

Stylianou, M., Kulinna, P. H., & Naiman, T. (2016). '...Because there's nobody who can just sit that long': Teacher perceptions of classroom-based physical activity and related management issues. *European Physical Education Review, 22*(3), 390–408. https://doi.org/10.1177/1356336X15613968

Substance Abuse and Mental Health Services Administration (SAMHSA). (2024, December 3). Child trauma. Author. https://www.samhsa.gov/mental-health/trauma-violence/child-trauma

Supekar, K., Iuculano, T., Chen, L., & Menon, V. (2015). Remediation of childhood math anxiety and associated neural circuits through cognitive tutoring. *Journal of Neuroscience, 35*(36), 12574–12583. https://doi.org/10.1523%2FJNEUROSCI.0786-15.2015

Sutton, R. (2005). Teachers' emotions and classroom effectiveness: Implications from recent research. *The Clearing House, 78*(5), 229–234.

Sutton, R., & Wheatley, K. (2003). Teachers' emotions and teaching: A review of the literature and directions for future research. *Educational Psychology Review, 15*, 327–358.

Swartz, R. (2016). Mistakes as an important part of the learning process. In *From Socrates to Summerhill and beyond: Towards a philosophy of education for personal responsibility* (pp. 269–278). Information Age Publishing.

Tate, M. L. (2009). *Mathematics worksheets don't grow dendrites: 20 numeracy strategies that engage the brain, PreK–8*. Corwin.

Taverno Ross, S., Hasson, R., Johnson, M., Nocera, V., Sallis, J., Simon, L., Wheeler, L., & Kaushal, N. (2020, September). The urgency of now: Achieving equity in school physical activity policies and practices during the COVID-19 pandemic. *American College of Sports Medicine.*

Teodoro, S. D., Donders, S., Kemp-Davidson, J., Robertson, P., & Schuyler, L. (2011). Asking good questions: Promoting greater understanding of mathematics through purposeful teacher and student questioning. *Canadian Journal of Action Research, 12*(2), 18–29.

Terada, Y. (2018). How mistakes help students learn: Guessing is useful for students' ability to recall information—Even when the guesses are wrong. *Edutopia.* https://www.edutopia.org/article/how-mistakes-help-students-learn

Thomas, K. (2021, January 6). New review says ineffective "learning styles" theory persists in education around the world. Swansea University. https://www.swansea.ac.uk/press-office/news-events/news/2021/01/new-review-says-ineffective-learning-styles-theory-persists-in-education-around-the-world-.php

Thomas, M. S., Crosby, S., & Vanderhaar, J. (2019). Trauma-informed practices in schools across two decades: An interdisciplinary review of research. *Review of Research in Education, 43*(1), 422–452. https://doi.org/10.3102/0091732X18821123

Tichenor, M., & Tichenor, J. (2019). Collaboration in the elementary school: What do teachers think? *Journal of Curriculum and Teaching, 8*(2), 54–60.

Tomporowski, P. (2003). Effects of acute bouts of exercise on cognition. *Acta Psychologica, 112*(3), 297–324. https://doi.org/10.1016/s0001-6918(02)00134-8

Tugade, M., Fredrickson, B., & Barrett, L. (2004). Psychological resilience and positive emotional granularity: Examining the benefits of positive emotions on coping and health. *Journal of Personality, 72*(6), 1161–1190. https://doi.org/10.1111/j.1467-6494.2004.00294.x

Turnaround for Children. (n.d.). Stress and the brain. Author. https://turnaroundusa.org/wp-content/uploads/2020/03/Stress-and-the-Brain_Turnaround-for-Children-032420.pdf

Uzunboylu, H., & Hürsen, Ç. (2011). Lifelong learning competence scale (LLLCS): The study of validity and reliability. *H.U. Journal of Education, 41*, 449–460.

Van de Walle, J. A., Bay-Williams, J. M., & Karp, K. S. (2022). *Elementary and middle school mathematics: Teaching developmentally* (11th ed.). Pearson.

van Oers, B., & Duijkers, D. (2013). Teaching in a play-based curriculum: Theory, practice and evidence of developmental education for young children. *Journal of Curriculum Studies, 45*(4), 511–534. http://dx.doi.org/10.1080/00220272.2011.637182

Vander Elst, O. F., Foster, N. H. D., Vuust, P., Keller, P. E., & Kringelbach, M. L. (2023). The neuroscience of dance: A conceptual framework and systematic review. *Neuroscience and Biobehavioral Reviews, 150*, 105197. https://doi.org/10.1016/j.neubiorev.2023.105197

Vetter, M., Orr, R., O'Dwyer, N., & O'Connor, H. (2020). Effectiveness of active learning that combines physical activity and math in schoolchildren: A systematic review. *Journal of School Health, 90*(4), 306–318.

Vogt, F., Hauser, B., Stebler, R., Rechsteiner, K., & Urech, C. (2018). Learning through play: Pedagogy and learning outcomes in early childhood mathematics. *European Early Childhood Education Research Journal, 26*(4), 589–603. https://doi.org/10.1080/1350293X.2018.1487160

Walker, S. H., Walker, D., & Widaman, K. (2020). The ABCs of math attitudes: Reliability and validity of the three-factor model. *Journal of Studies in Education, 10*(1), 1–17. https://doi.org/10.5296/jse.v10i1.15792

Wallace, C., & Russ, S. (2015). Pretend play, divergent thinking, and math achievement in girls: A longitudinal study. *Psychology of Aesthetics, Creativity, and the Arts, 9*(3), 296–305.

Ward, Z., Bleich, S., Cradock, A., Barrett, J., Giles, C., Flax, C., Long, M., & Gortmaker, S. (2019). Projected U.S. state-level prevalence of adult obesity and severe obesity. *New England Journal of Medicine, 381*(25), 2440–2450. https://doi.org/10.1056/NEJMsa1909301

Watanabe, T. (2003). Teaching multiplication: An analysis of elementary school mathematics teachers' manuals from Japan and the United States. *The Elementary School Journal, 104*(2), 111–125. https://doi.org/10.1086/499745

Weight, E., Harry, M., Lewis, M., Jensen, J. A., Popp, N., & Osborne, B. (2018). *The walking classroom: Classroom testing study*. Oak Foundation.

Whitehead, J. R. (1993). Physical activity and intrinsic motivation. *Health and Human Services Department, Office of Public Health and Science, 1*(2). https://www.govinfo.gov/app/details/GOVPUB-HE20-PURL-LPS21124

Williams, J., & Roth, W.-M. (2019). Theoretical perspectives on interdisciplinary mathematics education. In B. Doig, J. Williams, D. Swanson, R. Borromeo Ferri, & P. Drake (Eds.), *Interdisciplinary mathematics education: The state of the art and beyond* (pp. 13–34). Springer Open.

Williams, L. E., Huang, J. Y., & Bargh, J. A. (2009). The scaffolded mind: Higher mental processes are grounded in early experience of the physical world. *European Journal of Social Psychology, 39*, 1257–1267. https://doi.org/10.1002/ejsp.665

Williams, T., & Williams, K. (2010). Self-efficacy and performance in mathematics: Reciprocal determinism in 33 nations. *Journal of Educational Psychology, 102*(2), 453–466. https://psycnet.apa.org/doi/10.1037/a0017271

Wong, M., & Evans, D. (2007). Improving basic multiplication fact recall for primary school students. *Mathematics Education Research Journal, 19*(1), 89–106. https://doi.org/10.1007/BF03217451

Zacarian, D., & Alvarez-Ortiz, L. (2020). *Teaching and supporting students living with adversity* (quick reference guide). ASCD.

Zakaria, E., & Nordin, N. (2008). The effects of mathematics anxiety on matriculation students as related to motivation and achievement. *Eurasia Journal of Mathematics, Science and Technology Education, 4*(1), 27–30. https://doi.org/10.12973/ejmste/75303

Zaslavsky, O., Nickerson, S., Stylianides, A., Kidron, I., & Winicki-Landman, G. (2021). The need for proof and proving: Mathematical and pedagogical perspectives. In G. Hanna & M. de Villiers (Eds.), *Proof and proving in mathematics education* (Vol. 15). Springer.

# Index

The letter *f* following a page locator denotes a figure.

# About the Authors

 **Suzy Koontz** is a founding board member and current vice president of the National Math Foundation (NMF) and the creator of Math & Movement. She has spent more than 25 years helping students achieve academic success through a movement-based approach to mathematics and literacy education. As a trained actuary and lifelong advocate for inclusive learning strategies, Suzy has created more than 200 teaching tools that have been adopted by schools nationwide and has authored over 20 books for learners both young and old. She actively leads professional development workshops for teachers and administrators across the country to support the implementation of movement-based mathematics and literacy strategies.

As a national presenter and keynote speaker at schools and conferences, Suzy weaves research, lived experience, and heartwarming stories of how movement can increase teacher and student self-confidence and, in turn, transform the way students learn and retain knowledge. Suzy's vision is for movement- and play-based learning to be incorporated during the school day, in after-school programming, and in summer learning programs.

 **Kirby Schoephoerster, EdD**, is the senior program director at the National Math Foundation (NMF) and an ardent advocate for the (re)design of educational spaces to foster positive learning identities for all students. Kirby received his doctorate in education at Vanderbilt University. His recent work at the NMF has involved facilitating organizational strategy development, coordinating educational research projects with community partners, and designing and implementing professional learning events for mathematics educators and school leaders across the country. Kirby has presented extensively on the topics of movement-based instruction, the science of learning and the brain, professional learning implementation, and the development of positive mathematics attitudes. Kirby's years of educational leadership experience lie within the fields of grant and research management, professional learning design, and nonprofit administration, blending his passion for improvement sciences, the relationship between organizational design and behavior, and supporting educational institutions with the evidence-based tools to create and sustain systems-level change for the learning communities they serve.

As a vocal proponent for lifelong and lifewide learning, Kirby's vision is to bridge research and practice around the effective implementation of inclusive, systems-oriented educational design so that *every* learner has access to transformative educational experiences.

## Related ISTE+ASCD Resources

At the time of publication, the following resources were available (ASCD stock numbers in parentheses).

*Conquering Math Myths with Universal Design: An Inclusive Instructional Approach for Grades K–8* by Jenna Mancini Rufo and Ron Martiello (#124004)

*Games and Tools for Teaching Addition Facts (Quick Reference Guide)* by Jennifer Bay-Williams and Gina Kling (#QRG118020)

*Games and Tools for Teaching Multiplication Facts (Quick Reference Guide)* by Gina Kling and Jennifer Bay-Williams (#QRG119016)

*Math Fact Fluency: 60+ Games and Assessment Tools to Support Learning and Retention* by Jennifer Bay-Williams and Gina Kling (#118014)

*The School Leader's Guide to Building and Sustaining Math Success* by Marian Small and Douglas Duff (#118039)

*Teach for Authentic Engagement* by Lauren Porosoff (#123045)

*Teaching Students to Communicate Mathematically* by Laney Sammons (#118005)

*Total Participation Techniques: Making Every Student an Active Learner, 3rd Edition* by Pérsida Himmele and William Himmele (#125031)

*Why Are We Still Doing That? Positive Alternatives to Problematic Teaching Practices* by Pérsida Himmele and William Himmele (#122010)

For up-to-date information about ISTE+ASCD resources, go to iste-ascd.org. You can search the complete archives of *Educational Leadership* at ascd.org/el. To contact us, send an email to memsupport@iste-ascd.org or call 1-800-933-2723 or 703-578-9600.